Designing VR Stressors for Occupational Simulation Training in the ICU Context

Dr.-Ing. Sebastian Weiß

Bibliografische Information der Deutschen Nationalbibliothek:
Die Deutsche Nationalbibliothek verzeichnet diese Publikation in der Deutschen
Nationalbibliografie; detaillierte bibliografische Daten sind im Internet über
http://dnb.dnb.de abrufbar.

Zugl.: Oldenburg, Univ., Diss., 2024

Verlag: BoD · Books on Demand GmbH
In de Tarpen 42
22848 Norderstedt

Druck: Libri Plureos GmbH
Friedensallee 273
22763 Hamburg

ISBN: 978-3-7597-8593-0

Zusammenfassung

In den letzten Jahren ist die Zahl der Menschen, die sich für den Pflegeberuf entscheiden, zurückgegangen. Gleichzeitig verlassen immer mehr erfahrene Pflegefachpersonen ihren Beruf, weil sich die Arbeitsbedingungen verschlechtern. Einer der Gründe, insbesondere auf der Intensivstation, ist der allgegenwärtige Stresspegel. Chronischer Stress kann zu gesundheitlichen Problemen bei den Pflegefachpersonen führen, ihre Entscheidungsfindung beeinträchtigen und fatale Folgen für die Patienten haben. Das Stressniveau wird durch verschiedene Stressoren erhöht, wie beispielsweise häufige akustische Alarme, Zeitdruck, oder emotionale Beziehungen zu Patienten und deren Angehörigen. Es gibt jedoch Möglichkeiten, den richtigen Umgang mit Stress zu erlernen, welche bereits in der Pflegeausbildung eingesetzt werden können.. Der Status quo verwendet sowohl Rollenspiele im Klassenzimmer als auch detaillierte Szenarien in so genannten Skills Labs. Da beide Lernformen mit Nachteilen wie beispielsweise Verfügbarkeit oder niedrigem Realismus verbunden sind, soll in dieser Dissertation in einem partizipativen Ansatz erforscht werden, welche Stressoren aus der Intensivstation in die virtuelle Realität (VR) implementiert werden können. Ein weiteres Ziel ist es zu erforschen, welches Potenzial zur Stresssteigerung bei den Teilnehmenden im Hinblick auf ihre Nützlichkeit im Stressimpfungstraining besteht. Ziel ist es, VR als Lehrmittel zu positionieren, das einen Kompromiss zwischen dem Realismus von Skills Labs und den niedrigschwelligen finanziellen Belastungen von Rollenspielen abbildet und mit der hohen Verfügbarkeit und den vielfältigen Einsatzmöglichkeiten der VR-Technologie kombiniert. Auf Basis einer umfassenden Bedarfsanalyse wurde ein Studienapparatus aus vier Komponenten entwickelt, die in verschiedenen Nutzendenstudien zum Einsatz kamen.

Unsere Ergebnisse zeigen, dass die virtuelle Nachbildung von Alarmbelastung, Zeitdruck und moralischer Verletzung einen Einfluss auf das Stressniveau der Teilnehmenden haben. Dies wurde sowohl durch objektive als auch subjektive Messverfahren, d.h. Veränderungen der Vitalfunktionen und Fragebögen, nachgewiesen. Darüber hinaus deuten die Ergebnisse auf eine hohe Präsenz während der Experimentierphasen hin. Durch einen Vergleich der virtuellen Intensivstation mit einer den wahren Gegebenheiten nachempfundenen Laborumgebung (Skills Lab) zwecks ökologischer Validierung konnte auch gezeigt werden, dass zwischen den beiden Realitätsstufen kein signifikanter Unterschied im Bezug auf die verschiedenen Dimensionen des Simulationsrealismus aufweist. Es lässt sich festhalten, dass VR als kostengünstiges Schulungsmittel einsetzbar ist, das die Vorteile aktuell genutzter Lehrtechniken verbindet.

Die in dieser Arbeit durchgeführten Studien zeigen, dass die VR Technologie ein vielseitig einsetzbares Tool mit einer hohen Validität in der Stressinduktion sein kann. Die zahlreichen Möglichkeiten zur Simulation machen VR zu einer sinnvollen, kostengünstigen und als realistisch empfundenen Alternative zu Skills Labs zur Unterstützung der momentanen Pflegeausbildung. Zukünftige Forschungsarbeiten sollen den Einfluss verschiedener Interaktionsmöglichkeiten innerhalb der VR evaluieren und die Effekte von Multi-User Szenarien genauer betrachten. Auch die mögliche Integration in den Pflegeunterricht sowie stresssenkende Effekte und Einfluss auf die Wissensretention bieten weitere Forschungsansätze.

Abstract

In recent years, the number of people opting for the nursing profession has decreased. At the same time, more and more senior nurses are leaving the profession because of deteriorating working conditions. One reason, particularly in the intensive care unit (ICU), is the ever-present level of stress on a ward. Chronic stress can lead to health problems for nurses, impair decision-making, and have fatal consequences for patients. Stress levels are increased by various stressors, such as frequent audible alarms, time pressure, emotional relationships with patients and their families, and others. Yet, there are ways to learn how to deal with stress more appropriately and these can be applied as early as during the nursing apprenticeship. The status quo uses both role-playing in the classroom and detailed scenarios in so-called skills labs. Since both forms of learning are associated with disadvantages, such as availability or low perceived realism, this dissertation uses a participatory approach to explore which stressors from the ICU can be implemented in virtual reality (VR) and what potential exists for increasing stress in participants concerning their usefulness in stress inoculation training. The aim is to position VR as a teaching tool that combines the realism of skills labs and the low-threshold financial burden of role-playing games with the high availability and diverse application possibilities of VR technology. Based on a comprehensive requirement analysis, we developed a study apparatus comprising four components, which were utilized in different user studies.

The results of our user studies show that the virtual replica of alarm stress, time pressure, and moral distress have an impact on participants' stress levels, as demonstrated by both objective and subjective measures, i.e. changes in vital signs and questionnaires. In addition, the results indicate a high level of presence during the experimental phases. By comparing the virtual ICU with a laboratory environment modeled after real-world conditions (skills lab) for ecological validation, we were also able to show that there is no significant difference between the two reality levels within the different dimensions of simulation realism. It can be concluded that VR can be used as a cost-effective training tool that combines the advantages of currently used teaching techniques.

The studies conducted in this thesis show that VR technology can be a versatile tool with high validity in stress induction. The broad possibilities for simulation make VR a useful, cost-effective support for current nursing training that is perceived as real. Future research should evaluate the influence of different interaction possibilities within VR and take a closer look at the effects of multi-user scenarios. The possible integration into nursing teaching as well as stress-reducing effects and influence on knowledge retention also offer further research approaches.

Acknowledgements

For the better half of the last decade, I was able to work with inspiring researchers in a multi-national, multi-disciplinary team of inspiring people, all sharing values like friendship, openness, and an interest in all things HCI. During this time, I became not only a researcher, but also a project manager, lab administrator, and VR enthusiast. My supervisor Susanne Boll helped me navigate the scientific seas and supported me with ideas, feedback, and words of encouragement. For this, and for the trust and recognition she extended to me, I would like to express my gratitude!

I want to extend my thanks to Wilko Heuten, who kept making sure I wasn't getting lost in specifics or following the wrong research idea. Wilko was a boss and a mentor who turned into a friend and co-founder.

Many people were helping me on this journey, as I am right in the middle between two generations of researchers in the HCI group of Oldenburg. I want to express my gratitude to Vanessa Cobus, Shadan Sadeghian Borojeni, Andrii Matviienko, Thorben Wallbaum, Uwe Grünefeld, Tim Claudius Stratmann, Abdallah El Ali, Marion Koelle, Erika Root, Heiko Müller and many more for welcoming me into the group, showing me the ropes, and thus giving me a head start into an area I was very new to. Special thanks also to Tobias Krahn, Pascal Hinrichs, and Christian Kowalski who started PIZ with me and with whom I exchanged insights and ideas, and shared many many meeting minutes. Over the years, the faces changed. Simon Kimmel, Frederike Jung, Sophie Grimme, Saja Aljuneidi, Hatice Sahin-Ippoliti, Michael Chamurnowa, and Mikolaj Wozniak were always available for coffee, discussions, and a good pun or two. Within this newer generation at OFFIS, I met my loving wife, Ani Weiß, who made sure I stayed on track, dotted the is and crossed the ts. I couldn't have done a better job without you.

And finally, I am grateful to my parents Werner and Monika Weiß who enabled my education, and my brothers Daniel and Frederik who have supported me for the past 36 years (on the day, by the time of this writing) and are the reason I am where I am today. Thank you!

Contents

"VR creates routine,
routine creates certainty,
certainty creates trust."

-P13

1 Introduction

Nurses are a vital pillar of the healthcare system, and their profession belongs to the most stressful professions one can choose as a career path. This is true even more so for the intensive care unit (ICU), a safety critical ward for patients recovering from life-threatening issues. The environment and working conditions for ICU staff are inherently stressful, especially during extraordinary situations (cf. Figure 1.1[1]). The primary sources of stress are physical overload, emotional situations involving patients and their families, dealing with dying and death, and little interaction with colleagues or support from supervisor(s). The stress that ICU nurses are exposed to has a great impact on both their professional and private lives. There is an extensive body of research linking occupational stress to reduced job satisfaction and patient care, higher staff turnover, worsening performance on the job, burnout, and absenteeism [RF11, MJM12, KM00].

Even though short-term stress can improve focus, task efficiency, and cognitive abilities, prolonged stress can have serious consequences [GDM11]. It can negatively affect feelings of self-worth, create feelings of inadequacy, and contribute to intercollegiate conflict. Stress can have negative effects on nurses' health, including heart disease, depression, burnout, and in severe cases, post-traumatic stress disorder (PTSD). In fact, Mealer et al. show that nurses in the ICU are more prone to suffering from PTSD than other subgroups in the profession [MSB+07]. In addition, the stress increases the risk of inattentiveness and involuntary negligence, which in turn puts patients at risk. It is safe to say that the nursing profession is one of the most stressful ones. The percentage of members of the workforce suffering from stress and illness is noticeably higher (between 14% and 18%) when compared to the general population [KPGW16].

Chronic stress in an ICU is one of the major reasons for staff leaving the workforce early. Considering the increasing number of elderly people and thus a growing number of people in need of care puts the health care system under strain. For Germany, it is estimated that the number of patients (in the long-term care sector alone) will grow by 70% by 2050 [RKM+15]. To deal with this increase in patients, more nurses are required. Similarly, the American Association of Colleges for Nursing describes that nursing schools have had problems in the past with low enrollment numbers for nursing college programs, citing staff shortages and insufficient clinical placements [Ros]. These numbers demonstrate that securing care will be increasingly difficult and poses one of the greatest challenges of the future. To support nursing staff, the development and implementation of mental health programs, i.e. reducing stress and thus improving job satisfaction and overall health, could prove beneficial [CBH+06].

---

[1] https://www.healthcareexecutive.in/blog/stress-for-healthcare, last accessed December 2nd, 2023

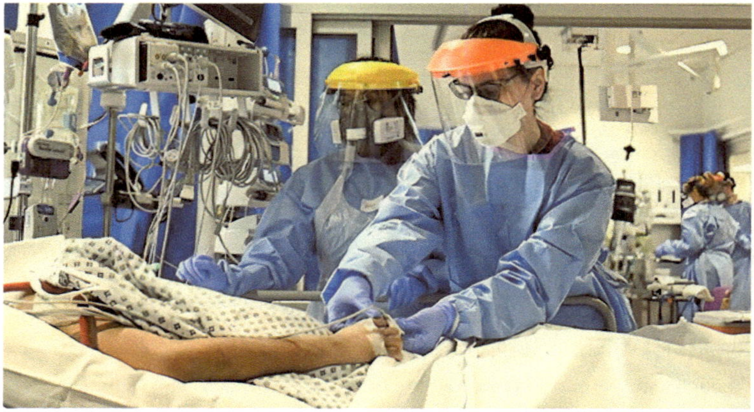

Figure 1.1: Two nurses in full personal protective gear tending to a COVID-19 patient.

Policymakers on both governmental and institutional levels need to implement a range of approaches that include both short- and long-term solutions to counter a pending nursing shortage. This includes improvements on the management level to increase job satisfaction, such as flexible schedules, or the utilization of modern technologies to help relieve some of the burden, both physical and mental. For nurses to respond more effectively to occupational stressors, i.e. to boost resilience, both professional and mental resources need to be increased. In the organizational context, resilience means the ability to respond to stressors in an appropriate and timely fashion [VR21]. Fortunately, dealing with stress can be learned and trained, so the investment in mental health can start as early as during the apprenticeship.

Over the years, several individual interventions to decrease occupational stress as well as coping mechanisms have been used and taught in nursing. In a review of these techniques, Velana and Rinkenauer found and investigated 27 publications working on this topic. The research presented in their review most commonly applied technology-delivered interventions for stress management, using websites or mobile phone apps. Other forms can be classified into mindfulness and spirituality interventions, cognitive-behavioral approaches, and physical approaches [VR21]. Most of them, however, do not fit into the educational context or have to be repeated at regular intervals (physical approaches like massages or acupuncture). Approaches that employ mindfulness and spirituality require nurses to dedicate some time during the day (mantras, breathing exercises). A sensible approach would thus be to teach nurses the necessary skills to cope with stressors before the stress becomes overwhelming. Velana and Rinkenauer include one study in their review that uses a smartphone-based approach for self-help stress management called stress inoculation training (SIT) [VGC$^+$13]. SIT is a general, framework-like approach in which stressors are simulated so one can learn to cope with them before handling the non-simulated stress. As simulations, i.e. mimicked versions of real environments or entities [EAHB15], they can be implemented into the education of nursing apprentices, as teaching in the classroom is not only carried out in the form of traditional frontal teaching. Other forms of simulation, such as role-playing, are also employed.

Role-plays are called experiential learning that can be delivered in different degrees of reality. They can be used with students individually (one-to-one) or as group role-plays [RS10]. Participants take on a role and follow a designated script. Role-plays can range in realism from scenarios in which only roles are taken on, to classrooms that are partially rearranged and equipped with medical equipment for greater realism, to so-called skills labs, specially equipped laboratories in which sometimes professional actors play a role. Role-playing can immerse learners in a simulated real-life situation that is experienced in an implicitly safe environment. They are highly adaptable and cost-effective, in contrast to simulations or standardized patients which can be expensive and require training to be used correctly [BC23]. Simulations focus more on the general situation as well as problem-solving and aid in the development of awareness for the environment students will work in. While in the late stages of the apprenticeship, students learn in the field, this is not the case for first or second-year students, where simulation techniques are most commonly implemented. As role plays are often conducted during classes, they happen mostly in classrooms, at times temporarily rearranged as makeshift patient rooms.

In some cases, educational facilities have set up a clinical skills laboratory (CSL), or at least have access to one. CSLs are rooms modeled after real clinical environments. In the early 2000s, they became an educational tool wherein students could learn and try their newly acquired skills in an implicitly safe simulation environment. Safety is one of the best arguments for CSLs, as it helps to remove pressure from students as well as protect patients [EAHB15]. The acquisition of practical skills in the CSL is organized in various ways, using different educational approaches and simulation levels. The simulation fidelity may vary, ranging from low- and medium-fidelity simulation, to high-fidelity simulation where different healthcare scenarios are built with computerized models [Har10], see Figure 1.2. Using simulations, one can create replicas of certain aspects in varying degrees of fidelity and provide students with learning opportunities in a safe environment until competency in a particular skill is achieved [SN21].

These approaches all have their benefits and drawbacks. Schools, in many cases, have to fall back to using training based on role-play in re-purposed classrooms for financial reasons, which may lack the necessary realism for safety critical or stressful situations [HRP13]. Furthermore, the CSL would only operate during the opening hours of the school, thus students are limited in their ability to learn in their spare

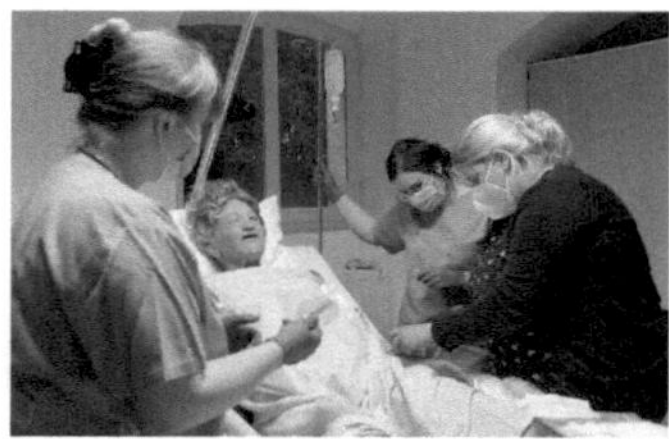 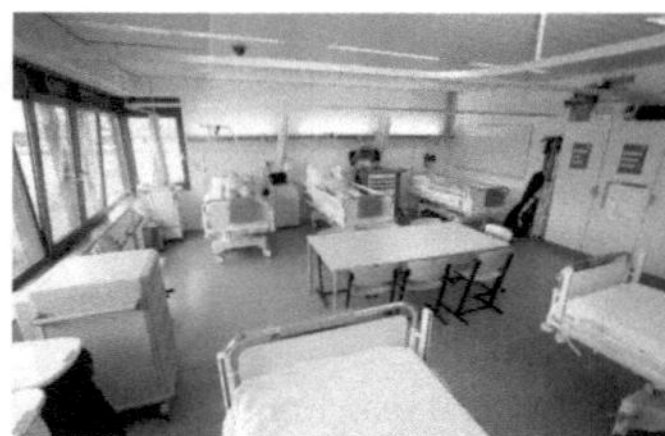

(a) Nursing students (left, right) engaging in role-play, under instruction by the nursing practice instructor (center). With friendly authorization from Friesland Kliniken gGmbh.

(b) A skills lab featuring several workstations for simultaneous learning of different skills. With friendly authorization from www.skills-med.de

Figure 1.2: Provisionary patient rooms in a classroom (left) and a highly realistic skills labs are at opposing ends of possible realism for educational environments.

time. Using virtual reality, one could not only combine the advantages of both of these teaching methods but at the same remove the disadvantages.

Virtual Reality, VR for short, is defined as "a computer-generated digital environment that can be experienced and interacted with as if that environment were real" [Jer15]. For this dissertation, we consider head-worn displays as a means of experiencing VR, even though there are other modalities. Using computer-generated environments, it is possible to create highly realistic depictions of hospital rooms, as well as the acoustic atmosphere. Through the application of virtual characters or multi-user applications, role-play scenarios can be experienced, even at a distance. It further allows creating rare, but critical situations, such as dementia patients or aggressive patient families. These situations can then be experienced in an inherently safe virtual environment (VE). Modern VR systems are mobile, so students can use them at home and continue learning in their spare time. Additionally, consumer devices are affordable and thus available on a low budget. The immersive capabilities of virtual reality make it a viable and powerful tool in nursing education. Another advantage of VR simulations is the high repeatability and reproducibility of training scenarios. In these training scenarios, one can combine simulations and role-play in a game-like experience. Games can be an engaging, highly authentic learning experience. The timely feedback provided in games supports the student's grasp of a subject and supports the application of learned skills in real situations [CG09].

The idea is to create a VR skills lab where students can use SIT within a virtual ICU. This way, they can become familiar with the inherent stress of their profession and the right coping strategies. Research shows that VR as an ecologically valid simulation environment has been successfully used as a tool for SIT simulation in other disciplines [FKD+18a, CJH+19]. Until now, the application of this combination has not been specifically used in the nursing profession. There is a lack of implementation of (intensive) care stressors in VR and evaluation of their ability to generate stress. This dissertation contributes to the implementation and demonstrates the effectiveness of virtual stressors for use in stress training.

1.1 Challenges and Opportunities

The challenges of inducing stress through VR experiences are discussed in this section.As related work has demonstrated, VR has been successfully used as a powerful simulation tool in other safety-critical professions, such as medicine [GBW+16], aviation [VCJ17], as well as police [BMC15] and firefighting [GJ21] operations. There is also existing research that combines VR with SIT as part of pre-deployment training for emergency medical technicians [PWD+19a]. By using SIT in VR, it could be possible to support nurses in acquiring the right coping skills or developing stress resilience through different trainings.

However, the literature in the field shows several factors that need to be considered to make SIT usable for nurse education. To the best of our knowledge, there is no published research specifically combining VR and SIT for nurses. It is therefore not currently known what is required of the virtual ICU environment to be perceived as real, or what stressors can and should be used to apply SIT. Yet, SIT is only an effective anti-stress tool if utilized correctly. This also includes using potent stressors, as otherwise, a stress reaction can not be evoked, rendering the intervention pointless. Furthermore, related work has only in a few cases compared the realism or stress-inducing capabilities with non-HMD results, e.g. [CJH+19]. To position VR as a useful solution, however, it is crucial to compare results to the status quo.

Creating an Immersive Environment

Establishing a robust connection between the simulated situation and how students perceive its fidelity and realism is crucial to creating a truly authentic scenario and poses the first challenge. Immersion and realism are key to drawing students to the technology and committing to learning with it [MMP+18, NBR13]. It has been shown that perceived realism influences both the attainment and retention of knowledge. This methodology allows the creation of fictional environments that replicate real situations. The more realistic the situation presented and perceived, the better the participants can immerse themselves in the simulation and achieve the learning and training objectives [CMPMSI+23].

Stressors Need to be Effective

The second challenge is the design and implementation of the stressors in VR, which must closely resemble their real-life counterparts for SIT to succeed. Further, the stressors used in the training need to increase the stress level of the trainee. To ensure this, the change in stress level during the experience must be measured. On the one hand, this is important to demonstrate that virtual stressors influence stress levels, and on the other, to enable teachers and students to evaluate progress in the development and application of stress-coping skills.

From the Lab to the Classroom

The third challenge is being able to estimate on how closely the stress that has been created in such a VR simulation resembles the stress that is being experienced by trainees in a skills lab. By achieving similar stress levels in both situations, one could argue for the financial benefits of VR simulations without the low realism levels of a classroom role-play, and the bonus of availability and mobility of modern VR systems.

1.2 Research Goals and Contributions

The aforementioned challenges are the starting point for the research presented in this dissertation. This section serves to more closely describe the challenges and formulate the research questions (RQs) we have been contributing to. As presented, it is paramount to help nurses cope with occupational stress not only in their own interest but also in the interest of patients and to relieve the burden on the healthcare system.

Research has shown that while several coping strategies are available and have been used, many of them fall short of delivering long-term effects or require several weeks to take effect. Current VR headsets can cost-effectively deliver highly immersive environments and have shown to be an effective tool for SIT. Nevertheless, related research has tested only the stress-inducing capabilities of their scenarios in isolation. We strive to create a more holistic experience that takes into account both nursing teachers and students, to show that it is an effective tool for stress inoculation and that it could serve as an additional simulation tool to CSL. Following the Human-Centred-Design Process [ISO19], the first research question, therefore, deals with the requirements of prospective end users:

RQ1: What are the requirements for VR software to be used as a stress management tool in nursing training?

We make the following contributions: First, we collect organizational and technological requirements by synthesizing data from shadowing sessions, focus groups, expert interviews, and an online survey. Second, based on these requirements we develop an apparatus and virtual environment that is suitable for educational institutions. Third, we identify relevant stressors that are named frequently as major contributors to occupational stress: time pressure, task interruption, and moral distress. Finally, we provide a measurement toolbox to measure the change in stress levels both on from an objective and a subjective point of view.

SIT can only develop a positive effect on stress coping when the simulated stressors evoke a stress reaction from the participants. If a stressor is ineffective, the nervous system will not react and there is no need to apply coping mechanisms. Therefore, the major part of this thesis deals with the analysis of the effects of the implemented stressors, covering different stressor categories to address the second research question:

RQ2: How can different occupational stressors from the nursing profession be replicated in VR and what effect do they have on users?

We address this question by researching the effect of three different stressors. Through participatory design, we iteratively conceptualize virtual versions of the stressors and subsequently implement them into the virtual ICU. By exposing study participants to these stressors and collecting information about their stress levels pre- and post-experiment, we demonstrate that the mimicked stressors have a stress-inducing ability and can thus be used as part of an SIT. We further present insights on the mental workload of the experiment.

Having investigated the efficacy of the stress-inducing capabilities of the virtual software, the last research question aims at the ecological validity of the experiment, as factors such as novelty and usability of the VR system may influence the stress reaction. This is investigated in RQ3:

RQ3 To what extent are VR stress and real stress comparable when using a full simulation?

To make statements about the ecological validity of the VR environment, we create a new scenario encompassing all three previously measured stressors and implement it in both VR as well as our own skills lab. We contribute the results of objective and subjective stress measures, as well as the comparison in simulator realism of both environments as measured by the ProRealSim questionnaire [CMPMSI+23]. The results of this study thus provide important insights into the perceived realism of our VR scenario when compared to an equal scenario that is presented in a skills lab. We show that VR can mimic the realism of a skills lab.

1.3 Methodology

As we aim to develop for a specific professional group, we need to ensure that our research takes into account the very particular needs and requirements associated with the profession and its training. To achieve results that meet these requirements, we follow the Human-Centred Design (HCD) process described in Chapter 7 of the DIN-ISO 9241-210 standard. The HCD process is an iterative cycle of four inter-linked human-centered design activities [ISO19]. However, before we started the implementation, we carried out comprehensive requirements engineering. With this process, we identified stakeholders and their needs. The process also includes analysis, communication, and the subsequent implementation [Sut02]. In short, requirements engineering ensures that we are "designing the right thing" [Boe81]. Because of this, we involve the target group in the processes early on to emphasize that both the development and the evaluation of the experimental scenarios are strongly supported by nurses and nurse educators. Throughout our research, we collected feedback on the studies and adopted the suggestions in the virtual skills lab in an iterative manner.

For this thesis, we used a mixed methods approach with an exploratory sequential design, i.e. we implemented a series of different VR scenarios based on extensive expert knowledge. Subsequently, we evaluated the scenarios with members of the target group to gain insight into the effects the scenarios have on users, which is in line with the concept of "research for design". To contribute to the first research question, we collected requirements and design ideas in the form of multiple semi-structured interviews, focus groups, and shadowing in both professional and educational contexts. These approaches provide a deep insight into the professional environment, e.g. how an intensive care unit is structured, what tasks are involved there, and further how students are currently educated, what methods are used, and what problems arise. In doing so, we created an extensive knowledge base from which we built the different building blocks used in these studies, i.e. a laboratory for mixed reality research, the virtual skills lab, and the stressors and scenarios used during the experimental studies. We further combined an established storytelling technique with suggestions gained from expert interviews. The resulting VR scenarios as well as the research artifacts are examined in user studies concerning their stress induction capabilities and various other qualities.

The combination of quantitative and qualitative research methods allowed us not only to investigate the effectiveness of the stressors but also to acquire feedback in the form of questionnaires. These questionnaires were used to gain insight into other relevant factors such as felt presence (IPQ [SFR01], the task load [HS88], and realism [CMPMSI⁺23]). We executed several experimental studies to investigate the effect of several isolated stressors specifically. In the user studies, we utilized both physiological and subjective parameters to quantify the stress responses of participants thus contributing to the second research question. It should be noted, however, that although laboratory studies make it possible to exclude confounding factors, the results should not be regarded as universally valid. For this reason, the final study aimed to answer the third research question by investigating how participants' responses differed between the virtual ICU environment and a skills lab.

The combination of these methods makes it possible to draw holistic conclusions about the stress response and perceived realism within the virtual skills lab as opposed to the status quo in education. Based on these findings, we derive recommendations for the design and implementation of similar environments and experiments for practitioners and give an outlook for future research.

1.4 Thesis Outline

In this section, we provide an overview of the contents of each chapter of this dissertation. A graphical representation of the general content structure can be found in Figure 1.3.

Chapter 1 aggregates knowledge about the major topics of this dissertation: stress, nursing care, and virtual reality. We introduce what stress means in nursing and how caretakers receive education. Further, this chapter briefly describes how stress management can be integrated into education and what role VR can play as a part of simulation and role plays. The chapter also deals with the challenges that come with the research goals. Subsequently, we describe our general research approach, summarize the contributions made, and end the chapter with a list of the published research.

Chapter 2 lays the knowledge foundation about stress, its triggers and consequences, and why stress is particularly critical in the nursing context. Furthermore, we describe stress coping mechanisms, specifically SIT. The chapter also describes how stress can be measured. It further provides a basic understanding of VR technology and its underlying concepts. We show the results of an extensive literature review on previous work using VR to induce stress and derive ways how stressors from the nursing context could be transferred into VR. We also outline current applications in nursing education. Ultimately, the chapter highlights how VR is already being used in stress management.

Chapter 3 provides contributions to RQ1, as it discusses the user research we performed to collect the requirements for VR-based SIT training in the educational context. Further, we present the development of the overarching study system we used to create and evaluate the stressful scenarios described in Chapters 4, 5, and 6: a mixed reality laboratory, the virtual environment used in the studies, a scenario control software, and the measurement battery we employed to quantify the stress response in our participants.

Chapter 4 and Chapter 5 contribute to RQ2. Chapter 4 demonstrates the research on the environmental stress present in an ICU ward, what stressors are involved, and how they can be replicated in VR. We describe in detail how we designed and evaluated a user study comparing the effect of both time pressure and task interruption as these are very prevalent stressors in the intensive care unit.

Chapter 5, on the other hand, explores the effects of a mental stressor: moral distress. A moral violation occurs when people are asked to act contrary to their knowledge or their moral compass. We create a storyline along the three-act structure for storytelling, focusing on a moral violation. We employ artificial characters, to de-

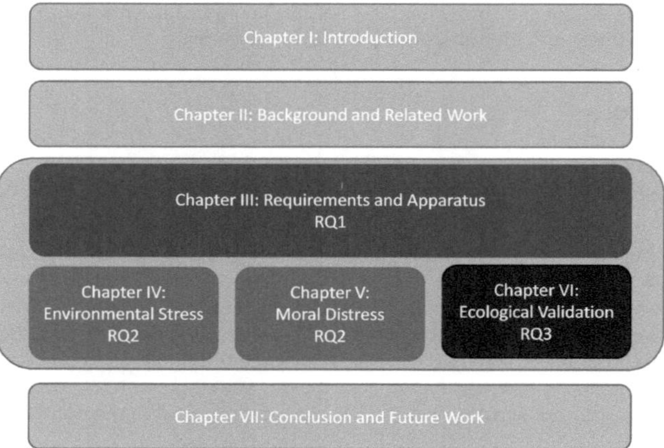

Figure 1.3: Structural setup of this document. Chapters I and II introduce the reader to the topic and provide background knowledge. Chapters III to VI comprise the research part, as they describe the approach, the study apparatus, and the results of studies conducted to contribute to research questions 1-3. Chapter VII concludes this work and offers an outlook for future research.

mand a specific course of action from trial participants, against their better judgment and measure the effect this has on their stress levels.

Chapter 6 investigates the ecological validity of the VR situation in a comparative study with a skills lab and therefore contributes to RQ3. We combine the stressors from the previous chapters to create a general test scenario. We present an upgraded storyline for moral distress and outline improvements in the details of the virtual environment. Expert knowledge is used to evaluate the artificial situation with respect to the degree of realism and the stress-inducing qualities in both the virtual and the laboratory simulation. The goal is to gain insight as to whether VR is capable of acting as a mobile, highly available skills lab.

Finally, Chapter 7 aggregates and highlights the contributions of this work and gives recommendations on how to conduct similar studies. Additionally, we discuss the systems' limitations and map out future research directions that have been discovered based on the results of the studies presented herein.

1.5 Contributions

The results of this work make several contributions. First, we present the systematic design and implementation of a specialized system for conducting studies in the context of intensive care with a high degree of realism, from requirements gathering to implementation. Secondly, we show how to design a stress induction and measurement apparatus using commercially available sensor technology and VR hardware. These results are highly relevant to other researchers in the field, as they can rely on the results to set up their study apparatus. The time-consuming process of designing a lab environment and selecting the right hardware can be greatly reduced.

The third contribution of this dissertation is the ecological validation of the results using a real-world scenario. Our results show that the virtual ICU environment is equivalent to a skills lab in terms of simulation quality. This shows that VR is a cost-effective, highly available alternative for simulation-based training. These results may be relevant for educators who do not have access to highly specialized skills labs, or for expert training that cannot take place on-site. Many important scenarios can be repeated and practiced by students as needed in a risk-free, self-directed manner.

Parts of this work have been published in scientific, peer-reviewed journals and conferences with a focus on human-computer interaction. The following list iterates over these publications, sorted by date, in ascending order. References will also be given in the respective chapters of these works are referenced in.

- Weiß, S., & Heuten, W. (2023, April). Don't Panic!-Influence of Virtual Stressor Representations from the ICU Context on Perceived Stress Levels. In Proceedings of the 2023 CHI Conference on Human Factors in Computing Systems (pp. 1-15).

- Weiß, S., Busse, S., & Heuten, W. (2022, March). Inducing emotional stress from the intensive care context using storytelling in VR. In 2022 IEEE Conference on Virtual Reality and 3D User Interfaces (VR) (pp. 196-204).

- Weiß, S., & Heuten, W. (2019). Exploring Stress Creation in VR for Task-Based Training in Nursing. Mensch und Computer 2019-Workshopband (pp. 1-6).

- Weiß, S., Cobus, V., & Heuten, W. (2021). Mixed Reality Collaboration Environment — It's a MiRaClE. In 4. Clusterkonferenz. Zukunft der Pflege (p. 1).

- Weiß, S., Bongartz, H., Boll, S., & Heuten, W. (2018). Applications of Immersive VR in Nursing Education—A review. In 1. Clusterkonferenz. Zukunft der Pflege (pp. 174-179).

- Weiß, S., Cobus, V., & Heuten, W. (2020). Bedarfe für Virtual Reality Basierte Stress Trainings in der Pflege. In 2. Clusterkonferenz. Zukunft der Pflege (pp. 1-4).

- Weiß, S., Lindt, D., & Heuten, W. (2023) Usability of PC-based Dashboards to Control Virtual Reality Training Situations. In 6. Clusterkonferenz, Zukunft der Pflege (pp. 99-103).

Other works, that do not appear in this dissertation but have been contributing to idea generation and its outcome, are listed below.

- Weiß, S., Klassen, N., & Heuten, W. (2021, December). Effects of image realism on the stress response in virtual reality. In Proceedings of the 27th ACM Symposium on Virtual Reality Software and Technology (pp. 1-10).

- Weiß, S., Kimmel, S., Cobus, V., Boll, S., & Heuten, W. (2023). Virtuelle und Erweiterte Realitäten für den Einsatz in der Pflege. Springer Books 73-95.

- Weiß, S., Withöft, A., & Heuten, W. (2020). aVRaid of Heights?-Exploring Integrated Non-Invasive Sensors For Stress Testing. In 2020 IEEE International Conference on Healthcare Informatics (ICHI) (pp. 1-10).

- Müller, L. M., Mandon, K., Gliesche, P., Weiß, S., & Heuten, W. (2020, November). Visualization of Eye Tracking Data in Unity3D. In Proceedings of the 19th International Conference on Mobile and Ubiquitous Multimedia (pp. 343-344).

- Weiß, S., Kimmel, S., Withöft, A., Jung, F., Boll, S.,& Heuten, W. (2022). Elevating Stress Levels—Exploring Multimodality for Stress Induction in VR. Mensch Und Computer 2022 (pp. 338–342).

- Gliesche, P., Weiß, S., Gerdes, A., Heuten, W., & Hein, A. (2022). Suitability of Virtual Reality for Eye Tracking Studies in a Nursing Context. In 5. Clusterkonferenz Zukunft der Pflege (p. 12).

Further research is currently undergoing review:

- S. Weiß, D. Lindt and W. Heuten: Heart Rate Variability-Based Stress Detection in Virtual Reality Scenarios for Caregivers Using Machine Learning.

- S. Weiß, S. Kimmel, H. Sahin-Ippoloti, V. Cobus, W. Heuten: A Systematic Review of Stress Induction and Measure in Virtual Reality.

2 Background and Related Work

This chapter lays the foundation for all relevant topics that are part of this dissertation. After introducing the concepts of "stress" and "stressors" (see Section 2.1), we show how stress can be dealt with, focusing on stress inoculation (cf. Section 2.1.4). We explain ways to quantify stress, both subjectively and objectively, and discuss the challenges thereof (see Section 2.2).

We further cover VR as a concept and as a technology, providing insight into the key theories of presence and immersion (see Section 2.3). In addition, the related work in the field of VR-based stressor research is shown (see Section 2.4). From there, we map out the possible applications for stressors from different categories in the field of nursing.

To show how VR can be used as a teaching tool, Section 2.5 also introduces the status quo in current nursing education, touches on the field simulation-based training, and illustrates how VR can combine the advantages of role play and skills labs. Lastly, we present related work that shows existing research on the application of VR in healthcare simulation.

Parts of the material in this chapter have been published in Weiß, S., Bongartz, H., Boll, S., & Heuten, W. (2018). Applications of Immersive VR in Nursing Education—A review. In Tagungsband der 1 Clusterkonferenz (pp. 174-179). Further work is currently under review for publishing at ACMs Journal for Computing Surveys (CSUR).

2.1 Stress and Stressors

There are ample definitions of the term stress. It has first been used in a mechanical context as a measure of material fatigue, describing the results of forces acting on an object. In the biological context, Walter Cannon coined the term to describe the fight-or-flight response in mammals [Can29]. Hans Selye, who is also known as "the father of stress", used the term in the context of behavioral science, describing an individual's perception of threat, resulting in anxiety discomfort, emotional tension, and difficulties in adjusting [Sel76]. Stress reactions vary depending on several factors, and they differ among individuals. Because of this, recent studies have shifted towards an individualized approach to defining stress: according to Kim and Diamond, stress is not dependent on the physical variables of environmental stimuli, but on how an individual reacts to them [GSVP16, KD02]. The authors proposed a coarse, three-component definition of stress [KD02]:

1. Stress requires increased arousal, measurable through EEG, motor activity, or neurochemicals.

2. The experience must elicit a negative response (distress, as opposed to eustress).

3. The situation is affected by a lack of control since having control is a potent mitigating factor for a stressful experience.

In this context, external factors, experiences, and situations can be of either positive (eustress) or negative (distress) nature. Eustress describes "good" stress, e.g. a feeling of euphoria, and distress refers to "bad stress" due to the negative influence on body and mind [Sel76].

These influences are commonly referred to as "stressors". A stressor is defined as an external condition that requires a change in the system for it to adapt. This adaptation is called the stress reaction. Kaluza et al. differentiate between performance stressors (e.g. time pressure, exams, quantitative or qualitative overload), physical stressors (e.g. noise, excessive temperature), social stressors (e.g. competition, isolation, conflict, separation, and loss), and bodily stressors (e.g. injury, pain, hunger) [Kal18].

These different descriptions of the term "stress" are still linked to the original definition by Selye, as they all describe a process in which "environmental demands tax or exceed the adaptive capacity of an organism, resulting in psychological and biological changes, that may place persons at risk for disease" [CKG97].

2.1.1   The General Adaptation Syndrome

Selye's work also included the general stress adaptation syndrome (GAS) that unifies several physiological processes and pathological events. Selye defines the GAS as an "integrated syndrome of closely interrelated adaptive reactions to non-specific stress itself" [Sel50]. It is a three-step process, beginning with the alarm reaction (AR), continuing with the stage of resistance (RS), and terminating in the stage of exhaustion (ES). In each of these stages, the sympathetic nervous system (SNS) purposefully reacts to counteract the adverse stimuli. For an illustration of the GAS, refer to Figure 2.1.

During the initiation of the stress adaptation, the SNS activates adrenals glands to release the hormones adrenaline and nor-adrenaline, which in turn regulate the function of internal organs. The release of these hormones increases the heart rate, activates bowel movements, and controls sweat glands. This is often referred to as the fight-or-flight response.

Throughout the resistance stage, symptoms from the AR are reversed or disappear in case of a successful adaption to the stressor. Otherwise, they will reappear in the exhaustion stage. Throughout the RS, the body will try to overcome the initial stress response and will return vitals to normal if the adaption is successful. A prolonged stay in the RS can cause symptoms such as insomnia, digestive problems, and irregularities in the cardiovascular system. Should the stressor be persistent, hormones will be continuously secreted and the organism will reach the exhaus-

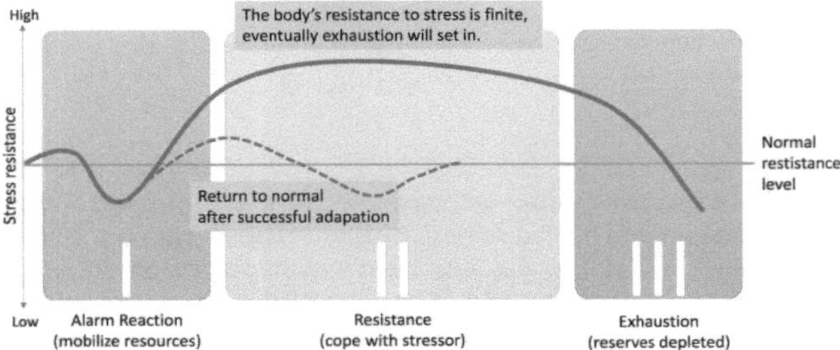

Figure 2.1: The three phases of the general adaption syndrome, adapted from [PBW06].

tion stage. Continued stress will inevitably lead to the exhaustion stage and result in fatigue and even burnout. This happens due to the strain that long-lasting stress puts on one's resources.

2.1.2 Stress in Nursing

As pointed out in the introduction, the nursing profession has been identified as a very stressful one, based on "its very nature" [SVBG21]. In this section, we want to give an overview of the stressors in nursing and how they affect staff.

Over the years, researchers have investigated the sources of stress both in the general hospital environment [CTMS18, HDRS+13, FBJ+13, MRB03] and in specific hospital wards, such as in palliative care [SVBG21], neonatal ICUs [LTFL+16], and palliative pediatric wards [LD08]. Further research has also been conducted in intensive care units (ICUs) [FZSBC90, VE69, DMTC+19, PTP+07, MHS+03, RHK15]. Laurent et al. summarized studies on occupational stress in nursing and further collected several nursing-specific stress questionnaires. Figure 2.2 shows the distribution of different stressors in questionnaires targeting specific settings.

Stressor Groups

Although the literature shows questionnaires about occupational in specific settings, they agree on the factors causing or influencing stress levels as well as on the consequences occupational stress carries. Based on the literature alone, several key sources of stress can be determined: poor working conditions such as low job control and high job demands, lack of support through management and colleagues, lack of essential resources, and frequent dealing with death and dying.

The identified key sources form the basis for the workshops in the requirement analysis (see Chapter 3), where specific stressors from the ICU environment will be selected with the help of experts. These stressors will be replicated in VR so the resulting software can be used as a stress induction tool, and help in decreasing the detrimental effects stress has.

Consequences

On the individual level, persistent stress among nurses can lead to physical ailments such as headaches, fatigue, and heart disease [CL20] and generally lower the body's self-defense capabilities [SG12]. It is also associated with hypertension and obesity [Fin17]. Mental consequences are also part of the issue: stress can trigger nervousness, anxiety, and burnout [HM00, CTMS18]. At the professional level, stress can contribute to conflicts within the staff and lead to reduced job satisfaction, absen-

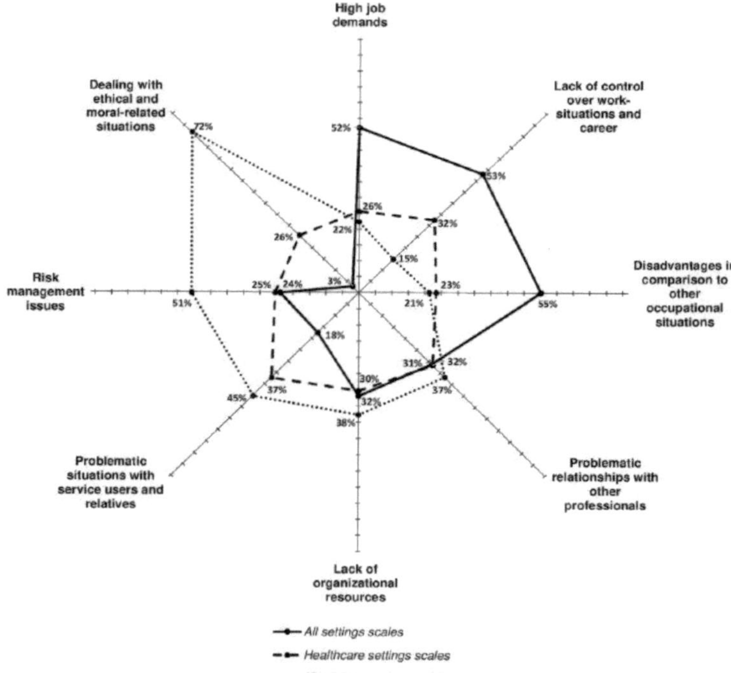

Figure 2.2: Stressor distribution over different wards and the frequency they are mentioned in nursing questionnaires, cmp. [LLG+20].

teeism, and high staff turnover [CTMS18]. In addition, patients also suffer from this problem. Stressed nurses show lower productivity, which affects the quality of care and the fulfillment of patients' needs [KDG+21]. Erroneous decisions or treatment errors caused by stress can hurt or even kill patients, which in turn will cause the nurse to suffer from feelings of guilt and second-victim syndrome.

2.1.3 Stress Coping Mechanisms

Lazarus and Folkman define coping as "thoughts and behaviors that people use to manage the internal and external demands of situations that are appraised as stressful" [LF87]. An individual who perceives changes in their social or physical environment initiates the process of coping to deal with the stress resulting from these changes. Coping mechanisms can be both positive (listening to music, socializing, getting busy, writing, etc.) or negative (self-negativity, overuse of nicotine, alcohol or other substances, impatient driving, etc). The selection depends on the individual circumstances [LA10].

According to Lazarus and Folkman, coping mechanisms can be classified as either problem-focused or emotion-focused [LF87]. Problem-focused coping involves taking actions to address the stressor itself, such as finding ways to remove it, evade it, or reduce its impact if it cannot be avoided. On the other hand, emotion-focused coping aims to minimize the distress that arises from stressors. Emotion-focused coping can take several forms, including self-soothing techniques like relaxation and seeking emotional support, expressing negative emotions like yelling or crying, focusing on negative thoughts, and attempting to escape stressful situations by using methods such as avoidance, denial, or wishful thinking [CCS10].

In a review of nurses' strategies for coping in nurses, Healy et al. found a correlation between occupational stress and mood disturbances, as well as a positive relationship between stress and job satisfaction. The use of avoidance strategies was a strong predictor for mood disturbances [HM00]. For nursing students, several studies have shown that problem-solving is the preferred coping strategy, while avoidance is the least applied. The problem-solving approach further proved to be beneficial to learning and professional performance, whereas emotional strategies are unhealthy [LMPG+16].

Several interventions have been developed and successfully applied to reduce stress on an individual level. The goal is often to increase the individuals' awareness of their stress levels and at the same time decrease the (subconscious) application of negative coping mechanisms. Common strategies to combat stress include mindfulness-based programs, physical training, and cognitive-behavioral techniques such as rational emotive therapy, cognitive restructuring, behavioral rehearsal, and stress inoculation therapy [VGC+13, VR21]. Cognitive-behavioral techniques can be extremely helpful in cases of burnout as they enable individuals to overcome unrealistic expectations and false hopes. Research has shown that some of these individual-level strategies are effective in reducing burnout. For instance, stress inoculation training can help individuals process information about stressful situations more productively and identify effective coping mechanisms to alter unproductive reactions, which can ultimately lead to a reduction in burnout levels [VGC+13]. As an example, West, Horan, and Games showed the efficacy of stress inoculation training on work stress management among 60 nurses [WHG84]. Stress inoculation training has already been proven to be an effective tool in the reduction of stress and has also been used in combination with VR. This conjunction promises to be a versatile tool for counteracting stress early on, as a cost-effective add-on to the current education styles. The next section introduces SIT in more detail.

2.1.4 Stress Inoculation Training

Stress induction is the process of gradually exposing people to stressors, thereby hoping to achieve a resilience-increasing effect, similar to how a vaccination works. To this end, the Canadian psychologist Donald Meichenbaum has developed a procedure called Stress Inoculation Training (SIT) [Mei77, MN85]. This structured, three-phase training can be applied in a self-instructional manner and preventive manner to help develop internal moderation that helps to regulate the coping response [VGC+13]. Due to countless combinations of stressors that can influence individuals or groups, SIT has to be tailored to these individuals or groups. It is furthermore meant to be used as a supplemental tool in conjunction with other therapeutic approaches [MN85].

Phase I: Conceptualisation

Initiating SIT, the practitioner usually interviews both the SIT participant and their family, asking questions about stressful incidents and creating assessments on the psychological and environmental factors. This stage serves as a familiarisation to tailor the following phases to the recipient of SIT and their situations. In this phase, recipients are educated about their stress patterns, the causes as well as effects, and are asked to reflect and reframe stressors in order to create opportunities to solve the problems associated with stress.

Phase II: Skills Acquisition

The second phase of SIT involves teaching the required coping mechanisms to handle their stress and anxiety. Once again, the therapist applying SIT considers the individual circumstances of the cases and adapts SIT to their client. Skills taught include - but are not limited to - exposure therapy, problem-solving skills, self-calming mechanisms like focused breathing, and diversion techniques. Clients are furthermore being taught how to deal with stressors out of their control, and how to make use of existing social support. As a last step before the third phase, clients shall consolidate the acquired skill-set and rehearse them with the therapist, discussing possible barriers and obstacles.

Phase III: Application and Follow-through

During the third and final phase of SIT, participants are exposed to stressors in a graduated manner and apply skills and mechanisms from the first two phases. To this end, the therapist either asks the client to imagine or visualize a stressful situation or creates a role-play scenario in which the stressors in question are included. A third possibility is engaging participants in in-vivo exposure, i.e. a real-world or (virtually) simulated scenario.

For SIT to be successful, the stressors used must be effective, i.e. they have to increase the stress level and feel real. Furthermore, the outcome of the intervention also needs to be verified. For this reason, the stress levels need to be quantified. The next section introduces several techniques that are used to measure stress.

2.2 Stress Measures

Given that stress is a complex, multidimensional sensation that influences physiology, behavior, and cognition, quantifying it is no straightforward task. The scientific community uses two broad categories: subjective and objective stress measures [AV13]. In the past, stress has been evaluated through human assessment, which involves people rating their stress levels on a scale or with questionnaires such as Brief Symptom Inventory [Der75], or the State Anxiety Inventory [Spi10]. Utilizing standardized questions or validated questionnaires, the subjective stress response of participants can be collected, which is why these measures are called subjective measures. Subjective measures have been shown to depict an accurate stress level [GSVP16].

As the physiological/physical stress reaction is controlled by the sympathetic branch of the autonomic nervous system (ANS) [SG12], it can be measured using devices that quantify the stress reaction via changes in the cardiovascular system or hormone levels. However, physiological reactions can also arise in contexts unrelated to stress, resulting in the problem of separation. Acquiring additional subjective measures is considered a sensible approach [SMS+20]. Thereby, the validity of the acquired physiological stress measurements can be assured.

To make an educated selection of stress-quantifying tools in a virtual environment, we executed a literature review of research that applied different stressors and stress measures in VR. Figure 2.3 visualizes the PRISMA[1] flow diagram, showing the process of search-and-review that was applied for paper selection. We categorized the stressors we identified in selected papers into a modified version of

---

[1] http://www.prisma-statement.org/ [PMB+21], last accessed October 5th, 2023

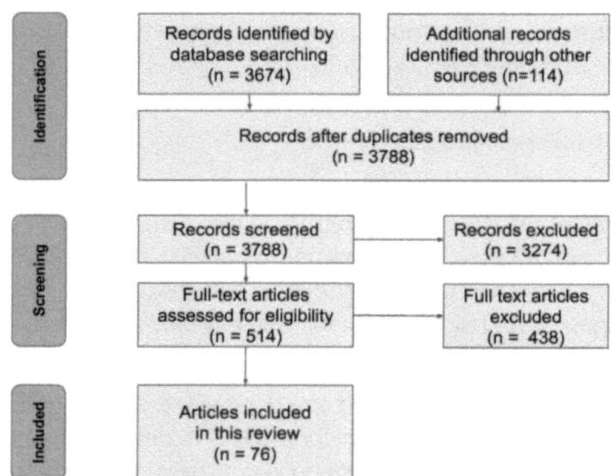

Figure 2.3: PRISMA flow diagram, visualizing database record research and inclusion process.

Kaluza's stressor categories. Considering that the act of wearing a virtual reality headset (see Section 2.3) is already a physical stress factor, we excluded the category "bodily stress", replacing it with the category "anxiety/phobia/fear". In the following subsections, we present both the various subjective and objective measurements that have been used by other researchers.

2.2.1 Subjective Measures

From the 76 publications covered in our review, twelve relied solely on measuring physiological reactions, and 49 employed these in combination with subjective and other stress measures. 15 of the analyzed research papers solely applied subjective and other outcome measures to quantify stress responses.

In contrast to the physiological measures, subjective/other measures were employed in a hardly individual and context-sensitive manner. On the one hand, this is highlighted by the fact that custom measurements are employed most frequently in each stressor category (see Figure 2.4). On the other hand, the same becomes apparent when one emphasizes that 36 different measures were used in 64 papers in which subjective and/or other measures were deployed. It should also be pointed out that 30 of those constructs were applied in just two or fewer papers. The measures included not only quantitative approaches such as Likert scales (e.g. [CWZ17, KZA$^+$20, KBL19, PLJS20]) or visual analog scales (e.g. [AGSM$^+$15, FTA19, GWKJ19, LLRJ15]), but additionally qualitative [WM18, LKHI21] as well as observational methodologies [LKHI21].

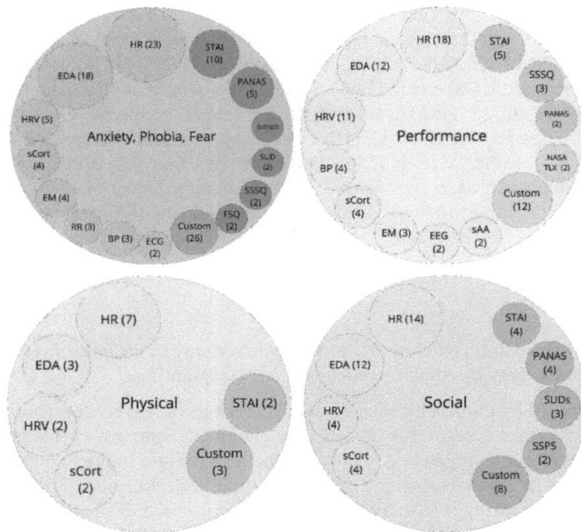

Figure 2.4: The circles show both the amount of objective and subjective measures applied per category. The diameter of the inner circles denotes frequency.

Apart from custom measures, the State-Trait-Anxiety-Inventory (STAI) developed by Spielberger et al. [Spi70, Spi10] was most frequently used (e.g. [AVS+20, BHB+18, CHO+17, LLRJ15, MMCK20, QNBB19]). The questionnaire was employed in a variety of different versions and different languages [Spi70, Spi10, MLO10, Jul11, MB92].

Other subjective measuring constructs recurring in a multitude of papers include the Positive and Negative Affect Schedule (PANAS) designed by Watson et al. [WCT88] (9 times, e.g. [AVS+20, DPLB17, DCBL18, BEW+21, KCE+14]), Subjective Units of Discomfort Scores (SUDS) created by Wolpe et al. [Wol58, Wol69] (5 papers, i.e. [BBH16, GWKJ19, JPKC+18, HKM+14, LB17]) and the Short Stress State Questionnaire (SSSQ) developed by Helton et al. [HN15] as a short version of a construct design by Matthews et al. [MSP+13] (e.g. [CJH+19, GWM+19, FKD+18b, WWH20]). The SSSQ was mostly employed in performance-related papers, while SUDS was only applied in contexts related to social and anxiety/phobia/fear-inducing stressors.

2.2.2 Objective Measures

The second major category in this dichotomy is the objective way to measure stress, i.e. the changes in physiology by which stress levels can be quantified.

The changes are caused by the ANS, as it is responsible for the stress reaction and in turn for the occurrence of measurable involuntary activities. Stressful events or emergencies cause dynamic changes in ANS, where the activity rate in the Sympathetic Nervous System (SNS) increases and the Parasympathetic Nervous System (PNS) activity decreases. During rest, activities in the PNS dominate. SNS and PNS regulate electrodermal activity, cardiovascular activity, and brain waves. Changes in these activities can be quantified and constitute the most commonly applied measures for stress used in literature. The regulation of the stress reaction through the ANS is classified as objective because it is involuntary and thus not influenced by an individual's perspective.

Objective measures can be subdivided into physiological and physical measures. Physical characteristics are features that change visibly and can be seen without specialized equipment, whereas physiological measures require sophisticated sensors to be quantified. Common physiological signals used in stress research include heart rate (HR) and heart rate variability (HRV), electrodermal activity (EDA), and alpha-amylase content in saliva samples. Figure 2.5 shows where on the body the respective signals may be obtained.

In our review, we analyzed how researchers monitored the impact of a VR environment on participants' stress and presence levels. In the 76 contributions, we identified 18 different physiological measurements being used in 61 publications. Roughly 70% of the analyzed contributions applied more than one measure simultaneously. Figure 2.4 also includes the measurement technologies for the stressor category they have been applied in. We found that HR has been used in about 25% publications dealing with the stressor category of Performance stressors, and up to about 50% in the category Social stressors. Furthermore, EDA sensing technology has been utilized in around 27% of papers in the Anxiety/Phobia/Fear category, and about 20% in both Performance and Physical categories. Except for the

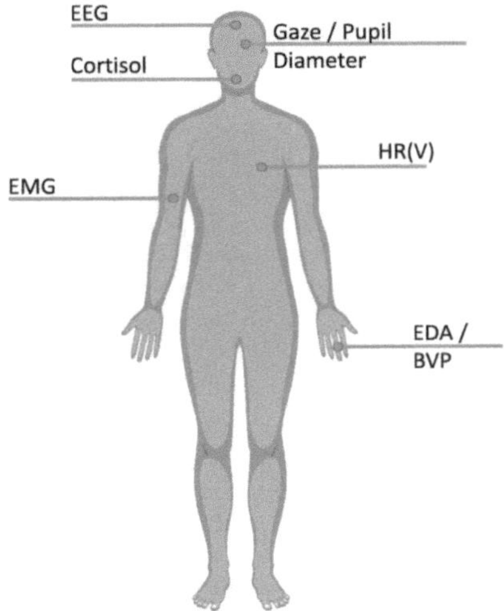

Figure 2.5: Frequently applied objective measures and their measuring site on the body. Adapted from [SG12].

Social stressors category, HR and EDA are the most frequently applied measuring techniques. Further, participants' HRV was also often observed (e.g. [SKM+20, SMS+20, RSS+20, LKHI21, GHP+19]). It was used in approximately 20% of Performance and Social stressor papers. In the categories Anxiety/Phobia/Fear and Physical, it was only used in about 10% of the reviewed publications. Moreover, salivary cortisol (sCort) levels were assessed in nine, blood pressure (BP) in six, and salivary α-amylase (sAA) and eye movement (EM) each in four of the reviewed studies as means to measure participants' stress response (e.g. [CZGZ20, DMK20, DPLB17, SZMD20, HEK20]). Finally, measures from the respiratory system have also been used to assess the stress levels of individuals [KCE+14, PLJS20, WWH20].

Measurement devices monitoring participant's brain activity, i.e. electroencephalography (EEG) were only employed very few times, and functional Near-Infrared Spectrum (fNIRS) was only used once. Salivary hormones have been tested for alterations throughout the experiment in 12 cases. Test kits for these hormones are widely available, and getting samples is not invasive, but it requires high standards in sterility and hygiene.

In general, it can be summarised that cardiac activity (HR, HRV, and BP) and EDA are the most frequently measured physiological characteristics in our review. They can be recorded with non-invasive sensors and easily analyzed with pre-written software libraries in various programming languages. More non-invasive measures can be collected from the respiratory system [THPC17, SAS+80].

Heart Rate

The HR is calculated as the mean heart contractions (beats) per minute. Because HR is controlled through the ANS, sympathetic stimulation, i.e. in response to stress or trauma, increases the HR, while parasympathetic activity decreases it. Although the exact numbers depend on the individual and their cardiac fitness level, a faster heartbeat is generally a sign of stress [SG12].

Heart Rate Variability

HRV is defined as the variation of the period between consecutive heartbeats over time and is thus dependent on the regulation of the HR. It can be used to assess the heart's ability to adapt to changing circumstances. The HRV has already widely been used as a primary measure for stress, as it is very useful in understanding the status of the ANS. A high HRV is a sign of a healthy heart, as it shows that the heart can quickly respond to external influences [GGG+19]. That also means that lower HRV is a sign of stress. In our studies, we report the root mean square of successive RR interval differences (RMSSD), a time domain measure of the HRV.

Electrodermal Activity

EDA is an umbrella term for measuring techniques that quantify skin conductivity or resistance. These values have been used as an indicator of stress in humans. In stressed individuals, an increase of moisture on the skin surfaces increases the conductivity of the skin. Conversely, in calm individuals, this conductivity decreases. Measuring EDA is highly suitable for monitoring activities of the ANS, as the sympathetic branch is dominant during stressful situations and solely controls the activity of the sweat glands [GGG+19].

Respiratory System

The minute ventilation (V_E (measured in l/min) increases as part of the stress response to a variety of stressors [THPC17]. The respiratory frequency (RF), measured in 1/min, is one part of the equation that governs the minute ventilation. The breathing volume, or tidal volume V_T, is the second part of the breathing mechanism contributing to V_E [THPC17]. The increase in V_E can be caused by hyperopnae (adequate increase in frequency and volume for metabolic needs), hyperventilation (exaggerated increase for the metabolic needs) or tachypnea (shallow breathing, RF < 20/min).

These measures can be recorded continuously throughout an experiment, enabling researchers to collect real-time information about the subject's stress response [GSVP16]. More importantly, they can be measured using non-invasive methods, which makes them suitable candidates for use in scientific experiments [RPF+19].

2.2.3 Challenges in Stress Quantification

When measuring stress, it is important to consider the environment and the context in which it is measured, as well as the feasibility of different questionnaires and measurement technologies.

There are several general and specialized questionnaires available in the stress literature. Many of them are specific to certain fears (dentist fear survey [KKA73], social phobia scale [MC98]) or are targeting anxiety instead of stress (e.g. STAI). While there are specific questionnaires for nurses, e.g. the nursing stress scale [GTA81], these tend to ask questions with respect to situations that cannot be covered in a virtual environment (e.g. lack of administration, having to work through breaks). A lot of research covered in our review opted for custom items that were specific to their setting, but not validated. While not included in our review, we found the PSQ20 [FRA+09] to be a good fit for our research. It has a manageable amount of questions and is kept general without covering topics aside from stress. However, the PSQ20 covers a period of four weeks, as do many standardized questionnaires. For this reason, we added a single 7-point Likert item as a second, instantaneous subjective measure. The question in the Likert item is "How stressed do you feel at this very moment?".

Practicability must also be taken into account in the objective measures. An EEG needs to be worn on the head and thus is impractical for our research, as we plan on working with head-worn VR devices. Eye-tracking can be done in certain VR headsets, but as stimuli and lighting conditions change unrelated to stressors, the data would be very noisy. Hormonal measures cannot be collected in real-time and are therefore also impractical The application of sensors for HR(V) and EDA is simple, and collecting data is both continuous and possible in real-time. Furthermore, there are high-quality sensing devices available on the market. Lastly, the analysis of the data is straightforward.

However, neither subjective nor objective measures are capable of providing a complete overall picture. Objective measures record all influences, even the physical strain of walking or wearing the VR device for a prolonged time. The same is true for the excitement due to the feeling of novelty for some users using VR for the first time. It is impossible to calculate the influence of a single factor towards the overall change in stress level. On the other hand, questionnaires do not quantify stress levels in real time and might be over- or underspecific. Moreover, answering them takes time which leads to a break in immersion between experiments.

Goyal et al. describe subjective measurement methods as the most reliable source for capturing stress, as objective measurement methods always rely on validation by subjective ones [GSVP16]. Nevertheless, to gain an accurate understanding of the stress responses, we make use of a combination of the two and consider other factors like the task load index and presence, both of which are predominantly measured with questionnaires. These will be introduced in Section 3.3.

2.3 Virtual Reality

Virtual reality, or VR for short, has been around since 1957, when Morton Heilig introduced his multimedia device "The Sensorama" [Hei92]. The technology behind what we now call VR only reached a form factor and price point that made it attractive to the consumer market in 2014. Since then, the term has been used in pop culture to describe the artificial, computer-generated - and hence digital - worlds that can be experienced through a head-mounted display (HMD) and interacted with through tracked controllers. To be more exact, the online dictionary Merriam Webster defines VR as an "artificial environment which is experienced through sensory stimuli (such as sights and sounds) provided by a computer and in which one's actions partially determine what happens in the environment"[2]. Freina et al. differ between two different pronunciations of the technology: immersive and non-immersive. While the first term describes the commonly used idea of VR which is a technology that "gives the perception of being physically present in the world", the second term characterizes the more simple concept of a "computer-based environment that can simulate places in the real or imagined worlds" [FO15]. These different forms of VR can also be sorted using Milgrams Virtuality Continuum, a concept introduced in 1994 [MK94] which is visualized in Figure 2.6:

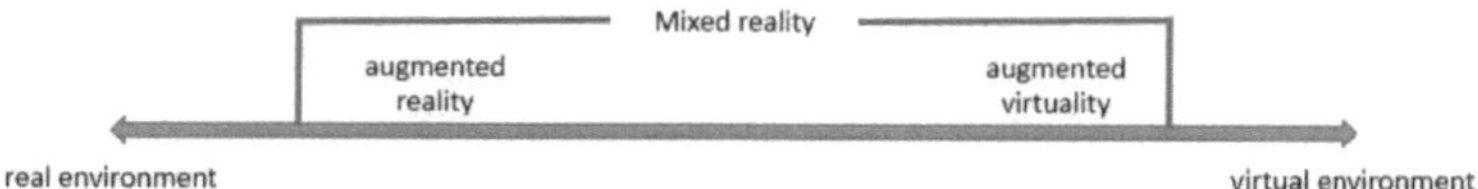

Figure 2.6: The virtuality continuum, adapted from [MK94].

This concept places different technologies on a spectrum that includes all possible forms and compositions of real and virtual objects. The left-hand side of the continuum describes our physics-based reality, but when moving toward the right side, more and more virtual content is added. First, we get to augmented reality (AR) where digital content is added to the real world. Often, this means visual content (e.g. Pokemon Go[3], an AR game released on July 6th, 2016), but can also mean audible enhancements (audio augmented reality, AAR [YBB22]). The next step towards

---

[2] "Virtual reality." Merriam-Webster.com Dictionary, Merriam-Webster, https://www.merriam-webster.com/dictionary/virtual%20reality. Accessed 22 May. 2023.
[3] https://pokemongolive.com/?hl=en

"true" virtual environments is augmented virtuality, where real objects are brought into the virtual space, such as using existing planes as a virtual tabletop game. A "virtuality", a wholly virtual reality, that lets users physically interact with objects and be fully present would fulfill Ivan Sutherland's description of the "ultimate display" from 1965: "The ultimate display would, of course, be a room within which the computer can control the existence of matter. A chair displayed in such a room would be good enough to sit in [...]"[S$^+$65]. However, this concept has been criticized in the past for its inexact wording concerning continuity, firstly because true virtuality can never be achieved and secondly because it limits the concept of what is now commonly understood as mixed reality (MR). However, it is embraced by the community and eases the understanding of augmented and virtual reality as well as the technology conveying these concepts to users.

In this thesis, we use VR as a term to describe a computer-generated environment that reproduces light and sound to make the user believe they are located in an ICU, and that they can freely move around and interact, whilst being on-site in our laboratory.

The concept of VR encompasses three important characteristics: Immersion, Presence, and Interactivity. These are described in the following paragraphs.

Immersion

The effect VR has on the users' minds and their perception of the virtual environment as a real one is primarily mediated through Immersion. In the context of VR, immersion is defined as the technical ability of the VR system (the combination of hardware and software) to stimulate visual, auditive, and haptic senses in a way that is extensive, matching, surrounding, vivid, interactive, and plot informing [SUS94, Jer15].

Extensiveness describes the amount of sensory channels that a VR system uses to transfer data to the user. The most commonly used channels are visual and auditory, but haptic/tactile as well as olfactory devices have been conceived to increase the immersive capabilities of modern VR systems.

Matching describes how well a VR system establishes concurrency between modalities, such as the correct and simultaneous alteration of real and virtual locations when walking in the physical space.

The surroundness of an experience is influenced by the field of view (FoV) of a device, and how far the panoramic extent of the virtual content spreads. Further factors are the quality and extent of tracking and spatialized audio.

By improving the graphical fidelity in terms of realism (i.e. colors, lighting) and by improving technical factors such as frame rate, resolution, and audio bit rate, the vividness of VEs can be increased.

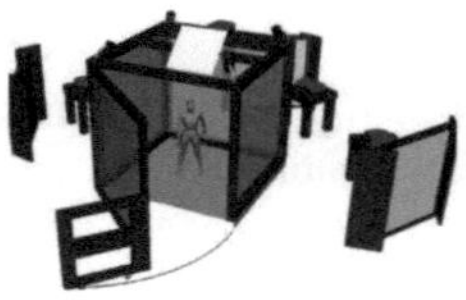

(a) A CAVE (cave automatic virtual environment) system, consisting of projections on several walls that surround the user [Muh15].

(b) Google Daydream, a head-mounted case that uses the display of compatible smart-phones to offer VR in 3 de-grees of freedom.

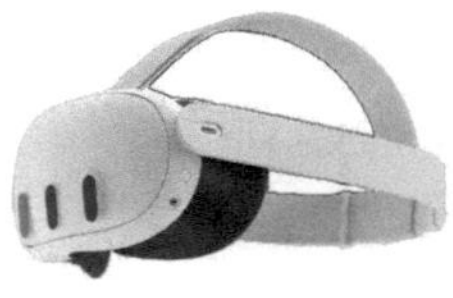

(c) Meta Quest 3, a 6 degrees of freedom HMD capable of mixed reality.

Figure 2.7: Different hardware solutions offering distinct degrees of immersion.

The more changes users can make to the virtual world, and the better the quality of the VEs response to those actions, the higher the resulting interactivity is.

The plot is the storyline of a virtual experience, defined by the consistency of the events happening in the virtual world, as well as the believable behavior of the entities within [Jer15].

Today, different VR systems on the market offer varying degrees of immersion. These differ most prominently in their display technology, as exhibited in Figure 2.7.

Presence

Immersion is the primary driver of a concept called Presence, although some researchers use these two terms interchangeably [OBW18]. Presence relates to "the subjective experience of being in one place or environment, even when one is physically situated in another" [WS98]. Several factors play a role in creating a sense of presence, see Figure 2.8. Throughout this work, we refer to this definition of presence.

Presence comprises several sub-dimensions, i.e. self-presence, telepresence, and social presence [OBW18]. Presence can influence emotional states [SUS94] as well as the behavior and reactions to stimuli in VR [RM19]. It is considered the defining factor for VR to work, meaning to fully enfold the illusion of being in another place [SAP+19].

The connotation of presence to being the subjective feeling of 'being there', however, does not fully describe the term. Slater et al. note that presence is rather rooted in the way users respond to the virtual surroundings and their ability to interact and modify them. According to them, presence arises when "there is the successful substitution of real sensory data by virtually generated sensory data" [SLASV09]. They further separate the term presence into two sub-components, namely Place Illusion (PI) and Plausibility Illusion (PSI). PI describes the type of presence that makes one feel like 'being there', despite knowing for a fact that this is untrue. PSI, on the other hand, is the illusion that the things that happen actually do happen, even if the recipient knows better. This includes physical plausibilities, such as gravity and collision [Sla09, WM18].

The concept of presence can be measured subjectively, similar to stress, using questionnaires. Objectively, one can use physiological signals (see Section 2.2) for presence measurement. Several different types have been identified, roughly divided into brain-related (with EEG being the most common measure) and brain-unrelated measures. However, physiological measures have often shown ambiguous results when measuring the presence, or the results could not be replicated [GL20].

Interactivity

The third characteristic, Interactivity, describes "the degree to which users of a medium can influence the form or content of the mediated environment" [Ste92, WS98]. These interactions are afforded by virtual elements and are mediated through

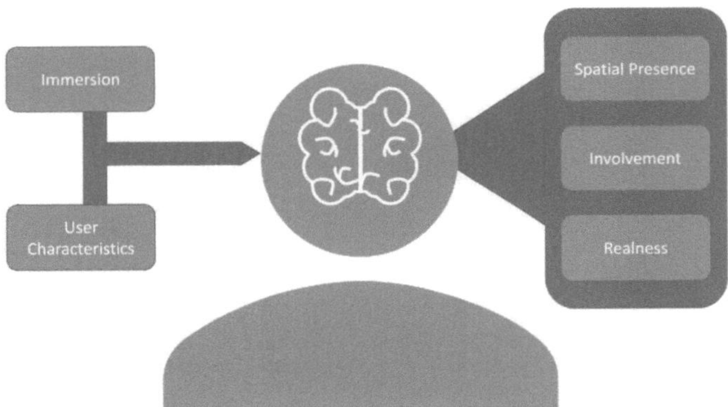

Figure 2.8: Presence as a psychological response to immersion influenced by the person's characteristics, adapted from [Mai18].

controllers [PPM22]. More generally speaking, the term refers to the user's participation in the information flow facilitated through computers, or in the case of modern VR, the HMD. Ippoliti et al. describe three different levels of interaction, the lowest of which is defined by the possibility of information selection, whilst the middle and highest levels add the insertion of content and the reaction of the environment to user input, respectively [ICCG].

2.3.1 VR Technology

Different technologies are commonly referred to as VR, generally as reality systems. These systems combine hard- and software to deliver content from the computing hardware to the user via a display and react to user input. The higher the degree of immersion a reality system offers, the better the users and their actions will blend into the experience. A (virtual) reality system comprises four different parts, two of which are input (tracking) and output (display). These can take several forms, e.g. world-grounded or tracked input, or visual, audible, or haptic displays. Together with application and rendering, these four parts are used by the user in the interaction cycle, as can be seen in Figure 2.9. Reality systems can take several forms, as the term is relatively broad: CAVE and AR devices are also referred to as reality systems, but the term VR commonly refers to head-mounted devices.

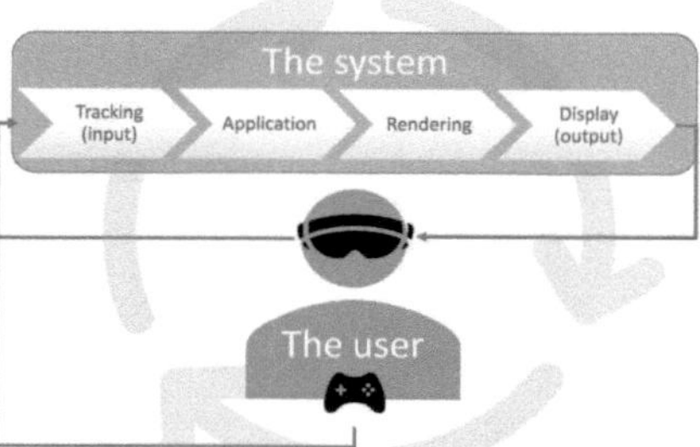

Figure 2.9: The user interacts with the VR system in a continuous cycle that includes user input, the application running on the VR system, the rendering process, and finally the updated output to the display. Adapted from [Jer15].

2.3.1.1 Head Mounted Displays

The first device that brought VR into modern pop culture was the Oculus Developer Kit I (see Fig. 2.10a), a wired and externally tracked headset, also called an HMD. HMDs combine visual displays and a sophisticated lens system in a wearable case. In some cases, the displays were "borrowed" from a smartphone (cf. Fig. 2.7b). The smartphone would separate the image into two different images with slightly different viewing angles, so the brain would be tricked into seeing a three-dimensional image. The case is then worn in front of the face, using a head strap. Some devices come with headphone jacks or a pair of speakers. Devices like the HTC Vive Pro[4] or the HP Reverb G2[5] are tethered devices. These devices are used to experience VR software that runs on an accompanying PC that takes care of the necessary calculations for rendering and tracking. Since then, the technology has gone through several revisions. Nearly 10 years later, Meta Inc. released the Meta Quest 3 in October 2023 (cmp. Fig. 2.10b). This is a lighter device with more modern lens technology, internal tracking, and enough processing power to run independently from a computer (note: it is not the first device with these features, we just use it as an example). It further is capable of mixed reality, i.e. rendering virtual objects into reality, using the device's cameras to show the environment on the display (video-see-through). This allows the users to bring the device along with them and use it independently from a PC. Users can freely roam around their play area without having to pay attention to a cable.

2.3.1.2 Tracking

There are several different technologies used in HMDs that track changes in the device's six degrees of freedom (DoF). These changes are forwarded through the device's operating system to the software, which then updates the user's location within the virtual environment. There are outside-in and inside-out tracking systems. Outside-in systems employ external hardware (e.g. cameras) that follows

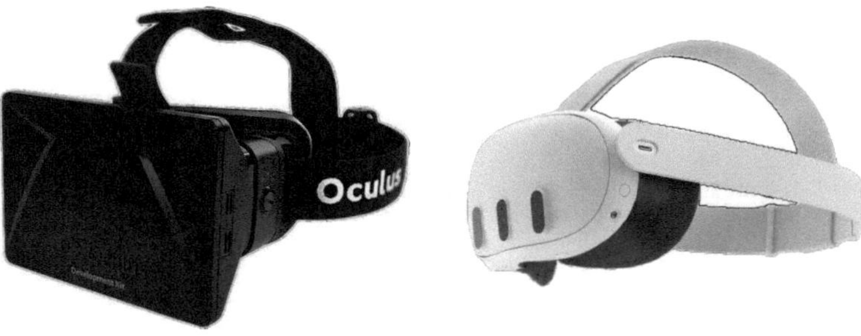

(a) Oculus Developer Kit, Version 1 (2013).   (b) Meta Quest 3 (2023).

Figure 2.10: Comparison between the Oculus DK1 and Meta Quest 3. Note the 10 year difference between the devices.

---

[4] https://www.vive.com/uk/product/vive-pro-full-kit/, last accessed Jan. 10, 2024
[5] https://www.hp.com/gb-en/vr/reverb-g2-vr-headset.html, last accessed Jan. 10, 2024

optical markers attached to the HMD and sends the position data to the application. Inside-out systems use feature tracking and a combination of sensors such as accelerometers and gyroscopes. These systems scan the ambient room for visual features, to create a coordinate system. The devices' relative changes in distance to these features, combined with inertia sensors, are calculated and subsequently translated into a change of position in the virtual world [DBGJ].

2.4 Stress Induction in VR

There is already a wide array of research investigating how stress can be induced in virtual environments. Virtual environments are implicitly safe as one does not deal with real stressors. Even more so, they are considered to be highly ecologically valid [MAF⁺19], which has a positive influence on training results. Results obtained from such training are considered to be comparable to those achieved using real-life training [AGSM⁺15, BBH16].

To get an understanding of the feasibility, diversity, and effects of applied stressors, we analyzed in our review (see Section 2.2) the types of stressors that have already been replicated in VR. To reiterate: the included publications were sorted into four categories, adapted and modified from [Kal18], see Figure 2.11 for a graphical representation of the results of this categorization. It is worth noting that the publications featured in this list have utilized a broad range of stressors, so we included each of them in all relevant categories, providing differing levels of detail for each sub-category in which they are applicable.

An in-depth analysis of all results would exceed the scope of this dissertation. Therefore, in the next sections, we will give examples of different stressors per category without going into excessive specifics. Figure 2.12 summarizes the different stressors from this section in a Sankey chart.

2.4.1 Anxiety/Phobia/Fear Stressors

This stressor category deals with the induction of stress in response to anxiety or fear triggers. Fear and anxiety are closely related, with fear arising in response to danger or threats, while anxiety is experienced when threats are unavoidable or uncontrollable [ÖLH93]. Anxiety disorders, also known as phobias, are caused by persistent or excessive fear of specific triggers, e.g. spiders (arachnophobia) or height (acrophobia) [Ass13].

After reviewing the 76 publications remaining after screening, we found that 41 works were using stressors that must be allocated to this category. The publications featured in this category use some form(s) of stressor(s) that may induce anxiety or induce a fear response in study participants.

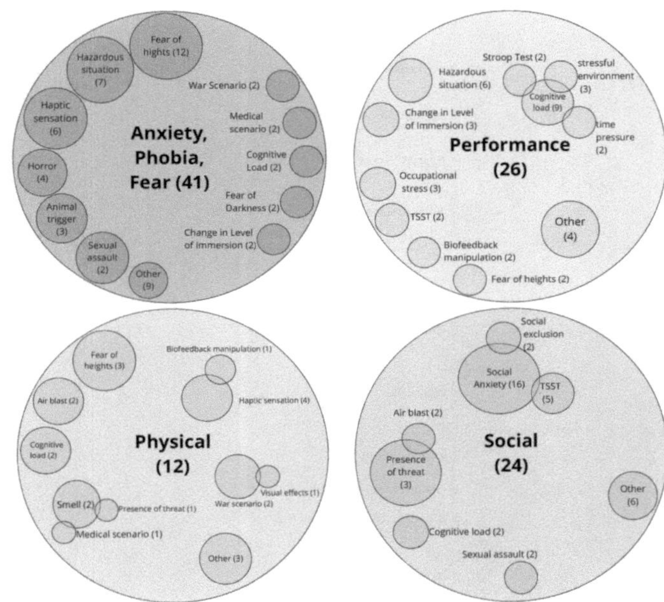

Figure 2.11: Visualization of applied stressors for each stressor category. The diameter of the inner circles denotes frequency.

In many cases, researchers use VR to approximate an ecologically valid environment to use in exposure-based therapy (ET) or similar fear-related interventions, e.g. acrophobia (e.g. [AVS+20, LLRJ15]), sexual and/or violent encounters ([KCE+14, LB17, SATS17]), post-traumatic stress disorder (PTSD, [MGS+20]), and others (e.g. animals or zombies [MWE19, KBBNZ20, MAS18, AGSM+15]). Notably, acrophobia has been the research focus in twelve publications [AVS+20, DLMZ16, FSZ+20, FKD+18b, FHF+18, LLRJ15, MAF+19, SAP+19, SATS17, TGCM19, WWH20, KvC21].

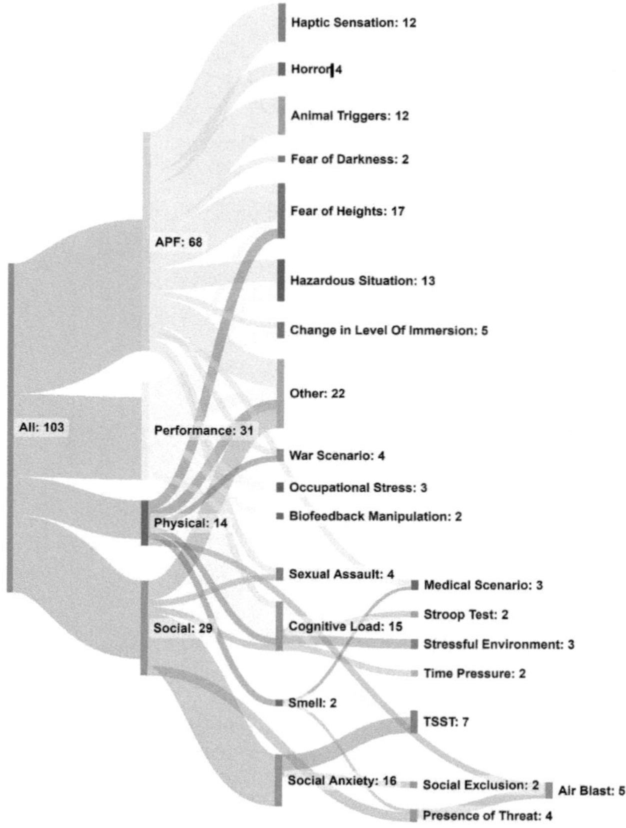

Figure 2.12: Sankey chart showing the distribution of stressors in stress categories. Note that some stressors fit into several categories.

One of the reasons for this may be that acrophobia can be easily recreated in VR, as it is highly reliant on the perception of height.

While these studies were used to intervene in existing fears or traumas, other research has investigated the use of to prepare subjects for stressful situations, such as medical procedures [GWKJ19, NKRB$^+$20] or hazardous situations [SZMD20, CWZ17, CZGZ20, TMG$^+$18, FKD$^+$18b, SMS$^+$20]. In hazardous situations, it is often the situation itself that creates a sense of fear. Researchers use virtual equivalences to invoke a sense of danger, such as fire or smoke [CZGZ20, SZMD20, SMS$^+$20] or rising water levels [HEK20, DLC$^+$15].

2.4.2 Performance Stressors

People perceive performance stress when they are placed under time pressure or experience an overwhelming amount of work. Performance stress also occurs for example when people are multi-tasking, partake in a competition, or await the outcome of an important exam [MHF15].

Researchers used a multitude of cognitive testing batteries to put participants under performance stress in 25 of the publications analyzed, e.g. [CHO$^+$17, FBS$^+$18, MLSRGR$^+$16, MBS$^+$20, RSS$^+$20, YYA$^+$20]. Other performance stressors were successful in eliciting stress by putting participants in emergencies, using simulated fire and smoke, accompanied by visual and aural effects [HEK20, SRN$^+$19, SRS$^+$18]. The same was reported in a study by Mosquera et al. [MGL$^+$19]. Dey et al. and Mosquera et al. showed that providing visual biofeedback in the form of a heartbeat in the software UI ([MGL$^+$19]) or in the virtual environment ([DCBL18]) can increase stress levels.

Performance stressors were also applied in research as a means to analyze stress elicited by occupational tasks. Scherz et al. [SMS$^+$20] highlighted the stress-inducing nature of completing a driving task. Das et al. [DMK20] implemented a crane simulation, showing that gaze behavior was significantly influenced by the perceived degree of danger. Studies conducted by Clifford et al. [CJH$^+$19] and Ferrandini et al. [FPETNFP$^+$18] both investigated whether tasks performed in VR can elicit similar stress levels as real-world tasks to evaluate the suitability of VR training in occupational contexts. In the reviewed publications, the research resulted in opposing results: while Clifford et al.'s aerial firefighter training elicited similar stress responses to regular training tasks, Ferrandini et al. monitored a decreased stress induction when comparing their health emergency VR training to clinical simulations. Induction of stress in a medical/emotional context was also researched by Prachyabrued et al. [PWD$^+$19a], who reported increased stress induction in medical training when presented in conjunction with social stressors.

2.4.3   Physical Stressors

Physical stressors are defined here as external factors largely beyond the control of the person experiencing them [Kal18]. These are included in - but not limited to - the following list:

- Visual Stressors. In virtual environments, it is possible to intentionally modify the way users perceive the surroundings. This can be accomplished by applying various alterations, such as vignetting, blinking, or blurring. It is important to note that we have excluded integrated environmental noises, such as wind. Our focus is solely on acoustic stressors, which are stimuli intended to cause stress through hearing.

- Haptic Stressors. Various sensory stimuli, such as vibrations, and real-world objects like fluids or planks, can induce stress in VR. Haptic stimulation can also administer electrical shocks to induce stress.

- Olfactory stressors. Using liquids or gases to induce stress by emitting certain smells, one can induce stress.

We found eleven contributions that used physical stressors. Misztal et al. compared different visual effects in a VR environment and their effect on intensifying the stress of a subject [MCZS20]. They implemented a VR scene in which participants interacted with objects in a shed while different events such as planes flying by or detonations could be seen through a window. Detonations were accompanied by visual effects like image noise, vignetting, and blur effects. The authors subsequently increased the intensity of alterations by adding added chromatic aberration as well as slight color grading. In a user study, they found that the perceived stress of the participants (n=6, using custom Likert scales) was more intense with visual effects than without. Moreover, their results indicate that these effects do not increase simulator sickness [MCZS20]. Other work that used visual stressors focused on simulating detonations, fire, and smoke is presented by Hirt et al. [HEK20], Shi et al. [SZMD20], and Schweizer et al. [SRS⁺18].

The most commonly applied acoustic stressors were simulated explosions or combat situations [HEK20, MGS⁺20, SRS⁺18, MCZS20]. We also found acoustic stressors that are closely related to the category Anxiety/Phobia/Fear (see Section 2.4.1), such as the noise of a dentist's drill [GWKJ19]. Even the sound of a beating heart in a multimodal set-up was mentioned to increase the perceived stress [MMCK20].

Three contributions used olfactory stressors to invoke stress in study participants. Schweizer et al. [SRS⁺18] used artificial fragrance to simulate the smell of smoke stemming from a car detonation. Gujjar et al. [GWKJ19] placed cotton wool soaked in clove oil around a dentist chair to create the environmental odor of a dentist practice for VR exposure therapy, thereby increasing the immersion in their multisensory VR environment.

Several studies suggest that combining different sensory experiences like sight, smell, and sound in VR settings can lead to increased levels of stress. However, there is a lack of research in the field of taste-induced stressors. Therefore, the use of smell and taste stimuli to induce stress has not been adequately explored. This represents a significant gap in research that should be addressed in future studies.

2.4.4 Social Stressors

Interacting with other individuals can create social stress. Responses to these stressors vary based on social skills and past experiences. Social stress can also evoke feelings of anxiety or fear.

The biggest common research item out of the 24 publications in this category was public speaking. We identified six publications that used a virtual equivalent of the Trier-Social-Stress-Test (TSST) [KPH93], a laboratory procedure to reliably induce (social) stress in participants [MBS+20, BBH16, DLC+15, KGG+21, ZWD19, MLSRGR+16]. Similarly, Brundage et al. investigated the utility of VR to examine the reactions of stuttering persons, giving a speech to a virtual audience, and subsequently compare the reactions to a similar situation but in an empty room [BBH16].

Several publications have explored the impact of violence and threats in VR [KCE+14, LB17, RPF+19, BHB+18, QNBB19]. These studies have focused on various scenarios, i.e. aggressive advances on female participants through a male-appearing artificial character, voiced by a real actor. The participants were then taught a breathing technique to manage their stress levels. Loranger et al. discovered that participants who experienced virtual sexual assault had a more pronounced response, suggesting an ecologically valid encounter [LB17].

In two studies, Reichenberger et al. [RPW+17, RPF+19] used virtual characters with offensive behavior (insults, spitting) to elicit stress. The spitting consisted of a sound with an accompanying air blast to the participant's neck. In their study from 2017, the authors showed that social fear conditioning in VR is possible, as indicated by differences in skin conductance. In 2019, they used the same paradigm to investigate the differences in gender of the virtual character and participants. While female participants reported higher fear ratings and also kept a higher distance from male agents, there were no differences in heart rate concerning stimuli, and only a gender difference in skin conductance [RPF+19].

Prachyabrued et al. [PWD+19a] show that an emotional bond with agents has a significant influence on the stress response of the subsequent loss of this agent. Participants were called onto the scene of a rescue mission. One group formed an emotional connection (EC) with their superior (the virtual agent) by having an informal, friendly chat before the emergency, the other group started the experiment in the ambulance on the way to the emergency, without the bonding (NE). During triage, the superior dies in an accident. Results show a significantly stronger stress response in the EC group.

2.4.5 Other Stressors

There is one publication by Higuera-Trujillo et al. [HTLTMLM17] that did not apply a stressor that would fit our categorization but rather measured the influence of the immersion level during the inspection of a supermarket aisle. The authors found significant differences in subjective and objective measures when they compared the reactions of participants to a standard photograph, a 360° photograph sphere, a physical environment, and a virtual environment with one another.

2.4.6 Summary

In our review, we found an extensive range of stressors that can be assigned to the four stressor categories. Based on the results, we identified the options available to us for the virtual representation of stressors from the care sector.

Fears and phobias are not typical nursing stressors. Although the fear of losing one's job was mentioned occasionally, this is not specific to nursing. These are therefore not taken into account in our studies. We exclude the use of odors to generate stress to ensure that the software is simple to use as it is also aimed at at-home use. This also applies to physical imitations of temperatures or heavy weights.

The use of visual and auditory representations of stressors allows us to simulate a high alarm load. These stressors are presumably easy to embed as they can be presented as part of the virtual environment. Several social and emotional stressors can also be easily simulated by integrating virtual characters and pre-recorded parts of conversations.

2.5 Nursing Education

The research in this dissertation deals with the development and testing of stress training that can be adopted in nursing education. For this reason, we introduce the organizational structure of the apprenticeship as well as common teaching methodologies.

In Germany, the content of the nursing apprenticeship is regulated by law, the Nursing Professions Training Act (Pflegegeberufeausbildungsgesetz). The three-year nursing training program in Germany consists of at least 2100 hours of theoretical instruction, role-plays, and at least 2500 hours of practical work under practical supervision. The content taught is defined in an internal school curriculum that needs to follow the legally set framework curriculum [Aus]. This legal framework was recently updated towards a generalistic apprenticeship to provide training for comprehensive care. Before that, students selected a specialization: nursing care (Gesundheits- und Krankenpflege), geriatric care (Altenpflege), or pediatric care (Gesundheits- und Kinderkrankenpflege). These fields are now combined, allowing nurses to work in all areas of care. However, it is still possible for students to select a deepening in a certain field, but this is not compulsory [Pfl23].

The required knowledge is attained in two different places of learning, at school and during practical placements. Apprentices learn the technical basics at school. However, the lessons are not purely theoretical. Various learning methods contribute to the transfer of knowledge. In addition to the usual text work for processing theoretical knowledge, problem-orientated learning (POL) is also used. This includes independent factual research, but also the use of role-play and skills labs, which are sometimes also referred to as a third place of learning.

During practical assignments in clinics or outpatient care facilities, students put the knowledge they have learned into practice. They are accompanied by practice instructors and practice supervisors. The practice instructors are employees of the facility and are responsible for the coordination of practical training. Practice instructors are required to have finished their apprenticeship in one of the German nursing professions (i.e. general care, geriatric care, children's nursing), and bring at least two years of professional experience. Further, they need to attend further training to qualify as practice instructors. In addition, they carry out selective practical guidance, i.e. they provide practical instruction to trainees according to their level of training. Practical supervisors, on the other hand, are employees of the nursing school. They work closely with the practical instructors and thus form the link between theory and practice. Their main task is to provide practical training for all apprentices they have been assigned. Like the practical supervisors, they are the point of contact for all issues relating to practical training [AA15].

2.5.1 Simulation-based Training

As outlined in the introduction, nursing education makes use of different teaching techniques to prepare students. However, newly graduated nurses often show a deficit between the clinical skills and the theoretical knowledge obtained, and further, they perceive a mismatch between the processes taught and the processes lived in the clinical environment. This "theory-practice gap" can be a safety risk for patients, negatively influencing job satisfaction and increasing job turnover rates [Bro19a, EAHB15].

To address this gap, educators make use of simulation-based training (SBT). Simulations or simulated experiences are interactive and meant to mimic real encounters, enabling repetition and reflection with minimal risk to oneself or the patient [Bro19a]. They reinforce practical skills, catalyze critical thinking, and help students to not only develop higher competence but also confidence [BJKB15]. Frequently used simulation techniques are role-playing and skills labs. These methods cover a range of fidelity from low to high fidelity simulation [PLS+21].

Both of these approaches have their advantages and disadvantages. The use of role-play may not provide the necessary realism for safety critical or stressful situations [HRP13, WCH19], whereas skills labs are expensive to maintain [Bro19b] and are not available 24 hours a day [WCH19]. Both approaches are described in the following.

2.5.1.1   Role Play

Role-play is an active learning technique and a form of problem-based learning. It is attributed to experiential learning, i.e. learning by doing [BC23]. Even though other options like standardized patients are available, they are comparatively expensive and require extensive training [SWS21]. Even as a low-cost technique, role-playing has been shown to make classes more engaging than frontal education and increases the cognitive processes involved in understanding and memorizing new concepts. Role-playing has further been shown to be reasonably adaptable, as it can be used to train mindfulness and soft skills such as empathy, respect, or patient-centered care. Especially when faculty staff is involved in role-plays, students report increased attention and participation [BC23]. Furthermore, students seem to better retain knowledge when comparing role-play with traditionally taught students. Nevertheless, role-play also has drawbacks. Due to a lack of realism, they might not fully engage the students, and students might lack the necessary sincerity when performing their roles [WCH19]. As role-playing includes at least two roles, it requires two students to perform the role-play which decreases flexibility. Furthermore, scripts must be learned beforehand, increasing the overall time required to execute role-play correctly.

2.5.1.2   Clinical Skills Labs

Clinical skills labs (CSL) are another form of simulation and are considered practical education at the school. As simulations, they are a protected and fault-forgiving space to learn in. Equal to role-play, they are classified as problem-oriented learning and are also attributed to experiential learning [EAHB15].

CSLs resemble a ward and are equipped similarly to patient-station rooms, including beds and utensils [AA15]. The fidelity - or realism - ranges from low to high fidelity simulations including mannequins, standardized patients portrayed by actors, and computerized models. Role-play, of course, can also be used within a skills lab. With the increased realism of skills labs, they create a bridge between the theoretical and the practical place of learning. As such, CSLs can be considered a key role in nursing education where procedural skills can be repeated and evaluated until minimum proficiency is developed [BN16]. CSLs are following a structured, supervised learning concept following methodological-didactic supervision.

In ideal cases, they create a highly real, yet anxiety- and risk-free environment for students to apply and increase their skills and knowledge [BN16]. The high realism of CSLs, however, comes at a cost. The equipment of a typical skills lab ranges from 40.000 € to 200.000 €. Furthermore, CSLs are usually not open during weekends or public holidays. This hinders students from learning in their spare time.

With a VR headset, the best of role-playing and skills labs can be combined. It is possible to create (several) virtual environments and apply role-plays with virtual characters. The mobility of the HMD increases flexibility and is less expensive in comparison to skills labs. In fact, there are already several approaches toward using this combination, as we will show in the following.

2.5.2 VR in Nursing Education

Recently, educational institutions have started to use VR simulations to train their students. VR simulations are part of SBT, which is widely used in safety-critical professions to safely train personnel. SBT has long been used with increasing accuracy in industries such as aviation and medicine. However, nursing educators have struggled to adapt new teaching methods due to strict safety regulations and reduced funding. In this context, less expensive solutions are needed to bridge the gap between the required training and cost-effectiveness (see also Section 3.2). VR has been identified as a solution, as it is a very versatile and cost-effective system. It has been applied to different topics covering the three domains of learning: cognitive, affective, and psychomotor [BKM84].

Concerning the cognitive learning domain, Blome et al. have developed a mixed-reality scenario with non-verbal guidance for reanimation skills. Haptic feedback allowed the researchers to simulate a pulse, and different training environments increased realism and showed the versatility of VR. A qualitative analysis of post-hoc interviews showed that students did not have trouble understanding non-verbal signs used to convey tasks during the scenario [BDR+17]. Farra et al. developed a VR-based training scenario to teach the required steps to be taken during a hospital evacuation [FSG+15]. They also compared the learning outcomes between students who learned using VR, students who learned using mouse and keyboard, and those students who received only written instructions. Students from the VR group claimed that they enjoyed the VR version despite technical issues. However, detailed results were lacking from the publication [FSG+15]. Moro et al. also compared the learning outcomes between different technologies (6 DoF VR vs. 3 DoF VR) in anatomy courses. While no statistically significant differences in learning outcomes were found, students using the 3 DoF system reportedly suffered from nausea and blurred vision [MSRS]. Shewaga et al. developed a serious game teaching epidural preparation and compared different ways of locomotion, using an HTC VIVE HMD. Participants were asked to fulfill tasks needed for the epidural either in seated or room-scale VR. Results show that room-scale VR leads to significantly higher immersion [SUQKA20].

For the affective learning domain, researchers have developed role-playing scenarios to improve students' communication skills with patient family [KPFF+14], when communication on an interdisciplinary level [PFSFL18], or when dealing with patients suffering from dementia [ELL16]. All studies report mixed results on knowledge retention: they claim that students generally prefer VR over less immersive options [KPFF+14], but also mention discomfort in nausea when in VR [PFSFL18]. Elliman et al. did not report on whether participants' results improved through repeated performance of the tasks in their study but were positive about the wireless implementation of their 3 DoF device, a Google Cardboard [ELL16].

Butt et al. developed a VR tool to practice urinary catheterization using an Oculus Rift, targeting the psychomotor learning domain. They compared metrics such as time on task, usability, and number of procedures in an hour of the VR system to the results of a mechanical simulator. The researchers note that the VR system was not only rated with better usability, but students were also more motivated to train as they used to system to practice significantly longer and more often. Further, there was no difference in the quality of a post-hoc skill demonstration, showing that the VR system was capable of delivering knowledge of the same quality as the mechanical simulator [BKEE18].

This related work clearly shows an increase in VR scenarios for nursing in different areas with different aims. The articles presented further corroborate a positive effect on student motivation. We can also deduce from this that special attention must be paid to the negative effects of VR, such as nausea and discomfort during prolonged use. We have not found research on stress-focused scenarios in the nursing domain. This highlights a clear research gap that we want to address in our work and investigate stress-related training for this occupation.

3 Requirement Research and Apparatus

To understand how VR software for stress inoculation needs to be designed and what features it needs to include for the education context, we present the methods used and how we applied them in Section 3.1, and outline the results in Section 3.2. In Section 3.3, we then introduce each component of the overarching system we built to execute our user research. examined the user requirements utilizing different methods. In Section 3.1 we outline the requirement analysis we are going to base our prototypes used in the research. Section 3.4 summarizes the contents of this chapter.

Some of the content in this chapter has been published in Weiß, S., & Heuten, W. (2019). Exploring Stress Creation in VR for Task-Based Training in Nursing. Mensch und Computer 2019-Workshopband (pp. 1-6) and Weiß, S., Cobus, V., & Heuten, W. (2020). Bedarfe für Virtual Reality Basierte Stress Trainings in der Pflege. In 2. Clusterkonferenz. Zukunft der Pflege (pp. 1-4) and Weiß, S., Cobus, V., & Heuten, W. (2021). Mixed Reality Collaboration Environment — It's a MiR-aClE. In 4. Clusterkonferenz. Zukunft der Pflege (p. 1) and Weiß, S., Lindt, D., & Heuten, W. (2023) Usability of PC-based Dashboards to Control Virtual Reality Training Situations. In 6. Clusterkonferenz, Zukunft der Pflege (pp. 99-103).

3.1 Requirements Analysis

For the custom VR software to act as a virtual skills lab where virtual stressors can be embedded, we need to identify the requirements of our users. Accordingly, we gather knowledge on the design of an ICU and what stressors are common in nursing and applicable in VR. Further, we want to analyze the context of use, i.e. how teachers and students perceive the possible use within the context of our education, and what factors are important when trying to embed the software into classes. To cater the experimental software to the needs of our target population, we need to understand their workflows and the given circumstances in the nursing profession. We followed the human-centered design process to best suit our prospective users' needs. According to the guidelines of the Human-Centered Design process [ISO19], the intended user of the software is included in the development process from the beginning. In adherence to these guidelines, we started with ethnographic research to get a deep understanding of the working and learning environment of nurses.

3.1.1 Accompany the User

Accompanying - in other words, shadowing - the user or the target group belongs to the ethnographic research methods. It gives researchers insights into how those accompanied go about their day, their tasks, and their social interactions. Shadow-

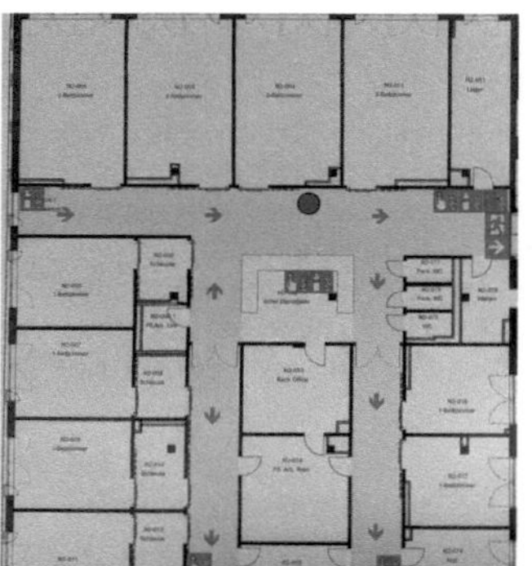

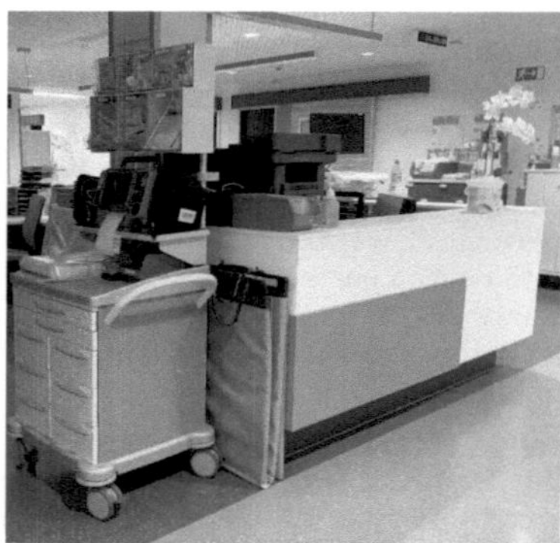

(a) Floorplan showing the arrangement of rooms for the ICU. Note the central location of the nursing room and the med prep.

(b) At the nurses' station, staff takes care of administrative work and can view digital replicas of patient-monitoring systems in each room.

Figure 3.1: The ICU includes ten patient rooms, four of which are two-patient. Of the remaining six single-patient rooms, four have a hygienic port. The rooms are arranged in a U-shape around the clean room, the back office, and the nurses' station.

ing sessions can range from being a silent companion to acting as a member of the target group and taking notes undetected. Doing so lets researchers better understand the needs of the user and how they perform their work, as they experience the profession firsthand. Moreover, one gets to experience cultural phenomena that might play a role. Understanding the hows and whys is crucial to the design of a prototype or product [LFH].

Intensive Care Unit

The first shadowing session took place in the intensive care ward of a local hospital.After contacting the hospital administration to get permission from both management and the head nurse, we agreed on a date and shift. During the morning shift from 6 a.m. to 2:30 p.m. we were shadowing two nurses during their everyday business. Before the shift began, we were dressed in scrubs and instructed on how to behave toward patients and other nurses. To record information, we equipped ourselves with a tablet computer for note-taking, drawing, and photo-taking. Note that for anonymity reasons no photos of people have been taken during the session. The ICU is capable of providing care for up to 14 patients simultaneously (see Fig. 3.1a for the floor plan). These were distributed in a U shape around the nurses' station, the back office, and the medication prep room. At the nurses' station, administrative work and documentation were done (see Figure 3.1b). Further, nurses could view digital versions of the in-room patient monitors, if necessary.

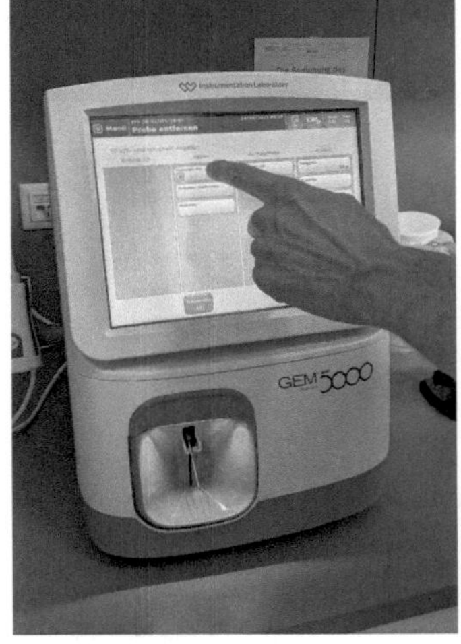 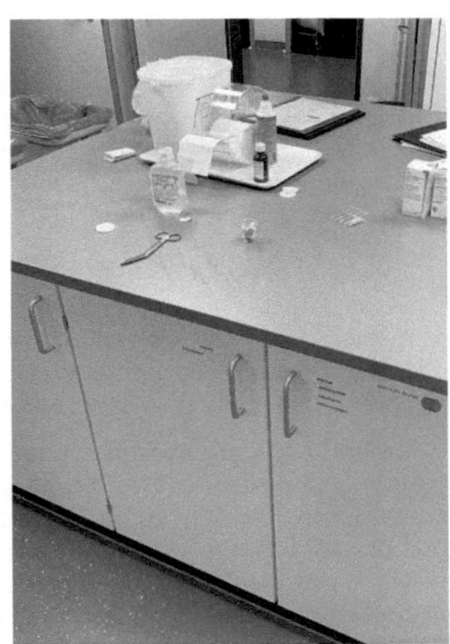

(a) A device for blood gas analysis. Blood samples (b) A nurse checks medication plans for patients
are mounted into the receiving slot of the device, and prepares dosages accordingly. Medication is
after which the device empties the content into an distributed on a regular schedule, as prescribed
analysis chamber and prints the results on screen or, in some cases, as necessary.
and paper.

Figure 3.2: Recurring tasks on an ICU.

The shadowing session began with a shift handover where nurses from the night shift informed the morning shift about notable events, such as new patients on the ward or whether patients had critical changes during the last shift. The handover further includes a general status update on each patient, their physiological stats, and their mental status. After the handover, nurses began the recurring rounds where vitals were recorded to keep the legally required documentation. We took notes on the tasks accomplished by nurses and the devices used for those tasks, unexpected events, and the interactions with their patients as well as with each other.

During the recurring rounds throughout the shift, there were several repeating tasks, including the withdrawal of blood and subsequent blood gas analysis (cf. Fig. 3.2a), the periodic recording of physiological stats of patients (heart rate, blood pressure, blood oxygen saturation), preparation and administration of medication (see Fig. 3.2b) and feeding patients. Any alarm was taken seriously but without haste, because nurses were able to interpolate the significance from previous occurrences and the general state of the patient that triggered the alarm. Except for moving a patient to standard care and accommodating another in the ICU, we were told it was a rather slow shift. Nurses were able to have private conversations with both colleagues and patients.

By shadowing two nurses during a full shift, we got impressions on several tasks and their execution, how a shift handover is executed, and how nurses respond to alarms. Further, we gained knowledge about the typical equipment and layout of an ICU patient room.

Classroom

Between May and August 2019, we shadowed several teaching lessons in different educational institutes in the greater Oldenburg area. The schools included an institute for continuous training as well as two nursing schools.

During a practical week in a nursing school, first-year students were tasked with accomplishing practice exercises that second-year students had prepared. Second-years further supported teachers by checking progress and the accuracy of the execution of role-plays. First-year students took turns taking the roles of the nurse and the patients when simulating bathing or feeding. It became apparent that not only did students interrupt the lessons by laughing at and with each other, but that they did not take these simulations very seriously either. We suspected that the lack of seriousness is grounded in the fact that the students knew each other, as well as in the lack of realism in the surroundings. The particular exercises were taking place in makeshift hospital rooms, with beds placed in the middle of the classroom, using tables as delineations between beds, as depicted in Figures 3.3a and 3.3b.

We executed a second shadowing session in an institute for continuous education and training. In contrast to the nursing school, students here had already collected several years of experience as registered nurses. The courses offered by this institute

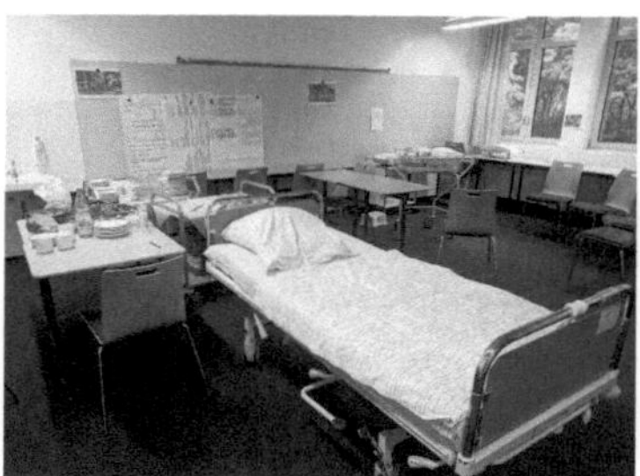

(a) A classroom used as a makeshift skills lab.

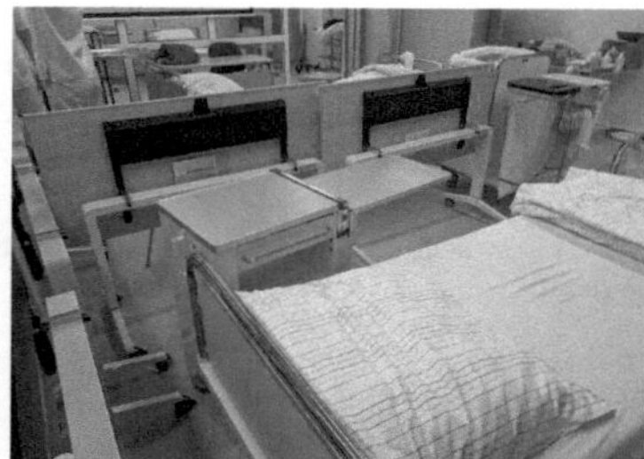

(b) Folding tables used as delineating devices between two simulated bed places.

Figure 3.3: Simulation environment during a training day at a local nursing education institute.

provide additional qualifications, such as specialist training for intensive and anesthesia care, emergency nursing, oncological nursing, and so forth. Whilst some of the lessons were designed as frontal education using a PowerPoint setup or blackboard, others were also executed as role-play. Even though the classrooms here were also not offering the reality degree a skills lab would, we noted that the participants of these courses took the matter more seriously than their younger fellows who were at the beginning of their apprenticeship.

We interviewed a lecturer their lesson on respiratory support ended, and they explained that the acquisition of knowledge about the operation of the specific respirator is often done in a way that only a single nurse gets selected by their superiors to partake in these introduction courses to compensate for time and travel costs. This nurse is then responsible for passing on the knowledge to other staff members. On the one hand, this procedure saves time and money as only one nurse needs to finish the course, but on the other hand, information gets lost due to the "Chinese whispers" principle: information is falsified or lost due to repeated forwarding of information over multiple. Because of this, knowledge is not fully available to every nurse, which might evolve into a problem later on.

A second class dealt with communication skills and de-escalation. This class adopted the technique of role-play, where students were required to apply previously taught knowledge to a conflict situation. Before the role-play started, course participants were asked to recollect memories of situations in which patients or patient families reacted aggressively. In a given example situation, a male family member of a patient accused a nurse of inappropriately touching the patient, started yelling, and finally shoved and punched the nurse before the hospital's security service escorted them off campus. While other examples were less extreme, they all demonstrated the necessity to learn about conflict management and deescalation.

The shadowing sessions in the lectures in both the school and the institute for continuous training underline the necessity for simulation-based training but also emphasize the disadvantages of role-play and how the realism or lack thereof influences training. As neither institution had a dedicated skills lab, they collected required devices in a classroom and prepared a make-shift version, at the cost of realism.

3.1.2 Ask the User

Surveys are a commonly used method to gain information from an individual, in the form of written questions and answers. In contrast to interviews, as they are usually self-administered, they do not require a researcher to be present. Surveys allow to generate an overview of people's thoughts with regard to the posed questions. They are appropriate to measure attitudes, awareness, intent, and user feedback on experiences [LFH].

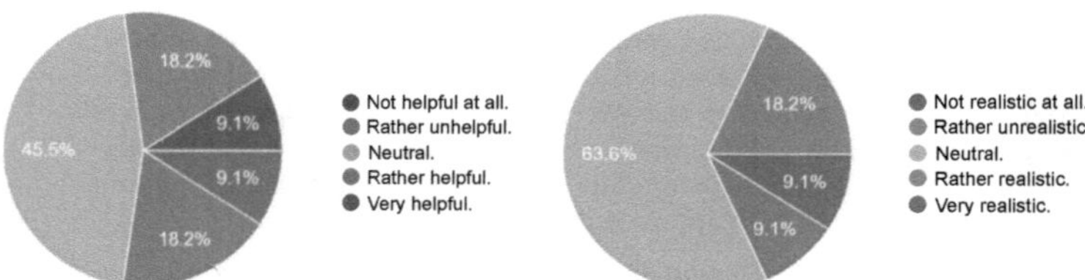

(a) Answers to the survey question: "How help-ful do you find role-playing games as a form of teaching?"

(b) Answers to the survey question: "How re-alistic do you think role-playing is as a form of teaching?".

Figure 3.4: Exemplary results from the student survey on virtual reality for roleplay as a form of teaching.

To learn about if and how students might want to apply VR in their learning pro-cess, we set up an online survey. The survey was sent to headmasters of the local nursing schools, who then shared it with the teaching staff, who in turn forwarded it to students using their respective e-learning platforms. The survey was made available over eight weeks after which response collection was closed and the re-sults were analysed. We collected survey results from 11 participants (age: 23 - 53, m=37.1 years, SD = 9.26). Over two-thirds (72.2%) were in their second year of the 3-year apprenticeship (1st year: 9.1%, 3rd year: 18.2%). The survey questions tar-geted experience with role-playing games in their education and their estimated realism. Only one of the participating students thought of role-play as very help-ful (see Figure 3.4a). Similar answers were given on the realism of role-play (see Figure 3.4b). We further asked about pre-existing knowledge of VR technology. Four participants had a definite idea, two had only a rough idea, three had heard the term VR, and two did not know VR at all. The survey included the question of whether students could imagine using VR as a tool for role-playing-based teaching scenarios in the classroom (4 yes, 5 maybe, 2 no) or at home (5 yes, 4 maybe, 2 no). Students also gave some ideas as to what they thought could be taught with and learned using VR. Figures 3.4b and 3.4a illustrate the indifference of our sample, the students are striking a middle-of-the-road attitude when confronted with the prospect of engaging in role-play.

The online survey showed that role-play is not perceived as real by many stu-dents. As we were able to see the circumstances under which role-plays are carried out during the focus groups, we believe that a more realistic environment might be beneficial. Many students would like to use VR in the classroom and even at home. We deduce that cost-efficiency and portability play a big role in the successful adop-tion of VR. Furthermore, it is important to increase engagement in this technique.

3.1.3 Discuss With the User

There are ways to more directly communicate with users than unsupervised surveys. Using interviews and (expert) focus groups, researchers may interactively converse with the target group and gain additional information, discuss prototypes, or brainstorm ideas using open-ended question questions. Whether to use focus groups or interviews depends on the formality and timing. Focus groups allow group discussions and thus provude an inexpensive tool to collect many opinions and experiences. Usually, groups between five and seven participants are deemed appropriate for in-depth conversations [LFH]. These groups foster interactivity and can compensate for non-talkative people, whereas single-person interviews may fail due to awkward dynamics. Nevertheless, using an interview allows for the interviewee to deep-dive into their specific line of answers without interruption, and one can elicit lots of information. Especially opportunistic interviewing increases understanding and deepening ideas.

Group Sessions with Teaching Staff

We executed focus groups with experts from other nursing school staff from the wider Oldenburg area. The sessions started with the introduction of VR technology and the demonstration of an early version of a virtual intensive care room to bring participants to a similar level of knowledge concerning the possibilities of VR. Participants were also educated about different interaction methods that can be used in VR.

The first session aimed at identifying stressors and groups to corroborate the literature (see Section 2.1.2). In the focus group, consisting of two registered nurses, two experts for nursing education, and two VR developers, several stressors were discussed. Together with the experts, we used card sorting [Spe04] and identified umbrella terms for the stressors found in the literature: "high job demands", "professional relationships", "ethics and morale", and "risk management". These terms aggregate stressors that we typically find in an ICU in more general categories.

As the experts were in unison in that the groups "high job demands" and "ethics and morale" were probably the most sensible to translate into VR, we tasked them with assigning the different stressors from the group "high job demands" a relevancy level and adding information as to what the underlying cause of these stressors are. The Venn diagram in Figure 3.5b shows the overlap between these factors. Lastly, under the guidance of the VR experts, participants discussed the feasibility of reproducing the stressors in VR. The results of this discussion were used in developing the apparatus, see Section 3.3.

With the resulting stressors from the first focus group, we conducted a second one. Participants were recruited from a nursing school teaching, where they were employed as practice instructors (n=5, 4f). The focus group was executed online using a conference tool. The goal of the focus group was to generate, collect, and

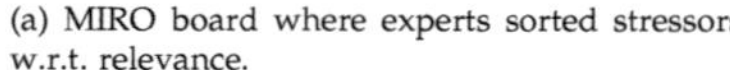

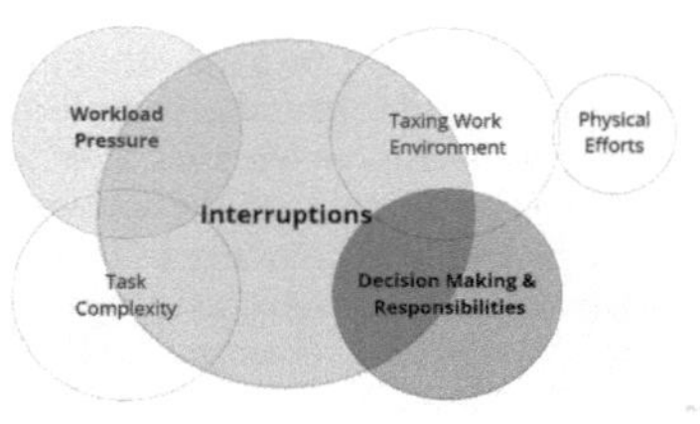

(a) MIRO board where experts sorted stressors w.r.t. relevance.

(b) Venn diagram of the stressors selected in the focus groups. Circle diameter denotes relevancy. Stressors belonging to the colored circles have been selected to be implemented in VR.

Figure 3.5: Interim and final results of the expert focus groups.

discuss ideas about typical tasks in the ICU and the feasibility of porting them into VR. In cooperation with the focus group, we defined two distinct, typical routine tasks: (1) refilling syringes for an infusion device and (2) collecting information from vital signs monitors to document in a patient chart. The development of the tasks is described in Section 3.3.

The focus groups showed that VR is not a common technology yet. We had to answer several questions related to the operating principles of the devices, their cost and availability, and possible applications. However, participants quickly gained a foundation that was sufficient to explain what they wanted from the system and how they thought stressors should be implemented. As a result, we were able to select three major stressor groups to investigate, as well as tasks we subsequently implemented to create an engaging and believable scenario

From One Expert To Another

To get a first impression of the requirements of the intended user groups, we conducted semi-structured interviews. This style of interview is guided by main questions but allows the interviewer to adapt to answers and guide the interview to further develop conversations on specific topics. To understand how VR might be incorporated into the existing curriculum, we invited three experts (teachers at nursing schools) for a telephone interview. The interviews were designed as semi-structured interviews to ensure that no important remarks and requests for clarification would be missed as would have been in the case of fully structured interviews. The interviews, which lasted about 1.5 hours, were recorded and transcribed in the next step. The analysis was carried out as a six-step thematic analysis as described by Braun and Clarke [BC06].

The questions in the interview address the experts' knowledge of VR, which scenarios in nursing are considered stressful, how these can be replicated, and what possibilities are seen for integrating these scenarios into everyday teaching.

Results show that our interview partners did not have in-depth knowledge about VR at the time of the interview. Further, we were told that even though funding might be available, there will be only little technical support in the setup and maintenance of the devices. The interviewees shared ideas about stressful scenarios, which largely matched the results from the focus groups, i.e. alarms from devices, and making decisions under time pressure. The experts further said that multi-user scenarios would be required to successfully integrate the technology into the classroom. Furthermore, they would need tools to administrate available scenarios and possibly create or at least adapt them to cover several situations and adapt to student abilities.

The insights collected using the methods described above constitute the base for the experiment apparatus. Our apparatus consists of four major parts, each of which was developed according to the requirements: a virtual environment with remote control software, a stress measurement apparatus, and a laboratory for experiment development and execution (see Section 3.3).

3.2 Key Findings

Several important topics emerged from the results which we summarized and grouped into clusters. This section serves to present the results in more detail and finally specify the requirements for both teaching staff and students, who represent our target users.

3.2.1 Levels of Knowledge About VR

From the results of the focus group, the expert interviews, and the online survey we can deduce that even though the term "VR" is already known to most participants, only a few have hands-on experience. More specifically, 27% of online survey participants reported either no interest in or no experience with the technology. On the other hand, 45% expressed interest in trying it out. Only slightly more than a quarter of all respondents (27%) have already used VR in a personal context. About one-third (36%) of the surveyed students claim to be interested in employing VR as a learning tool, whereas another 18% have an opposite opinion. The remainder of the participants were undecided. In stark contrast to the students, all teachers participating in focus groups and interviews were eager to at least try out the possibilities of VR in the classroom, hoping it would improve the learning outcome.

Considering the low level of prior knowledge, we note that the complexity of the proposed system should be kept to a minimum. The interviewed experts confirmed the availability of technical support in the school but also clarified that this is not the case for every institution. Additionally, students exercising at home can not count on technical support. Furthermore, to engage disinterested students, the software can incorporate methods from the field of serious gaming.

3.2.2 Virtual Environment

Nursing is a profession that requires a high level of dexterity and hand-eye coordination. In the focus groups, we discussed the use of haptic gloves (e.g. HaptX[1]) but found that the then-current generation was not able to simulate movements and haptics as accurately as the tasks would require. Instead, the scenarios should be designed to be realistic in the order of sub-steps and interactions with other people. As for immersion and the resulting user's feeling of being part of a real event, designers of software should strive to create a realistic reflection of the workplace during the simulation. Interview partners further stressed that the interdisciplinary nature of the profession requires the development of cooperative scenarios in which tasks must be solved as a team.

3.2.3 Integration into the Classroom

As mentioned before, about one-third (36%) of respondents expressed their willingness to try out VR in the classroom (No: 18%, Maybe: 45%). On top of that, 45% of respondents could even imagine using them at home (No: 18%, Maybe: 36%). Some of the apprentices argued in favor of the opportunity to experience the simulated scenarios through a first-person perspective, instead of just discussing them, and were also intrigued by the possibility of retrieving additional information about the scenario and its solution in real-time through the system. However, other students preferred the traditional learning method (P3) or stated they would feel uncomfortable using VR in the classroom (P11). On the contrary, the chance to use VR at home was met with more enthusiasm, as students liked the idea of minimized distractions during the experience (P5), and can facilitate more focused learning (P6). Teaching staff generally see opportunities for positive impact, but stress the importance of having the ability to create and manipulate scenarios as a prerequisite.

3.2.4 Financial Considerations

Commenting on financial constraints, teachers participating in expert interviews and focus groups stated that current federal funding for new media in schools is being used to equip teaching staff and classrooms. Thus, adequate funding should be available. However, when using new media in the classroom and at home, it is

---

[1] https://haptx.com/, last accessed January 4th, 2024

important to find a good compromise between realism and the capabilities of the system, as well as the associated costs. Autonomous VR systems (see Section 2.3.1) are particularly suitable for this purpose, as they do not require the purchase of additional computers. Furthermore, inside-out tracked HMDs improve immersion as they eliminate the interference of connection cables with the experience. Moreover, smartphones can also be used as software players in combination with cardboards[2], which serve as a holder and optical magnification system. This allows trainees to use their own handheld devices. However, this technology does not provide the opportunity to move around physically, resulting in lower immersion.

3.2.5 Requirement Classification

Summarizing the results described above, the requirements for VR software for stress training can be sorted into the following major categories.

- Organizational requirements

    - Low-cost solutions should be preferred, but the compromise made must consider both the immersive capabilities and the realism on the one hand, and the required existing knowledge and possibility for technical support on the other.
    - To create high-fidelity scenarios, detailed scripts must be written up in cooperation with staff, considering technological constraints.

- Functional requirements

    - Provide support for major device manufacturers to aid in adoption.
    - Mobile use is preferred over wired solutions.

- Usability requirements

    - As only little technical support will be available, the software should be handling errors itself or provide clear instructions.
    - To focus on stress training, keep other distractions low.

- Software requirements

    - To support several scenarios and scenario styles, both single- and multi-user scenarios should be supported.
    - Practitioners stated the need for a control tool to adapt the software.
    - Multi-modal user stimulation increases presence and can further contribute to user engagement.

---

[2] https://arvr.google.com/cardboard/, last accessed May 7th, 2022

- Requirements for experiments

  - The stress measuring apparatus needs to be compatible with an HMD.
  - The stress measuring apparatus must be able to consider both subjective and objective stress levels.
  - A setup of appropriate hardware and software is required to develop, test, and run the experiments.

Considering these requirements, we have developed an experimental setup with four major parts. Details on the overall system will be given in the next section.

3.3 Core Components for Inducing and Measuring Stress in VR

To satisfy the requirements we gained during our requirements analysis, we integrated several components into an overarching system, consisting of four major parts: (1) A mixed reality laboratory where experiments are developed, tested, and executed, (2) the virtual replica of an intensive care unit, including tasks and stressors, (3) a control dashboard for scenarios within the virtual ICU, and (4) the stress measuring apparatus. Figure 3.6 shows these four parts in an overview schematic. Participants are physically located in the mixed reality laboratory but immersed in the virtual ICU through the HMD they are wearing. Events in the virtual ICU are controlled using tablet-computer software. Objective measures are collected through the Zephyr Bioharness^{TM} and the SEEED Grove (cf. Section 3.3.4), while subjective measures have been realized as virtual questionnaires that can be answered whilst being immersed. The following subsections will go over the four parts in more detail.

3.3.1 MIRACLE

The experiment software that we used to investigate our research questions was developed and tested in a specialized mixed-reality laboratory using state-of-the-art hardware and software. We required an environment with the necessary hardware components and sufficient space. To this end, we set up the mixed-reality lab "MIRACLE" (Mixed Reality And CoLlaboration Environment) at OFFIS. The MIRACLE provides the necessary hardware and software to conduct mixed reality experiments. The VR-ready PC workstations are running on Windows 10 and are equipped with NVidia GeForce 2070 and 3060, respectively. To each PC, a head-mounted display (HMD, see Section 2.3.1) is connected. The currently connected HMDs are an HP Reverb Omnicept (wired, 6DoF, inside-out tracking) and a Vive Pro Eye (wireless, 6 DoF, outside-in tracking). Both HMDs feature eye-tracking and optionally facial tracking. Throughout the project, we updated the headsets used in the user studies to untethered devices, as they became available.

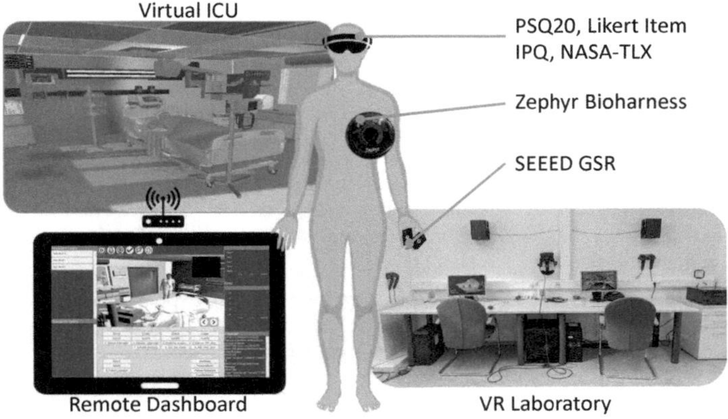

Figure 3.6: Schematic overview of our 4-part apparatus.

In the approximately 16 square meters large area available, an immersive experience for two users is ensured. The rear projection screen makes augmented reality (AR) experiments realistic and immersive with a variety of projected environments. Six projectors create a combined image with a total resolution of 4K onto a $1.8 * 3.2$m curved screen (coverage angle approx. 160°). For acoustic realism, a 5.1.2 surround sound system with Dolby Atmos is used. Figure 3.7 displays a panoramic view from the laboratory door into the room. The equipment described meets all requirements identified in the previous section.

The laboratory is versatile due to the wide range of technical equipment. However, the limited space is unsuitable for extensive environments. More considerable walking distances must be shortened in VR by employing teleportation techniques,

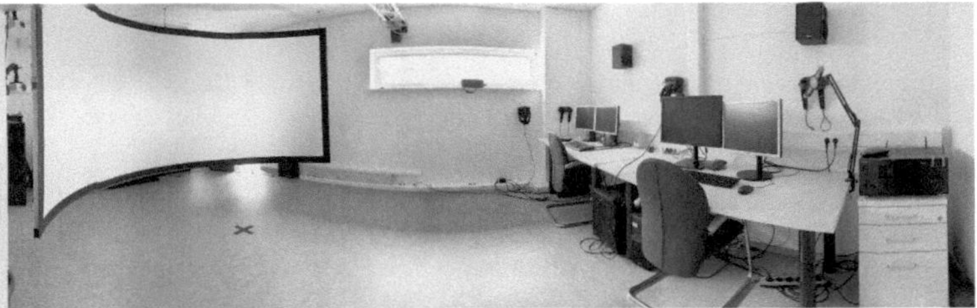

Figure 3.7: Panoramic view of the MIRACLE.

at the expense of immersion. The software developed was initially used locally, but with the availability of self-sufficient headsets, experiments can also be carried out location-independent.

3.3.2 Remote Control Dashboard

We have developed a Remote Control Dashboard to enable researchers and teachers to control a virtual scenario in real-time, remotely if necessary. Further, the tool includes capabilities for remote communication with the VR users, while they are immersed in the VR experience.

The software design is based on requirements gathered during expert interviews executed specifically for this application. It has undergone iterative design and implementation. Considering that not all teaching staff are proficient in handling computer software, it is crucial to design software that is easy to use to achieve high usability. Various tools can be used to evaluate and assess usability, including standardized questionnaires such as the NASA-TLX [Har06], the System-Usability-Scale [Bro96], or the Think-Aloud (THA) method [NH06]. When testing the remote control application, we collected data using all the tools mentioned above.

3.3.2.1 Requirement Analysis and GUI Prototype

We interviewed teaching staff (n=3) and UI/UX engineers (n=4) to gather requirements for our software. In a second step, that information was discussed with VR and UI experts, who were asked to create GUI sketches. An example of a sketch is shown in Figure 3.8a. The sketches were then iteratively refined, see Figure 3.8b.

We implemented the required features into a usable GUI prototype. The prototype uses a WebSocket connection to connect to client code running within our experiment software. The remote dashboard was developed using Unity3D's standard UI library as well as the TextMeshPro[3] library. This allows us to compile against web-based technologies, tablets, and PCs and thus offers a high degree of compatibility. The different functionalities included in the prototype are color-coded in the following manner (cf. Figure 3.9):

1. Events (blue): The event block enables interaction with the virtual ICU's door and window and provides control over movement and voice lines of artificial characters.

2. Tasks and Task Queue (red): Users can add or remove pre-programmed tasks like checking vital signs, exchanging medication syringes, and conducting a blood gas analysis. Tasks can be combined with stressors like time pressure or interruptions to make them more demanding.

---

[3] https://docs.unity3d.com/Manual/com.unity.textmeshpro.html, last accessed January 5th, 2024

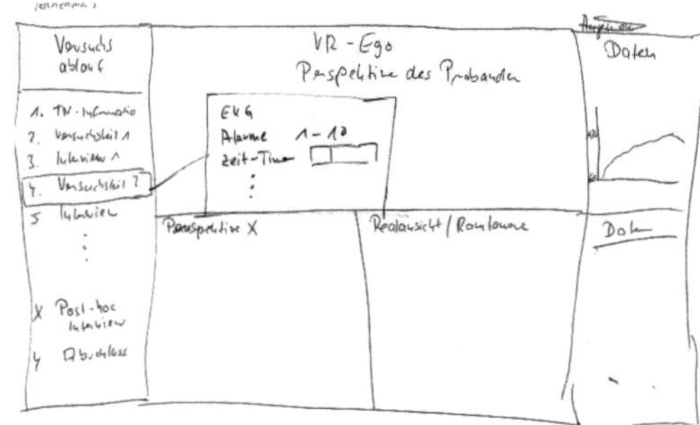

(a) Exemplary, hand-drawn sketch.

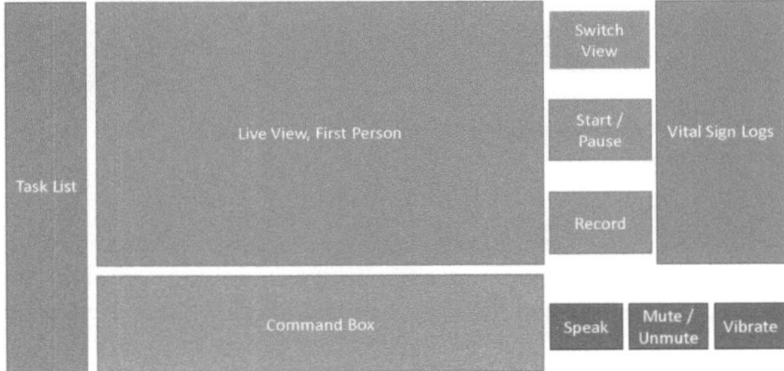

(b) Second iteration, wireframe mockup.

Figure 3.8: Examples from the sketch and wireframe design cycles for the RCD GUI.

3. Vital Sign Monitoring (purple): We use the Laboratory Streaming Layer protocol (LSL[4]) to display the HR and ECG of VR users in real-time. This increases the compatibility with a range of Bluetooth-enabled HR trackers. Using this information, the user can adjust the difficulty of each task based on the trainees' current stress level.

4. Communication (green): The application has communication features for both the trainer and trainee to contact each other. This includes an audio and video connection utilizing a webcam that is displayed on a monitor within the vICU and a chat function for written messages. The VR user can also communicate using voice chat.

---

[4] https://labstreaminglayer.org/, last accessed January 5th, 2024

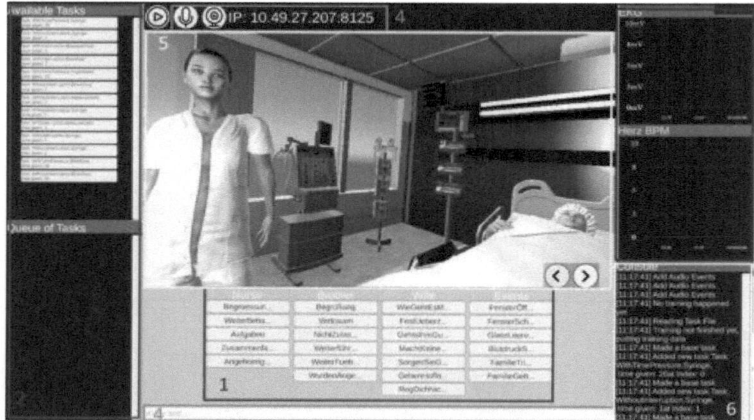

Figure 3.9: The GUI prototype in the stage the usability was tested in. Each colored block has a specific purpose.

5. Perspectives (yellow): The GUI includes buttons for the user to switch their perspective onto the VR. We added one perspective from each ceiling corner towards the room's center and further added the ability to take the VR users' first-person view.

6. Console (white): The console logs study events and errors throughout the runtime. Furthermore, it keeps a record of tasks already finished by the participant.

3.3.2.2 Usability Evaluation

We designed a user study to examine the usability of the remote dashboard and invited UI experts (n=6; 2f, 4m) to the MIRACLE for testing. We explained the experimental procedure and collected demographic data. After an introductory phase to the dashboard and some opportunity to test out functionalities and clarify questions, participants were provided with a randomized task list that they were to give to the VR user, embodied through one of the experimenters.

In addition to controlling the tasks, participants were also instructed to control the avatars for other roles in a given scenario (see Fig. 3.9, 1). To guarantee a consistent simulation experience for all users of the dashboard, we utilized a combination of tasks and stressors that we also use the user studies on the effects of stressors (see Chapters 4 and 5). During the experiment, another researcher took note of the participants' THA comments. After the session, participants completed the NASA-TLX and SUS surveys and left the laboratory.

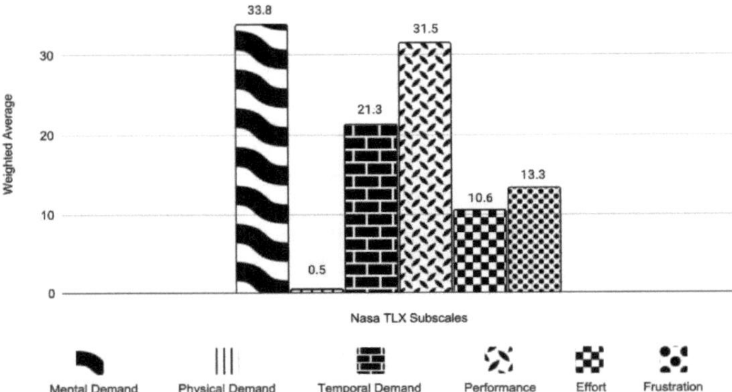

Figure 3.10: Task Load Index (TLX) results for n=6 participants.

3.3.2.3 Usability Results

We provide the quantitative analysis of both questionnaires. For a presentation of the qualitative data from THA, please refer to the next section.

NASA-TLX

The NASA-TLX results (cf. Fig. 3.10) indicate a relatively high Mental Load (mean= 33.8, SD=20.68). Moreover, participants rated the Performance required to use the software as moderately high (m=31.5, SD=16.12). The sub-scale Temporal Demand received a medium rating with a mean evaluation of 21.3 (SD=14.75). Effort (m=10.5, SD=10.86) and Frustration (m=13.3, SD=20.15), on the other hand, were rated at the lower end with a low impact. The Physical Demand was rated very low with an average score of 0.5 (SD=0.84).

Software Usability Scale

The SUS ratings of the tester were recorded and calculated according to Brooke [Bro96]. The resulting average weighted score was 32.5 (SD=17.46) and individual ratings of each participant are demonstrated in Table 3.1.

Qualitative Feedback from Thinking Aloud

Participants found the software slightly challenging to use but were generally satisfied with their performance. There was a learning curve, and some participants

P/ID	SUS Rating
1	20
2	62.5
3	25
4	22.5
5	40
6	45
Avg.	35.83

Table 3.1: SUS results for n=6 participants.

were frustrated by the lack of feedback from the software. Participants reviewed the GUI and tested out features such as camera perspectives and chat functions. While the possibility of following the VR user was generally considered useful, one participant found the "flying controllers" uncanny and suggested adding a semi-opaque render or using a third-person perspective to fix that issue.

Our subjects used the built-in chat and webcam only sporadically after the first use, likely due to proximity to the VR user. The task queue didn't meet P4's expectations as tasks had to be started manually, but they liked the ability to un-queue tasks.

Throughout the experiment, participants used the speaking and walking functions of non-player characters (NPCs, artificial characters) by clicking buttons randomly or repeatedly. We observed that the GUI should not allow users to access the NPCs' voiceovers before they enter the room, as noted by P1 and P4. Moreover, single-use events (such as being greeted by a colleague nurse or NPCs making statements) should be marked as used or even disabled after their first use. Similarly, the order of events needs to be carefully monitored, as participants often selected events in random order instead of following the Western cultural standard of top-bottom / left-right. P5 recommended that buttons should be either numbered or only enabled when they are relevant to the current situation.

Participants faced confusion due to the GUI's lack of feedback about remaining time, leading to overlapping voice lines and confusing both VR and GUI users. The absence of feedback was considered the major drawback of our GUI. To improve this in the future, we suggest using visual and auditory feedback for the GUI and auditory and haptic feedback for the user in the virtual environment to notify them about incoming tasks and chat messages. We further received feedback on the GUI that displayed the VR user's heart rate. P2 found it useful to know stress levels to adjust stressor events. P3 asked for notifications when the heart rate reached a predefined threshold.

Some participants frequently switched to a first-person view to observe VR users' activities but complained about the camera's quick movements. They saw the console window but paid little attention to it. P3 and P5 requested a timer in the GUI to estimate VR time.

3.3.2.4 Summary

The presented RCD was developed to aid in experiment execution and could be retargeted as a tool to remotely adapt learning situations to the current pupil. The results of our usability tests show room for improvement. The most requested feature was feedback on user actions. As participants found the general layout sensible, we will only make minor adjustments to text fonts and sizes to increase legibility, but will otherwise focus on functionality.

The software we have developed is designed specifically for our simulation procedure, and therefore cannot be used for other experiments in its current state. However, some of its features such as the LSL-based HR monitor, perspective-switching, A/V connection, and task queue can be reused in similar software. We are confident that the next iteration of the software, incorporating the improvements we have received from this initial usability test, will make the administration of the corresponding simulation software easier and save time for both professionals and laypeople.

3.3.3 Virtual ICU Environment

At the beginning of the implementation, the virtual ICU (vICU) consisted solely of a 3D asset[5]. In several iterations, we have improved the virtual space to align it as closely as possible with an existing skills lab, the Laboratory for Intensive Care Facility Experience (LIFE, OFFIS E66, cf. Section 3.3.6). The changes carried out included insertion and removal of (medical) devices, turning the layout of the room by 180°, and changing the location of the door frame. Figures 3.11a through 3.11c visualize the progress. The final vICU is presented in Figure 3.11d.

We added environmental sounds (e.g. phone ringing, monitoring standby sounds, ventilator, air conditioning, traffic from outside) and baked lighting for increased realism while decreasing the necessary computing power. All of the adaptations to the original 3D asset have been done in Blender3D[6] and the game engine Unity3D.

3.3.3.1 Task Development

The focus group described earlier in this chapter resulted in the selection of two basic, recurring tasks to be implemented in the vICU. Here, we describe how participants had to interact with 3D assets using the controllers. To ensure compatibility

---

[5] https://www.cgtrader.com/3d-models/science/medical/hospital-recovery-room, last accessed August 26th, 2023

[6] https://blender.org

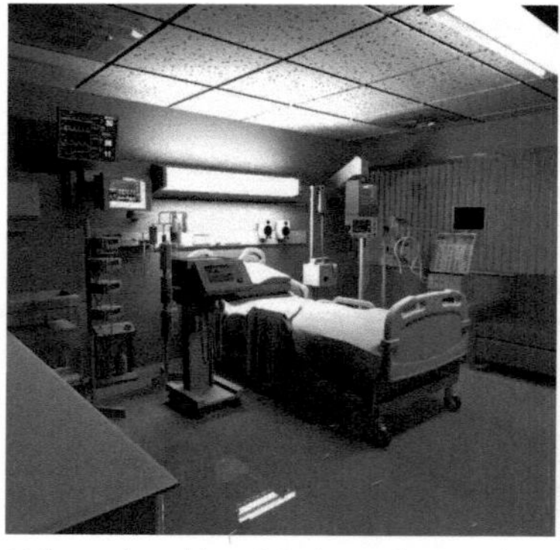 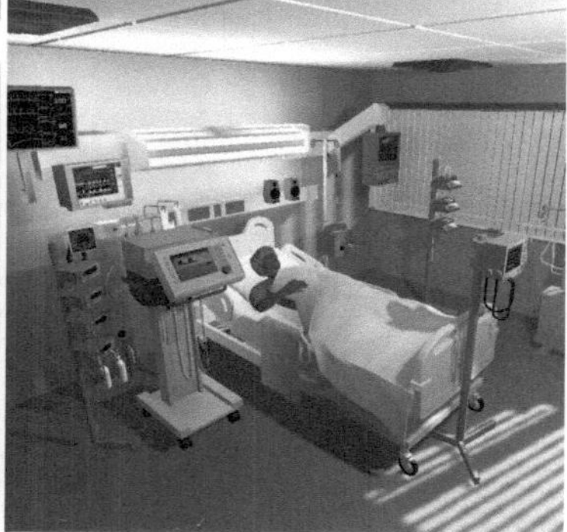

(a) Screenshot of the original asset the virtual ICU is based on.

(b) In the first iteration, we redid the lighting of the room, removed the couch, and added virtual characters for testing purposes. Some required assets were added as needed to finish the tasks.

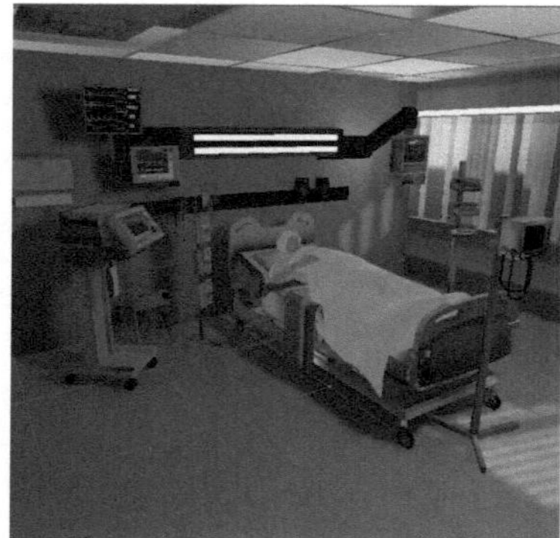 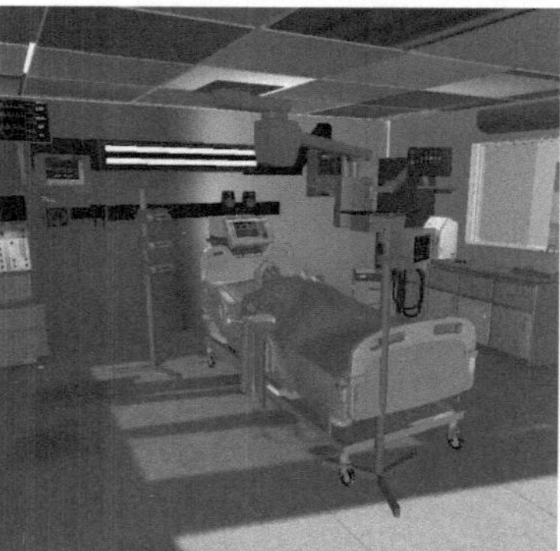

(c) The vICU design after the second iteration. We added environmental sounds and recolored the environment.

(d) After the third iteration, more required assets were added and room dimensions were changed to fit LIFE. The bed and other equipment have been positioned so that they face the opposite wall, in contrast to the previous versions.

Figure 3.11: The evolution of the vICU.

with several HMD manufacturers, we used VRTK[7] as a wrapper for the individ-

---

[7] https://vrtk.io, last accessed October 14, 2021

ual OEM drivers. Later on, VRTK was replaced by Unity's vendor-independent XR Interaction Toolkit[8].

Filling Syringes

For this task, we focused on the order of necessary sub-steps and not on the dexterity or haptic required for this task, as VR controllers do not support this. To complete the task, participants must use both the left and right VR controllers simultaneously. While the grip button on the controller shaft is utilized to grab items of interest, i.e. syringe and medication (see Fig. 3.12a), one needs to press the trigger button using the index finger of the hand to interact, i.e. activate the item functionality. No other buttons are required for the task.

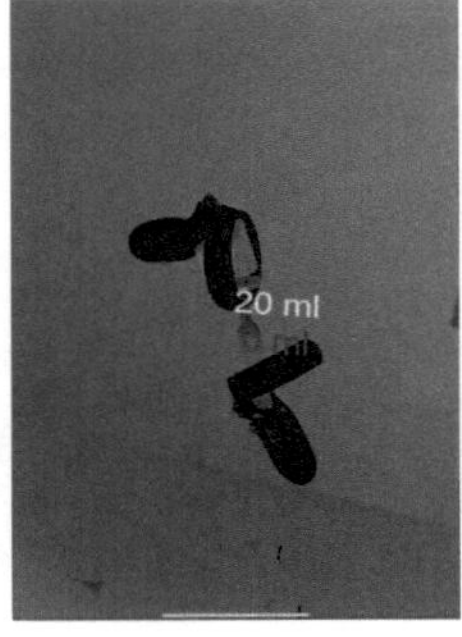

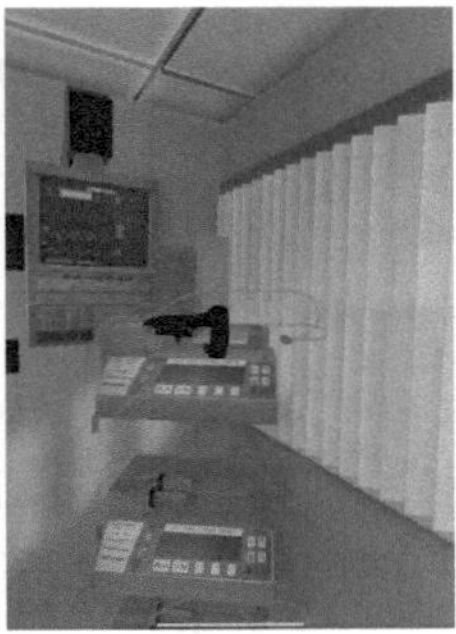

(a) The tools required for the syringe task. A medication vial, syringes, and two different needle caps are readily available for the participants to execute the task. The placement of the items resets after the task has been finished.

(b) Using the VR controller, participants grab the vial and syringe. The syringe is inserted into the upside-down vial and the medication is drawn by pressing the trigger button.

(c) As a last step, participants grab the empty syringe from the topmost perfusor with one controller and replace it with the new syringe they have just filled with medication.

Figure 3.12: Stepwise depiction of the syringe task. The task includes several sub-steps that participants have to execute in the correct order.

The "filling syringes" task involves several steps. Participants begin by reading the amount of medication required from a screen. For the sake of repeatability, this was always set to 50ml. They then attach a needle to the bottom part of the syringe and draw 50ml of air into it. Once air has been collected, the participant points the needle into the vial and presses the trigger continuously to mimic the process of creating pressure inside the vial. Then, another continuous push of the trigger

---

[8] https://docs.unity3d.com/Manual/com.unity.xr.interaction.toolkit.html, last accessed January 10, 2024

draws medication into the syringe. The required amounts of air and medication are displayed in white and blue numbers next to the syringe, respectively. Figure 3.12b illustrates this process.

Afterward, the syringe must be filled with the correct amount of medication. To insert it into the infusion device, the participant must first replace the needle part with a larger diameter slip tip to increase medication flow. The infusion device is located approximately three meters away from the syringes and medication vials. The participant removes the syringe occupying the slot in the device and replaces it with the one they just prepared, as depicted in Figure 3.12c. When the participant pushes a button on the infusion device, the pumping process starts, and they return to the task screen. To complete the task, the participant presses a button on the screen. If the participant makes any mistakes, such as filling the syringe with the wrong amount of liquid, forgetting to pump air into the vial before medication is drawn, failing to swap the needle caps, or neglecting to press the "pump" button, the task is recorded as incomplete or failed.

Documenting Patient Vitals

The second task observed during the shadowing and subsequently selected in the focus group was "the documentation of patient vitals". Nurses usually work in pairs or walk from the monitor to the desk, where the medical file of a DIN A3 size is unfolded. However, due to the distance between the desk and the monitor, the staff has to memorize the vitals until they can note them down. This task requires the nurses to be accurate and efficient in their note-taking, which is crucial for providing the right medical care to the patients.

During the VR task, participants were required to approach a monitor (as displayed in Fig. 3.13a) situated at the left side of the bed, approximately 1.9 meters above the ground. They had to remember a blood pressure reading that would only appear on the monitor when they were within 0.5 meters of it. Once they had read the value, participants were supposed to return to the task screen where several value pairs were displayed. From the displayed values, only one matched the value shown on the monitoring device (see Fig. 3.13b).

3.3.3.2　Stressor Representations

In the following, we describe the stressors selected in collaboration with experts during the focus group. Each stressor serves as an example of the stressor category they represent.

Time Pressure Stressor

During the experiment, the documentation and syringe tasks were assigned a time limit of 20 seconds and 30 seconds, respectively. This forced participants to increase

(a) The blood pressure would only appear when participants stepped within 0.5m distance to the monitor. The blood pressure must be memorized and then selected in a second step.

(b) Participants must select the correct value pair. Selecting one of the incorrect value pairs is logged as an error.

Figure 3.13: Patient monitor and task screen for the documentation of patient's vitals.

the speed of execution. In a real ICU, time pressure has been shown to not only reduce a nurse's ability to realize that an intervention is required [TDB$^+$08], but it also decreases the perceived quality of care in patients [THC10].

A short sound was played to inform the participants of the task's time limit, and the remaining time was displayed in red letters on the task screen within the environment, as illustrated in Figure 3.14a. If the countdown finished before the task was completed, it would end and the next task would start. Any incomplete tasks were logged as errors.

Interruption Stressor

In the ICU, tasks with a lower priority are often interrupted by tasks with a higher priority [DMSS19, FM10]. For instance, when a critical situation arises, such as a drop in heart rate or low blood oxygen saturation, alarms are triggered and lower-priority tasks are paused. In our experiment, we simulated task interruptions using a heart monitor placed at the foot-end of the bed, as demonstrated in Figure 3.14b. To resume the current task, participants had to acknowledge the alarm. Although the location of the heart monitor in our experiment does not reflect reality, we placed it there to increase the distance participants needed to travel to acknowledge the alarm. This also is closer to reality, as nurses are not in reach of the monitor immediately, but usually come there from another room. To handle the interruption,

(a) Participants were able to see the remaining time for the current task on the task screen on the back wall of the virtual ICU.

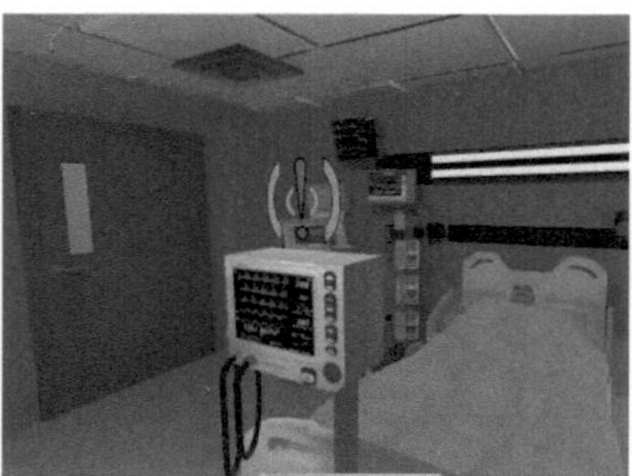

(b) The interruption was conveyed to participants by a visual signal on top of the patient monitor, as well as an alarming sound.

Figure 3.14: Visual representations of the stressors used during the experiment.

participants used a controller to interact with the device and confirm and silence the alarm.

3.3.4 Apparatus for Stress Quantification

As described in Section 2.2, both objective and subjective techniques are required to gain a complete picture of the participants' stress levels. Because of this, we have used sensing devices and questionnaires to collect information about the change in stress levels of our participants throughout our experiments. The selected measures have already been successfully used in similar experiments and can therefore be considered validated. This section explains the used devices in more detail.

Zephyr Bioharness

The Zephyr Bioharness™ (cmp. Fig. 3.15a) is a chest-worn device that integrates several physiological measures in a single system. The strap includes sensors for ECG and breathing. From these, we deduce heart rate, heart rate variability, tidal volume, and respiratory frequency. The device connects to a receiver using Bluetooth and can transfer data either in real-time or post-hoc, i.e. the device can store data on board and can later be transferred using a dock that connects to a PC using a USB-A connection.

SEEED GSR

The SEEED Grove GSR sensor, as shown in Figure 3.15b, is a device that senses skin resistance. It is based on the Arduino platform. The sensor uses two finger sleeves,

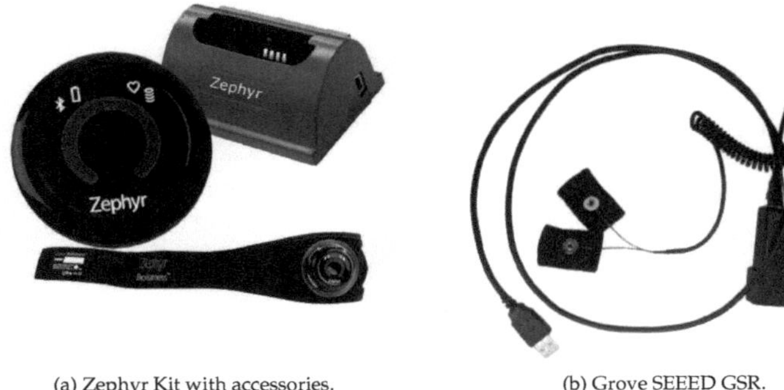

(a) Zephyr Kit with accessories.						(b) Grove SEEED GSR.

Figure 3.15: Sensing devices used to collect physiological information from which we deduce change in stress level.

each with an electrode, to measure electrical resistance. We turned the module into a wireless device by combining it with an Arduino base and a Bluetooth stack, and added a portable battery to increase mobility.

DeviceAPI

The software is designed to connect different sensors and has been developed in-house at OFFIS using the Java programming language. It is capable of reading, displaying, filtering, and saving multiple data streams simultaneously from both tethered and wireless sensors. We have successfully connected the Zephyr Bioharness^{TM} as well as the SEEED GSR sensor to the DeviceAPI. By using timestamps, we were able to match the data streams for further evaluation.

In the following, we introduce the subjective stress measuring instruments we have used throughout our experiments. Because our experiments take place in VR, we have created scenes in Unity that allow participants to answer the questionnaires in VR, using a controller (cf. Fig. 3.16). When answering questionnaires in this way, participants do not have to take off the HMD, keeping the presence high [SKHH].

Perceived Stress Questionnaire

The Perceived Stress Questionnaire (PSQ) is a 30-item questionnaire developed by Levenstein et al. in 1993 [LPV$^+$93]. It was validated with 230 participants in both English and Italian. For a test period of 12 to 24 months, the test-retest reliability was 0.82, while it varied by a mean factor of 1.9 over six months. The questions in the PSQ are meant to be answered w.r.t. the past month. We also translated other questionnaires in this manner.

Likert Item

As the PSQ and other questionnaires are meant to be answered with a longer time frame in mind, we do not use it as the only measure. To mitigate the problem, we added a single 7-point Likert item in addition to the questionnaire (see also [PWD+19b]): How stressed do you feel at this moment? We collected this information to get a momentary picture of the participants' stress levels pre- and post-hoc.

3.3.5 Other Measures

By collecting other information than stress levels, we obtained feedback about what participants thought of the VR software in terms of its immersive capabilities and how hard they thought it was to interact with the virtual devices within the artificial environment.

NASA-TLX

The NASA-TLX (Task Load Index) questionnaire was developed by researchers at NASA in the 1980s as a pen-and-paper tool to measure the subjective mental workload of operators working with human-machine interfaces [HS88].

The derivation of a task load is done in two steps. In the first step, subjects rate the task given on a multi-dimensional, weighted average on six sub-scales: Mental Demand, Physical Demand, Temporal Demand, Performance, Effort, and Frustration

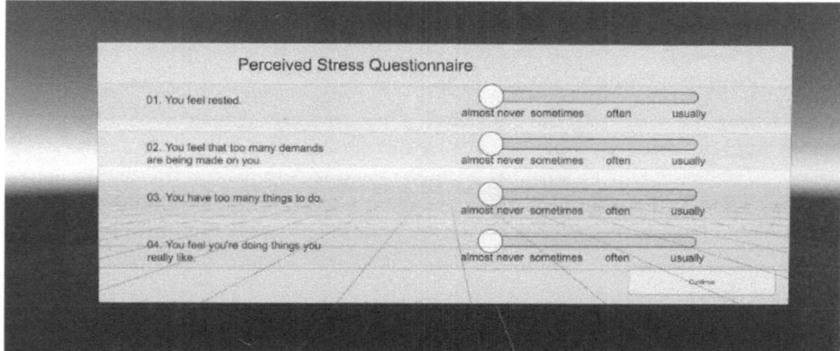

Figure 3.16: Screenshot of the PSQ in VR. Participants used the left or right controller to move the sliders, indicating their answer.

on a scale from "very low" to "very high". In the second step, test subjects create their individual weighting sheets by choosing the more important scale in several pair-wise comparisons. Instead of calculating the weighted score, one can omit the second step, which is referred to as the "Raw TLX" [Har06].

iGroup Presence Questionnaire

The iGroup Presence Questionnaire (IPQ) is a standardized questionnaire that lets developers evaluate the presence-inducing qualities of virtual environments [SFR01]. It was originally developed in German but is now available in several languages. The IPQ measures three different sub-scales of virtual environments (spatial presence SP, involvement INV, and realism R) and an additional general presence (GP) item by combining the answers to 14 questions. Each of these questions belongs to one of the sub-scales (SP=5, INV=4, R=4, GP=1).

ProRealSim

ProRealSim is a tool to assess the attained realism for simulations in the field of healthcare. Using the results of 53 indicators, one can assess the attained realism for three dimensions: Simulated Participant, Scenography, and Simulator. Each dimension contains several items. Most items are composed of scores for the naturality and accuracy (some items only have scores for the accuracy). The overall score is calculated by weighing the dimensions with 0.5, 0.2, and 0.3, respectively. The tool was developed by Coro-Montanet et al. [CMPMSI+23].

3.3.6   LIFE

The "Laboratory for Intensive Care Facility Experience" (LIFE) is a special room at OFFIS (E49) that is modeled after an ICU. It includes medical equipment and devices, a patient bed, and a ceiling support unit. It further features a desk, a lighting installation for natural lighting, a sink, and a care trolley. Figure 3.17 shows the first 3D sketch and the current state of the laboratory.

There are several use cases for this laboratory. On the one hand, researchers use it to test prototypes in a high-fidelity environment instead of a pure engineering lab. This allows them to make assumptions about their prototype in real-life settings. On the other hand, the laboratory is used to educate the public by showcasing not only technology that is already in the market but also prototypes of how researchers envision upcoming technology that can support professional caretakers.

For the context of this dissertation, this laboratory is used as part of the study and serves as a high-fidelity skills lab, in which the scenario will also be executed (see

(a) 3D-Sketch of LIFE.

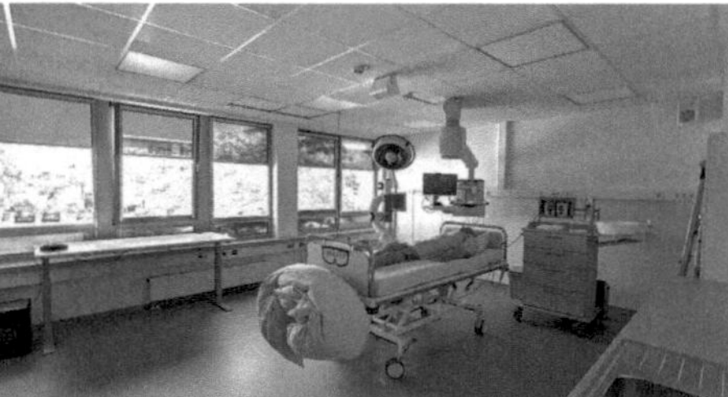

(b) Current state of the laboratory

Figure 3.17: Impressions of LIFE as a 3D model (left) and a photo taken from the door into the room (right).

Chapter 6). This is done to validate the effects of stressors in VR in a setting closer to education facilities' status quo.

3.4 Summary

In this chapter, we collected and analyzed user requirements using several techniques rooted in HCI. After summarizing and clustering the results from shadowing, interviews, focus groups, and a survey, we were able to create clusters of requirements. We subsequently created a comprehensive combination of hardware and software, tailored to satisfy these requirements. The major parts of our study setup comprise a specially equipped laboratory (MIRACLE), a virtual intensive care unit with remote control software, and a stress measurement battery. The MIRACLE is equipped with selected hardware to implement the experimental software. It was also used to run our user studies (see Chapters 4, 5, and 6), as it offered sufficient space.

The virtual ICU has been designed in collaboration with nursing teachers and practice instructors. We selected specific tasks and stressors and implemented them using platform-independent SDKs. We give details on how participants finish these tasks while immersed in VR. We also present the development of the remote software that is used to control the scenarios as well as a first usability study.

A measurement battery combining both objective and subjective stress quantification methods constitutes the fourth building block of our overarching study apparatus. We present sensors that measure certain physiological processes that are altered by the nervous system in response to stress triggers. The described virtual environment, the remote dashboard, the MIRACLE, and the described quantification tools constitute our experimental apparatus. In addition, we introduced LIFE, a high-fidelity laboratory for research in a hospital / ICU environment. The apparatus outlined here was adapted throughout our studies, reflecting the required changes in the apparatus for a specific use case. Details about alterations will be given in the applicable sections for the user studies in Chapters 4, 5, and 6.

4 Recreating Environmental Stressors in VR

The literature in stress research can be categorized into four groups of stressors: Performance Stressors, Physical Stressors, Bodily Stressors, and Social Stressors [Kal18]. Following the results from our second expert focus group (see Section 3.1), we investigate the effects of exemplary stressors from two groups, i.e. performance and physical stressors using a mixed methods approach. For this study, we use the term "environmental" for these stressors, as they are both part of the physical working environment of nurses.

In this chapter, we examine "Time Pressure" and "Task Interruption" more closely (cf. Section 4.1). We demonstrate how we investigated the effect of representations of these stressors in a virtual environment (VE) in an experimental study setup (see Section 4.2). We present the results of the user study in Section 4.3 and discuss our findings in Section 4.4.

Some of the material in this chapter has originally been published in Weiß, S., & Heuten, W. (2023, April). Don't Panic!-Influence of Virtual Stressor Representations from the ICU Context on Perceived Stress Levels. In Proceedings of the 2023 CHI Conference on Human Factors in Computing Systems (pp. 1-15).

4.1 Introduction

People perceive performance stress when they are placed under time pressure or experience an overwhelming amount of work. Performance stress also occurs for example when people are multi-tasking, partake in a competition, or await the outcome of an important exam [MHF15]. They include, but are not limited to time pressure, being quantitatively and/or qualitatively overwhelmed, exams, and athletic performance. On the other hand, physical stressors can be excessive temperature or noise, wetness, air quality, bright or very dim lights, etc., i.e. often environmental factors that one might have only limited influence on [Kal18].

4.1.1 Time Pressure

The term Time Pressure describes the lack of time for an individual to complete tasks [TH07]. People under time pressure tend to delay decision-making, filter existing information for a decision, and experience information overload [THC10]. Time pressure further increases sickness presence, i.e. going to work despite being ill.

Often, nursing staff is responsible for the identification of complications in patient care, making their ability to correctly recognize, assess, and make follow-up decisions critical. Their judgment is crucial for patient safety and, if erroneous, can be associated with suboptimal interventions and undue patient death. Thompson et al. point out that there are two influencing factors for nursing judgment: experience and available time [TDB⁺08]. While experience is generally positively connotated, time availability is viewed negatively. Both, however, are key drivers in judging risks and taking action. Time pressure is cited as the main reason for the inability to keep the care quality at a high level [BDU⁺05].

Based on the signal detection theory, there exists the idea of categorizing decision-making in a certain way. Depending on the level of knowledge and assessment skills, a response can result in one of four outcomes: true positive, false positive, true negative, and false negative, see Figure 4.1. Depending on the strength of the criteria a nurse is underlying their decision, they may assess a lot of cases correctly but will also label non-risk cases as risky and action-worthy. This creates overhead or causes the nurse to label action-worthy patients as non-critical, thereby maybe missing critical cases but minimizing false positives. This is referred to as the duality of error [Ham96]. Thompson et al. show in their study that putting nurses with critical care experience under time pressure for decision-making negatively impacts their performance in making the right decision. They call for educators to focus on teaching the value of information and how to set appropriate decision-making criteria [TDB⁺08].

For non-critical time pressure, i.e. not having time to complete their standard tasks, Duffield et al. illustrate that taking time for direct patient care positively contributes to a favorable patient outcome [DGCP08]. Having time to spare for patients is rare, as the amount of tasks to complete in patient care and administrative work puts nurses under time pressure, resulting in stress. This negatively influences correct decision-making and further fosters negative emotions and leads to exhaustion. Teng et al. show that time pressure also diminishes the perceived quality of care in patients [THC10].

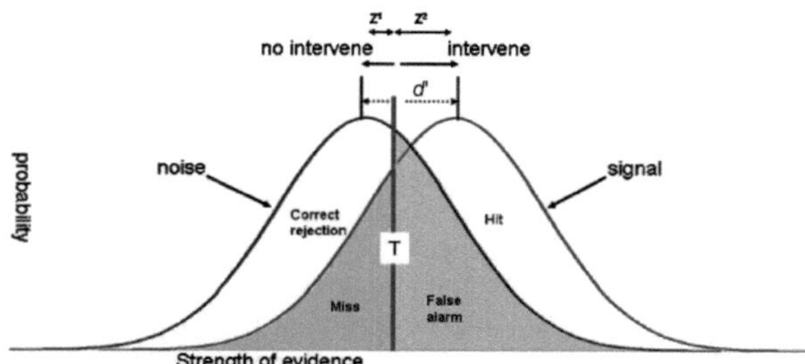

Figure 4.1: A simplified graph from [TDB⁺08]. Based on the strength of evidence and the probability of a required intervention, nurses decide on whether to take action.

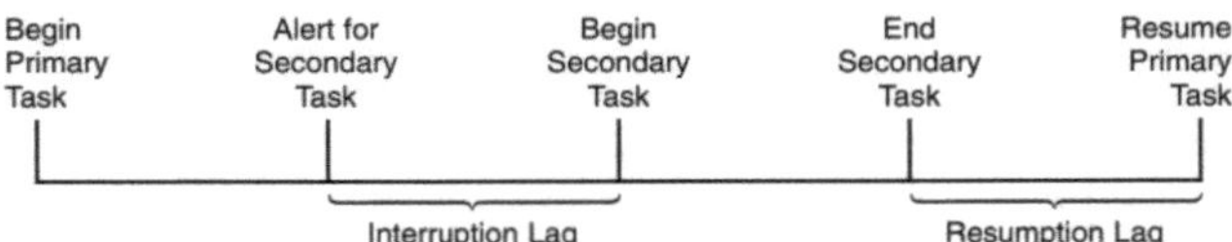

Figure 4.2: A task interruption timeline consists of five major events and two lag phases [TM07].

4.1.2 Task Interruption

The term Task Interruption is defined as a temporary suspension of an ongoing task (the primary task) in favor of performing another, usually unexpected secondary task [TM07]. One differs between externally initiated interruptions (e.g. phone calls, notifications) and internal ones (e.g. self-interruption, intrusive thoughts). Completion of the secondary task is commonly higher prioritized than the primary task, see Figure 4.2.

While it is established that interruptions have an impact on performance, the literature in the field of health care is complex, since the research is mostly field-based [Dre19]. Also, it is often investigated from the viewpoint of the research, which is why it is heavily biased [MSA17].

In nursing, as in other safety-critical professions, it is of great importance to finish tasks in the correct order. The self-control required to either not take up the secondary task or return to the primary task is a finite resource and can thus deplete [FM10]. Freeman et al. for example show that the frequency of interruptions in nursing tasks ranges from 0.3 to 13.9 interruptions per hour. Because the act of exerting self-control diminishes, the chance that subsequent attempts at self-control are successful decreases. Nevertheless, the closer one is to completing the original task, the stronger the detrimental effect an interruption has on self-regulatory and executive functioning [FM10]. There are two factors influencing how task interruptions are dealt with:

- The remaining time to task completion of the primary task when the interruption occurs: The less time remaining, the more one is poised to finish the primary task before beginning the secondary task [FM10].

- The amount to which a task is structured: The more structure, the more support the task lends to the memory process which subsequently leads to a reduced negative impact of the interruption. It can be assumed that unstructured tasks are more prone to task abandonment or omission of steps after the interruption [DMSS19].

We have selected the stressors presented above as representatives for their respective categories, as they are mentioned with a high frequency in the literature, and are also often featured in nursing-specific questionnaires (cf. Section 2.1.2). Our focus group also determined that they can be implemented with a feasible amount of effort and can be represented in VR while keeping the immersion to a high level.

4.2 Study Design

To best mix and match whole scenarios with different stressors and scenarios for later re-use, we were interested in the individual effects of the stressors. For this reason, we designed the experiment to be executed between subjects. Using Latin square, we prepared task lists to minimize task order effects. With the study, we investigate the following hypotheses:

- H_1: The use of the virtual stressors Task Interruption and Time Pressure in a virtual training environment increases the stress level in a subject significantly, as measured by the applied measuring technologies.

- H_2: The virtual stressor Task Interruption increases the stress level more significantly due to its multimodal presentation.

In this study, we investigated the independent variable Stressor Type in the conditions Task Interruption and Time Pressure by collecting information on the dependent variables "Heart Rate", "Heart Rate Variability", "Tidal Volume', "Respiratory Frequency", as well as the PSQ20 and a 7-point Likert item.

4.2.1 Apparatus

This study was run in MIRACLE using an HTC Vive HMD. Physiological signals were collected using the Zephyr Bioharness™ and the Groove GSR sensor (cmp. Section 3.3.4). The placement of the sensors is depicted in Figure 4.3. We chose not to inform participants about task completion status to prevent any potential frustration. However, we did inform them about the remaining time in case of the time pressure stressor. For the duration of those tasks in which time pressure was added, the time would be displayed in bold text and red color on the task screen within the ICU.

4.2.2 Participants

For this study 26 participants (11f, 15m, 0d; 19-50 years (m=29.46 years, SD=6.59)) from different professional backgrounds (nursing: 15, nursing practice instructor: 1, emergency medical technician: 2, HCI: 5, Other: 3) joined us on-premise. Test subjects did have little to no VR experience and normal or corrected-to-normal vision.

(a) Placement of the Zephyr Bioharness™. Note that the sensor would be worn under the shirt to enable skin contact, required for collecting data on cardiac activity using 1-channel ECG.

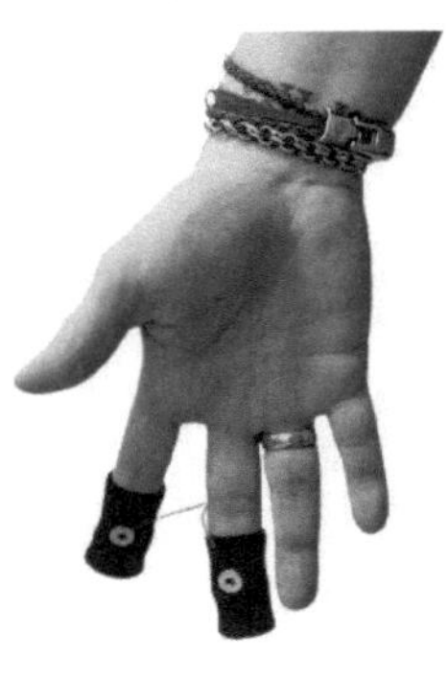

(b) Placement of the Grove SEEED sensing device used to collect EDA.

Figure 4.3: The correct placement for the stress measuring equipment used in our user study.

Attendees were compensated with 12 € for their participation. Having separated our participants into equal-sized experimental groups (n=13), we do not report a significant age difference between groups (t=0.63, p=0.54).

4.2.3 Experiment Procedure

The experiment procedure includes five phases, covering different aspects, see below. Before the first phase started, participants signed informed consent and put on the sensing devices. We collected additional data on "successful task executions" and "time to completion" in both task execution phases (three and four). A visualization of the study procedure is displayed in Figure 4.4.

1. During the first phase, a training session, participants learned locomotion and interaction. Experimenters instructed how the tasks were performed.

2. In the second phase, a baseline recording (BL) of participants' vitals was performed where they were shown a relaxing scene in VR while seated. The scene consisted of calming music in front of a starry background. This was done to return participants to a neutral stress level after the cognitive load from the previous

training and lasted for seven minutes, the last five of which were recorded. After the scene ended, participants filled out the PSQ20 and the Likert item for the subjective baseline.

3. During the third phase called No-Stressor-Phase (NSP), we asked participants to execute the given tasks without applied stressors. Tasks were carried out one after the other without a pause in between. We collected physiological data during and subjective data after the phase.

4. In phase four, the Stressor-Phase (SP), participants once again were asked to execute the tasks in a given order that differs from the previous phase. During SP, we applied either Time Pressure or Interruption stressors in 50% of the tasks in a pseudo-randomized fashion. We aimed to better mimic reality by adding stressors to only half of the tasks. Again, we collected physiological data during and subjective data after the phase.

5. The last phase was conducted after the experiment. We asked subjects to fill out the IPQ to understand how present participants felt in the VE. Finally, the NASA-TLX by [HS88] was employed to learn about the cognitive load each stressor put on the participants. Furthermore, we collected demographic data as well as information on occupation and experience. Moreover, we queried previous gaming and VR experiences and posed the open-ended question of what participants thought of the VE and the tasks.

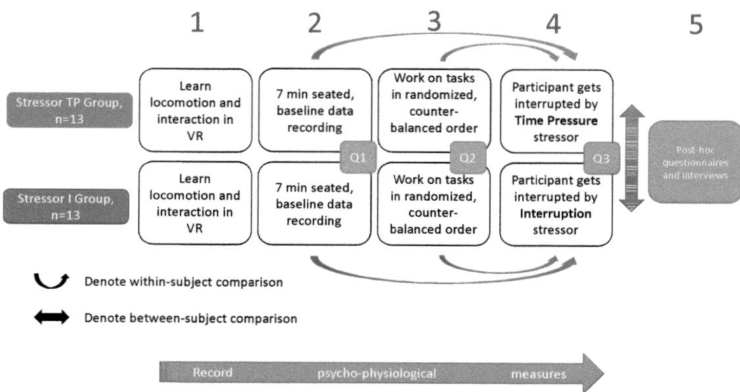

Figure 4.4: Abstract depiction of the experimental procedure. Blocks labeled Q1-3 indicate answering questionnaires. Participants from both groups underwent the same experiment procedure but were exposed to either Task Interruption (I) or Time Pressure (TP) stressor in the SP in phase 4.

4.2.4 Data Collection and Evaluation

To investigate H_1, the files containing physiological data of either group were cleaned and subsequently analyzed for statistically significant differences between phases. Additionally, the data from phase 4 was used to calculate unpaired t-tests, comparing the effects of the stressors with one another (H_2).

The results presented in the following are based on calculations performed on the average of each measure per phase averaged over all participants in each group (mean of means). The results reported in Table 4.1, show the percentual change between the two phases compared, for example to calculate change between NSP and SP we use the formula $[(Stressor - phase - No - Stressor - phase) * 100]/No - Stressor - phase$. This was done to normalize results and make them comparable. We tested for normality using the Shapiro-Wilk test and applied the repeated measures t-test or the Wilcoxon signed-rank test depending on the result. For comparing the two stressors in the last phase, we used the independent measures t-tests or Mann-Whitney-U tests. We focused on increases from baseline to the Stressor-Phase and from the No-Stressor-Phase to the Stressor-Phase. All GSR data had to be excluded from the study analyses due to technical errors.

Table 4.1: Overview of average percentage changes between baseline (BL), No-Stressor-Phase (NSP), and Stressor-phase (SP) of both stressors. Results in bold are significant.

	Interruption		Time Pressure	
	BL->SP	NSP->SP	BL->SP	NSP->SP
Heart Rate	11.37%	2.94%	8.86%	1.69%
HRV	-1.5%	-3.01%	-9.08%	-4.65%
Resp. Frequency	75.10%	4.38%	120.03%	4.39%
Tidal Volume	0.68%	1.17%	-0.04%	-1.16%
PSQ20	16.86%	0.38%	66.59%	22.45%
Likert Item	50.83%	82.08%	92.95%	104.64%

4.3 Results

For improved readability results are given in a textual format, while results of significance tests are displayed in Table 4.2. This table also includes information on whether the results support either H_1 or H_2. Moreover, we present findings from the questionnaires, i.e. the subjective stress level estimations. To simplify understanding, measures are always reported in the order of Baseline, No-Stressor-Phase, Stressor-Phase.

4.3.1 Change in Objective Stress Level

The following subsections include quantitative reports on the recorded physiological measures. There was no statistical significance between the baseline recordings of the stressor groups (HR: t=-1.0614, p=0.3036; RF: W=60.5, p=0.2205; BD: W=39.5, p=0.683).

Heart Rate

From phases 2 through 4, HR was increased in both stressors. All data was distributed normally. For Task Interruption we report 77.7bpm (SD=33.46bpm) for the baseline (BL) measure, 86.95bpm (27.41bpm) in the No-Stressor-Phase (NSP), and 89.5bpm (19.36bpm) during the Stressor-Phase (SP). In the participants of the Time Pressure group, HR increased from an average baseline of 90.69bpm (16.67bpm) to 92.55bpm (14.28bpm) in NSP and 98.78bpm (14.93bpm) in SP, respectively.

Heart Rate Variability (RMSSD)

For the participants in the Task Interruption group, HRV data was normally distributed. We report a mean RMSSD of 701.19ms (SD=174.1ms) in BL, and 670.441ms (122.77ms) for NSP and 690.63ms (170.69ms) for SP. In the Time Pressure group, RMSSD is as follows. BL: 710.39ms (158.6ms), NSP: 665.99ms (183.1ms), SP: 638.87ms (149.26ms).

Respiratory Frequency

In the Task Interruption group, we report the following mean and SD for phases 2 through 4 (BL, NSP, SP): 8.91 (SD=2.23), 17.10 (4.60), and 17.96 (2.96). Average RF and SD for Participants exposed to Time Pressure, were 9.64 (3.28) at BL, increased to 20.33 (4.27) in NSP, and further increased to 21.22 (4.09) in SP.

Tidal Volume

We computed the means and SD of tidal volume (V_T) for both stressors. For the Task Interruption group, average V_T was calculated at 511.27 (13.49), 508.82 (13.05), and 514.78 (8.78). Similarly, for the Time Pressure group, the V_T means were 516.68 (9.47), 522.52 (15.61), and 516.47 (18.14).

4.3.2 Change in Subjective Stress Level

Participants filled out both the PSQ20 and the Likert item at BL and after experiment phases 3 and 4 (cf. Section 4.4). Whether we can accept our hypothesis depends on the differences in the average percentual change between these data collection points, namely BL to SP and NSP to SP. Figures 4.5 and 4.6 present the normalized

Table 4.2: Significance test results for the increase of stress levels per measure, for each stressor, between phases. Significant results are in bold. The results are based on raw data, not on percentage changes.

Measure	Stressor	Phase Comparison	Test Result	Supports H_x
HR	TP	BL->SP	t(8)=-2.42, p<0.05	H_1
		NSP->SP	t(8)=-0.31, p=0.76	
	I	BL->SP	t(9)=-3.05, p<0.05	H_1
		NSP->SP	t(9)=-0.64, p=0.54	
	TP/I	SP	W=24.5, p=0.11	
HRV	TP	BL->SP	W=52, p=0.34	
		NSP->SP	W=48, p=0.55	
	I	BL->SP	t(9)=0.31, p=0.77	
		NSP->SP	t(9)=-0.85, p=0.42	
	TP/I	SP	W=43.5, p=0.5	
RF	TP	BL->SP	V=0, p<0.01	H_1
		NSP->SP	V=14, p=0.36	
	I	BL->SP	t(9)=-7.25, p<0.01	H_1
		NSP->SP	t=-1.2, p=0.26	
	TP/I	SP	W=27.5, p=0.16	
V_T	TP	BL->SP	V=18, p=0.65	
		NSP->SP	V=33, p=0.25	
	I	BL->SP	V=19, p=0.43	
		NSP->SP	V=20, p=0.49	
	TP/I	SP	W=45.5, p=1	
PSQ20 Overall	TP	BL->SP	t(12)=-3.04 p<0.05	H_1
		NSP->SP	V=16.5, p<0.05	H_1
	I	BL->SP	t(12)=-0.75, p=0.47	
		NSP->SP	V=35, p=0.78	
	TP/I	SP	t=0, p=1	
Likert Item	TP	BL->SP	t(12)=-3.77, p<0.01	H_1
		NSP->SP	t(12)=-2.92, p<0.05	H_1
	I	BL->SP	V=0, p<0.01	H_1
		NSP->SP	t(12)=-3.42, p<0.01	H_1
	TP/I	SP	W=62.5, p=0.26	
NASA-TLX	TP/I	post-hoc	t=1.15, p=0.26	

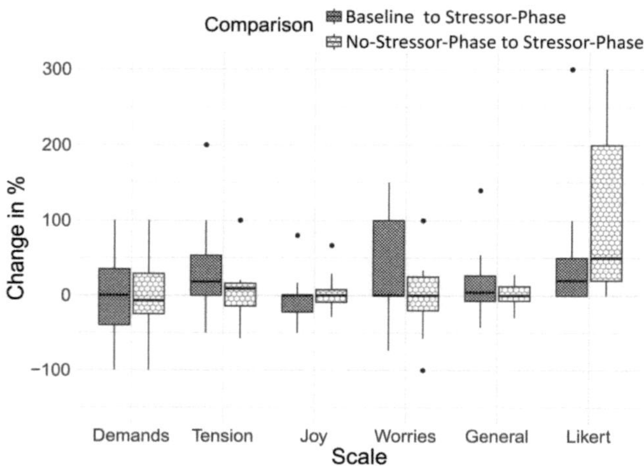

Figure 4.5: Result comparison of percentage changes between phases, for the Task Interruption.

results for all PSQ20 sub-scales (Worry, Tension, Joy, Demands) and its Overall Score, as well as the 7-point Likert-scale item.

Results of the PSQ20 and Likert Item

With few exceptions, subjective data was normally distributed (Task Interruption: $BL_{PSQ-Worries}$: W=0.81, p<0.05; BL_{Likert}: W=0.85, p<0.05; Time Pressure: $BL_{PSQ-Worries}$: W=0.85, p<0.05; $NSP_{PSQ-Demands}$: W=0.62, p<0.01; $NSP_{PSQ-Overall}$: W=0.79, p<0.01). The following significance tests are based on raw results.

Those participants who were exposed to the Task Interruption stressor did not perceive the SP significantly more stressful than the BL not according to the PSQ20 and its sub-scales: Worries: V=13.5, p=0.57; Tension: t(12)=-1.54, p=0.15; Joy: t(12)= 0.89, p=0.39; Demands: t(12)=-0.72, p=0.49; Overall Score: t(12)=-0.75, p=0.47. The difference in the Likert item is significant: V=0, p<0.001. Comparing the subjective measures in NSP to SP, we see that, again, the PSQ20 results are not significant: Worries: t(12)=-0.60, p=0.56; Tension: t(12)=0, p=1; Joy: t(12)=-0.22, p=0.83; Demands: V=37, p=0.91; Overall Score: V=35, p=0.78. The Likert scale shows a significant increase: t(12)=-3.43, p<0.01. Figure 4.5 visualizes the results.

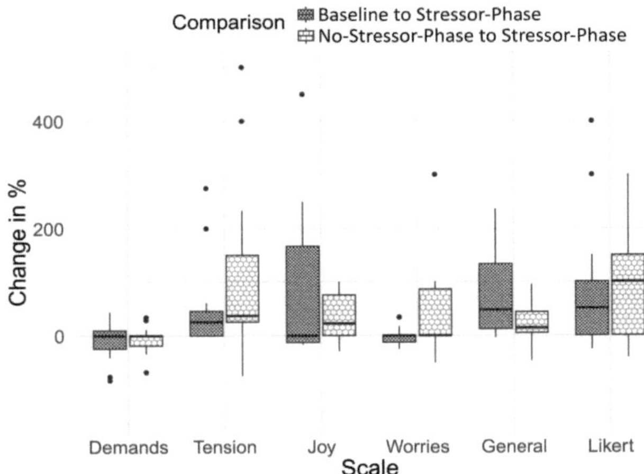

Figure 4.6: Result comparison of percentage changes between phases, for the Time Pressure.

In the Time Pressure group, we found significant differences between BL and SP in the PSQ20 Overall Score: t(12)=-3.04, p<0.01 (Worries: V=10.5, p<0.05; Tension: t(12)=-2.73, p<0.05; Demands: t(12)=-3.16, p<0.01). As the exception in the PSQ20 sub-scales, Joy did not show a significant difference (t(12)=1.1512, p=0.27). Ratings for the Likert item also showed a significant difference: t(12)=-3.77, p<0.01.

In the comparison of NSP and SP, the subjective measures of the Demands sub-scale (V=12, p<0.05), the Overall Score (V=16.5, p<0.05), and the Likert item (t(12)=-2.92, p<0.05) showed significant differences. Other sub-scales did not (Worries: V=10.5, p=0.085; Tension: t(12)=-2.17, p=0.051; Joy t(12)=1.72, p=0.11). For a graphical overview of the results, please see Figure 4.6.

To test H_2, we compared the stress levels induced during SP. The results demonstrate that the participants did not rate the stress-inducing abilities of the stressors differently (Worries: t(24)=-0.34, p=0.74; Tension: t(23)=0.53, p=0.6; Joy: t(23)=0.21, p=0.84; Demands: t(22)=-0.31, p=0.76; Overall Score: W=84, p=1; Likert Item: W=106.5, p=0.26).

Igroup Presence Questionnaire

The General Presence was rated at 5.81 out of 7 on average (SD=0.69), Spatial Presence at 5.91 (0.91), Involvement at 5.92 (0.85), and Experienced Realism with 5.80

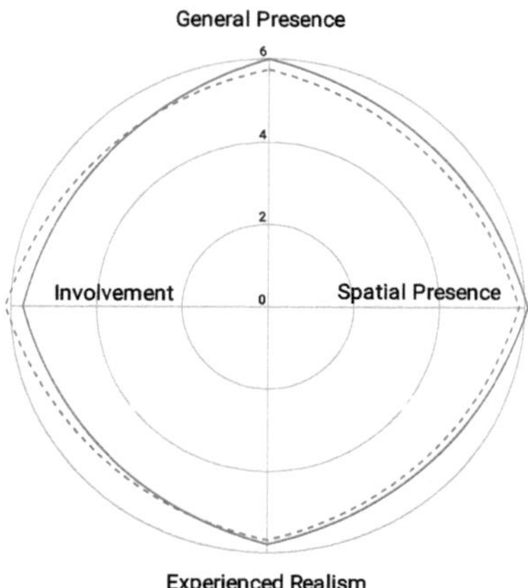

Figure 4.7: Radar chart showing IPQ results for both stressors. Time pressure is shown as a continuous line, and task interruption as a dashed line.

(1.00). There were no statistically significant differences in the average IPQ ratings between the stressors (General Presence: W=78.5, p=0.78; Involvement: t(90)=0.09, p=0.92; Spatial Presence: t(99)=-0.14, p=0.89; Experienced Realism: (49)=-1.01, p=0.32). Figure 4.7 shows the IPQ results in a radar chart.

NASA-TLX

We report means and SDs for the NASA-TLX sub-scales in the following. Mental Demand was rated at 31.23 (SD=22.16), Physical Demand at 12.38 (16.87), Temporal Demand at 39.46 (6.43), Performance at 29.46 (23.08), Effort at 27.58 (18.98), Frustration at 33.92 (31.92), and Overall Workload at 36.1 (2.31). While most data was normally distributed in both participant groups, data for the sub-scales Physical Demand, Frustration, and Effort were not. A visual representation of the results is illustrated in Figure 4.8. With the exception ofPerformance (t(18)=3.52, p<0.01), we report no statistically significant differences for any of the TLX sub-scales (Mental Workload: t(24)=1.25, p=0.22; Physical Demand: W=88.5, p=0.83; Temporal Demand:t(24)=0.19, p=0.85; Effort: W=58, p=0.19; Frustration: W=114.5, p=0.12, and Overall Load: t(22)=1.15, p=0.26).

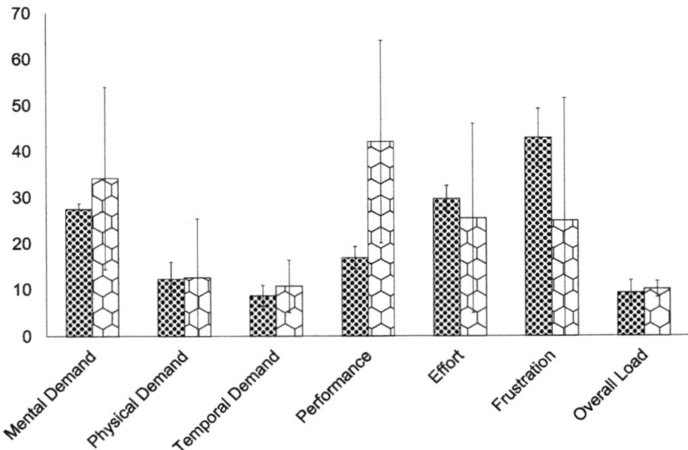

Figure 4.8: Results of the NASA-TLX post-hoc evaluation. Time pressure is shown as dotted bars, and task interruption with a comb structure.

4.3.3 Task Execution

Throughout the tasks, we logged both the required time as well as errors during task execution.

In the NSP participants from the Task Interruption group needed 4.58 minutes (SD=1.01) on average, and 5.8 minutes (2.39) in the Time Pressure group, respectively. During the stressor phases, participants were slower. On average, subjects from the Task Interruption group required 7.8 minutes (1.96), and participants from the Time Pressure group needed 7.2 minutes (1.6), respectively.

We have logged 2.2 mistakes on average (SD=1.39) during NSP and 2.56 (1.3) throughout SP for participants exposed to Time Pressure. This stressor did not lead to a significant increase in errors (V=10, p=0.27, r=0.09). Participants in the Task Interruption group, however, had 1.9 (1.1) errors logged during NSP, and 4.1 (1.79) in SP. There is a significant increase between the phases (V=14.5, p<0.01). In either phase, it did not make a difference to what stressor participants were exposed (TP$_{NSP}$ vs. I$_{NSP}$: W=38, p=0.58; TP$_{SP}$ vs. I$_{SP}$: W=67.5, p=0.07). Participants spent between t_{min}=23.5 and t_{max}=49.6 minutes (m=34.2, SD=6.9) on average in the virtual ICU.

4.3.4 Interview Results

The fifth phase of the experiment procedure consisted, among other things, of a semi-structured interview where we inquired about general opinions on the experiment. Further questions were about what influence participants believed their (technical) problems had, and in what way they imagined VR applications like the one they used during the experiment could be adopted into the curriculum.

Fidelity

Participating healthcare professionals rated the vICU considerably high in both simulation fidelity and graphical detail: "I had expected much less" (P2). Especially the correct task order the syringe task was positively commented on (P6, P8, P15). On the other hand, one nurse mentioned that the room was "too clean" and told us that it was missing "the little things", i.e. bandages, a box for syringe disposal, and a trashcan (P21). A few participants remarked on the little diversity in both stressors and tasks. Following the suggestions, we believe that we can increase the presence in the environment.

Interaction

Several participants reported difficulties of interacting with the VE using the handheld controllers. For example, P16 expressed frustration that she was better at grabbing objects during the training phase but struggled when the timer was introduced. These claims are consistent with the NASA-TLX measures, as both the mental demand and the frustration scale show high scores (see Fig. 4.8).

Curriculum

The question of whether participants thought VR could be a valuable tool in education led to mixed replies. P22 welcomed the future-orientedness of the experiment and further substantiated that with a comment on versatility. Others criticized the unrealistic handling and missing haptics, stating that correct hand-eye coordination is crucial to most tasks.

4.4 Discussion and Findings

The following discussion focuses on the stress-inducing capabilities of the system as well as the results of the NASA-TLX and IPQ, as they can be put into relation to one another and support the investigation of our first research question.

Our results demonstrate that using VR to mimic different stressors from the intensive care environment induces stress. We observed significant changes in some physiological stress levels (HR, RF) during the SP in both groups. Other measures at least show a trend of changing stress levels. The lower levels of HRV in the stressed phases are also a sign of increased stress levels [RAPJK+06]. The different increase between NSP and SP in the two pulmonary measures could be based on the mechanisms of breathing, as RF has a higher influence on the overall air intake than V_T, depending on the type of stressor [THPC17]. The difference in the overall PSQ20 score was significant in both comparisons for the Time Pressure group, but not in the Task Interruption, whereas the Likert item shows a significant increase in all comparisons. While this could be caused by the framing of the questions in the PSQ20 compared to the Likert item, it likely points to a stronger increase in subjective stress, which is supported by the performance and frustration scales of the Nasa-TLX.

We believe that the virtual environment and cognitive load of tasks already induced some stress which may have resulted in a ceiling effect, resulting in non-significant changes in stress level between the NSP and SP in both stressors. In comparison to the baseline, the stressors had a significant effect. While in the objective measures, this could be explained with physical activity, the subjective ratings also support H_1, which is why we accept H_1. VR is not yet a ubiquitous technology, but with increasing use, this ceiling effect will decrease. For this reason, we believe that our approach is capable of inducing stress in participants, supporting our research question, and providing a basis for future research.

The vICU was designed according to the requirements (see Section 3.2) and was able to evoke a strong sense of presence among the participants. The study's environment scored high in the IPQ scales General Presence and Experienced Realism. We observed that the stressor alone was not the only factor that determined the level of presence. The combination of virtual environment, tasks, and stressors played a bigger role in inducing presence than each component individually.

Due to the short average time spent in VR and the exclusion of physical props, temporal and physical demands were not rated high. In contrast, the mental demand scored higher. The 10-point difference between the stressor groups results from participants having to re-focus on the task after a task interruption, which is in line with related work [DMSS19]. To reiterate, the low pre-existing experience in VR is also a reason for the mental workload, which would decrease with more training.

The results from the NASA-TLX sub-scales of Performance and Frustration indicate the expected effects of our stressors. While the Task Interruption group was able to complete their tasks, the Time Pressure group had difficulties with this, as the timer often ended before tasks were accomplished. This demonstrates that the stressors had the intended impact. Also, the Task Interruption group made more errors during the SP, which is consistent with Coiera's work on communication and interruptions [CJH+02].

We have to reject hypothesis H_2 based on NASA-TLX, PSQ20, and objective results. Multi-modality of the Interruption stressor did not have a significant impact on induced stress but instead led to more mistakes. Further research must explore additional sensory modalities' impact. For instance, vibration could negatively affect performance despite conveying Time Pressure [CYL+13].

The tasks we defined were developed in collaboration with a local clinic, taking into account user research. However, they are limited to the specific processes established by the clinic, which means that their generalizability may also be limited. We did not vary the timings in our experiment procedure to ensure comparability, but since some participants lacked experience, experimenters had to intervene and provide assistance.

In the upcoming chapters, we will first immerse the participants in a story-driven scenario to investigate the effects of a moral dilemma and finally combine the stressors and evaluate their ecological validity.

5 Inducing Moral Distress in VR through Storytelling

Many intensive care staff members suffer from psycho-physiologic exhaustion due to organizational and environmental stressors such as understaffing, alarms, and time pressure. Emotional stressors further contribute to this problem. If left unattended, emotional stress can cause psychological distress, emotional discomfort (e.g., sadness, anger, and frustration), and physical consequences such as chronic sleep disturbances, loss of positive feelings, or lack of drive. These issues ultimately decrease the quality of care and patient interaction.

To investigate whether we can recreate emotional distress in VR, we designed and implemented a storyline for the vICU presented in Chapter 3. In this chapter, we explain the concepts of emotional stress generally and moral distress in particular (see Section 5.1), describe the development of our storyline and the accompanying scenario (cf. Section 5.2) using the three-act-structure by Field [Fie94]. Then, we outline how we conducted the experiment (see Section 5.3) and its results (see Section 5.4) before we end this chapter with the discussion of our findings (cmp. Section 5.5) and a summary (cf. Section 5.6).

The material in this chapter has been published in Weiß, S., Busse, S., & Heuten, W. (2022, March). Inducing emotional stress from the intensive care context using storytelling in VR. In 2022 IEEE Conference on Virtual Reality and 3D User Interfaces (VR) (pp. 196-204).

5.1 Introduction

Emotional stress is defined by the American Psychological Association (APA) as psychological stress and discomfort caused by situations that threaten personal security, or by inner conflicts, frustrations, loss of self-esteem, and grief [1]. The Encyclopedia of Behavioral Medicine describes emotional stress as a psychological stress response caused by changes in hormonal levels, which can affect the cardiopulmonary system [Men20]. Negative emotions such as fear, sadness, and anxiety can trigger those hormonal changes, leading to increased stress levels.

The level of stress caused by emotional stressors can vary from person to person, depending on their ability to cope with the situation. The presence of positive social support and the use of effective coping strategies, such as relaxation techniques, exercise, and cognitive strategies, are the most important factors in preventing emotional stress. These strategies have been shown to have positive effects.

---

[1] https://dictionary.apa.org/emotional-stress, last accessed Oct. 25th, 2023

5.1.1 Emotional Stressors in an ICU

According to Gélineas et al., emotional stressors in intensive care refer to those that cause direct emotional distress, differentiating them from environmental and organizational stressors. The constant exposure to the suffering of patients and their families requires a great deal of compassion [CLMM12]. However, if a caregiver becomes too involved on a personal level and absorbs the suffering, it can lead to a sense of helplessness and failure. Additionally, when treatment is unsuccessful despite maximum effort, one may doubt their competence, leading to feelings of powerlessness and inadequacy [Epp12a, MSU16]. Caregivers can experience emotional stress when they feel that they have not been able to provide enough care to a patient due to constraints in the organization, such as insufficient time or resources. This may be particularly true when caring for younger patients in palliative care, as it can make caregivers realize that mortality can also affect their own lives [CLMM12].

5.1.2 Moral Distress

Moral distress refers to a form of emotional stress that individuals experience when they are unable to act according to their fundamental values or what they perceive to be right. This is particularly true for caregivers who have limited decision-making power when it comes to patient treatment, compared to attending physicians. In the context of healthcare, one of the most common causes of moral distress is having to comply with the wishes of patients or their families, even when they conflict with the caregiver's moral values. For instance, caregivers may feel moral distress when they have to continue life-sustaining measures that are not in line with the best interests of the patient, or when medical staff (i.e., doctors) decide to discontinue life support for hopelessly ill patients. Another cause of moral distress is when caregivers have to assist doctors whom they deem incompetent [ECK05, Epp12b].

Research has shown that an emotional connection not only increases the stress level [PWD$^+$19a], but it also influences knowledge retention positively [DJBM$^+$10]. Both Prachyabrued et al. and Kleinsmith et al. demonstrated that it is possible to feel empathy towards virtual characters [PWD$^+$19a, KRGF$^+$15]. We build on these results by adding emotional and dramaturgic events, as dramaturgy increases the emotional presence [PCR$^+$13].

5.2 Development of a Storyline

To develop a scenario that confronts our study participants with moral distress, we needed to find an example and implement it into the existing VE. Furthermore, we wanted to create a believable story arc To that end, why we followed a standardized storytelling technique called the three-act structure, developed by Field [Fie94].

5.2.1 Storytelling Using Three-Act Structure

Every story follows a certain dramaturgic structure which represents the basic scheme for a screenplay. The scheme is composed of three parts, namely the beginning, middle, and finale. These are also commonly referred to as acts (cf. Fig. 5.1). Each act is assigned a specific task to advance the plot.

At the beginning, the exposition takes place, in which the story (the setup) is established in the first act. The base for the story is laid out here, including the necessary information about the story on which further plot can be built. The exposition consists of three basic elements: (1) the introduction of the main characters, (2) the clarification of the dramaturgic meaning, i.e. what the story is about, and (3) the introduction of the constellation, i.e. the circumstances that are connected to the plot. At the end of the first act, a plot point occurs, which is an intervening event in the plot. These events serve as fixed points that stabilize the paradigm and offer a new direction for the story.

The second act is the most significant part of the story as it contains the primary conflict or confrontation. It is crucial to establish the protagonist's objectives and create obstacles for them to overcome to achieve their goals. The second plot point, which occurs towards the end of the second act, is an essential plot twist that leads to the third act.

The plot culminates in the third act with the resolution of the main character's conflict, resulting in either their success or failure.

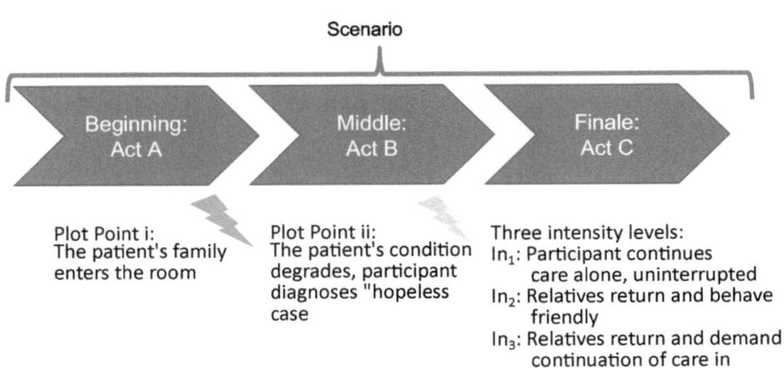

Figure 5.1: Schematic overview of the three-act structure in our scenario including both important plot points (i, ii) and intensity levels (In_1-In_3) of act C.

5.2.2   Development of a Scenario

To create a believable scenario, we involved users as much as possible in the development of our experimental software. We began by conducting a literature review to gain a better understanding of the emotional stressors experienced in an ICU. Following this, we interviewed experts in the field.

We used Mayring's qualitative approach [May15] on the results of literature research which we conducted in the scientific search engine Google Scholar[2] and the local university's databases. We utilized specific keywords such as "emotional stress", "psychological stress", "intensive care", and "intensive care unit" in our search to find relevant research papers. Both English and German papers were included to answer the question, "What are common emotional stressors in the critical care context?" After analyzing the collected information, we summarized and categorized it by bundling and paraphrasing the material.

We developed a set of interview guidelines for conducting semi-structured interviews. Our main objective was to gain deeper insights into emotional stress, expert knowledge, practical knowledge, and common practices in the ICU. We used the semi-structured approach to allow for flexibility in our questions based on the context of the conversation. This approach enabled the interviewees to share their experiences more freely, even if their specific case was not covered by the guidelines. The interview guidelines encompassed various questions related to the study objectives, e.g. What are the relevant emotional stressors that regularly occur in the critical care context? or If we address concrete situations, what is a typical sequence of these situations? Which actors are involved?.

During the interviews, we covered four main topics. Firstly, we asked the interviewees to describe situations that had caused them emotional stress in a general sense. Next, we inquired about their interactions with patients' families and how involved they were in the decision-making process for patient care interventions. Then, we questioned the participants about their interactions with colleagues, both medical and nursing staff. Lastly, we discussed how the respondents perceived moral conflict and moral distress. All questions were designed to help us gain a better understanding of their experiences and perspectives in these areas.

We conducted interviews with five ICU nurses (2f, 3m, 0d). Their ages ranged from 20 to 36 years (m=28.4, SD=6.58). All participants had professional experience that ranged from three to 15 years, with an average of seven years (SD=4.74). The interviews were conducted using an online conference tool software and were recorded after obtaining consent for future reference. We analyzed the recorded interviews using Mayring's qualitative analysis method, which focused on the experiences and situations of the participating nurses and their emotional effects. The analysis was based on the same questions as the interview guidelines and followed the structuring procedure. We used existing codes from the literature review and

---

[2] https://scholar.google.com, last accessed January 14th, 2024

Table 5.1: Stressors and the frequency in which they have been mentioned by the expert interview partners.

Stressor	Times mentioned
Incompetent medical staff	5
Fulfill family's requests	5
Relationship to patient	5
Conflict with colleagues	4
Taking care of younger patients	3
Taking care of hopeless cases	3
Feeling unqualified	2
Conflict between medical and nursing staff	2
Unnecessarily prolong dying	2
Unsuccessful in spite of best efforts	2
Feeling not to have done enough	2
Confrontation with the suffering of family	2
Disliking the patient	1

added new ones based on knowledge obtained from the interviews. The results are listed in Table 5.1 which summarizes stressors extracted from literature and mentioned stressors in expert interviews, ordered by frequency.

5.2.3 Scenario Development

We developed a scenario in three acts to investigate the effect of a stressor from the domain of moral distress, in which participants take on the role of a nurse. They interact with several NPCs that are also part of the storyline. One of these NPC characters is Yvonne, a nurse who is handing over the patient to the participant. Further NPCs in the scenario are relatives of the patient. We investigated whether the intensity of a stressor influences the stress reaction in our participants. The intensity of the stressor is driven by the family's behavior.

The scenario is split into three parts, namely Acts A, B, and C. We aim to investigate whether we can elicit varying levels of stress in our participants by changing the behavior of the patient's family towards them. These modifications are referred to as "Intensity I through III" (In_1-In_3) for Act C. Acts A and B remain constant for all participants.

Act A

At the start of the simulation, the NPC nurse updates the participant on the patient's condition. The first act takes place in an ICU and establishes the participant's role and background story. The NPC explains the consequences if the patient's health deteriorates and provides instructions on the tasks the participant must perform. The NPC then asks if the participant has any questions before leaving the room. Before departing, the NPC also informs the participant about the patient's wife and brother's imminent visit, which marks the start of plot point i. Please refer to Figure 5.1 for a visualization of the event timeline.

Act B

In the second act of our story, we introduce the main conflict. Additional NPCs arrive in the ICU, who are the adult relatives of the patient - his wife and his brother. After a brief greeting, the participant can explain the situation to them and inform them that continuous care may not be advisable if the patient's vitals worsen. However, both NPCs insist that treatment and life support should be continued in any case. Then, the wife and brother leave the room.

The second plot point occurs when the participant gets notified about the patient's decreasing blood pressure in the form of an audible alert. This marks the turning point of the story and highlights the central conflict, as the family's wishes now oppose the information about the meaningfulness of treatment continuation. This creates a moral obstacle for the participant, preventing them from providing the best possible care to the patient and acts as an emotional stressor.

Act C

The third part of the experiment (Act C) varies depending on the intensity level (In_{1-3}), whereas the first and second acts are the same for all participants. The first intensity level (In_1) serves as a control scenario without any relatives and was experienced only by group α. During this control scenario, the aim was to remove the impact of family presence on stress levels. As one of the interview partners stated, "It is much more stressful when the relatives are present, and their grief is also felt". Group β experienced the second intensity level (In_2) where the NPCs were friendly and understanding, while group γ encountered NPCs acting stubborn and agitated in the third intensity level (In_3).

In both In_2 and In_3, the relatives return to the room, but their reactions differ based on the intensity of the stressor. At first, the NPCs behave similarly in both intensity levels. The brother reveals that they are aware of the patient's status, and the wife explains that they know the situation is hopeless, as the nurse NPC informed them earlier that week. She then asks the participant for their personal opinion on how to proceed. However, the relatives' behavior starts to differ depending on the intensity level:

- In In_2, the family members accept and understand that further treatment would be futile. They express their trust in the participant and do not want their loved one to suffer any longer. Nevertheless, they remain present in the room but do not cause any additional moral distress to the participants of the study. Eventually, the scene concludes with the patient continuing their standard tasks while the wife requests the participant to take good care of her spouse. The family members remained calm and composed throughout the remainder of the experiment, leading to a neutral resolution.

- The highest level of moral distress among the participants, denoted by In_3, occurs when family NPCs insist on continuing care and express their wishes in an agitated and stubborn manner. For example, the patient's wife exclaims "We will not lose hope!" while the participant continues to carry out their tasks, or the patient's brother angrily states "I cannot allow the machines to be switched off! My brother would not give me up either!" In such situations, participants face a moral dilemma, as they have to provide a treatment that contradicts their knowledge and personal opinion, and there is no clear solution to the problem.

5.3 Study Design

We conducted a laboratory study with participants from intensive care and other occupations to investigate the impact of a virtual reproduction of this stressor. By measuring the participants' stress responses in both subjective and objective ways, we aimed to answer the following research question:

Moral distress can be caused by treating a patient to fulfill the request of relatives against one's own set of moral standards and one's own belief that it is not in the patient's best interest. How can this be induced using a VE?

We measured the impact of moral distress on participants experiencing different intensities of the stressor during Act C. We quantified stress levels using the test battery presented in Section 3.3.4. To perform this study, we designed a "Wizard-of-Oz" experiment, where participants were unaware that the NPCs they interacted with were being controlled by experimenters. Participants were informed that they could respond to the NPCs, but they would not respond. We decided that only NPCs initiated the conversations since the number of possible variations of answers would have created an unmanageable decision tree on what answer to give. For this experiment, we hypothesized the following:

- H_1: A higher stressor intensity of "emotional distress" leads to a more pronounced stress response than a lower intensity.

Virtual Environment

The scenario was set in the vICU presented in Section 3.3.3. We further utilized the same tasks as in Chapter 4, albeit in an adapted (i.e. simpler) form. This was carried out to decrease the cognitive load on the participant, decreasing its influence as a confounding factor in our stress measures. Two more tasks were added, which were also kept simple intentionally:

- Filling a glass with water. Water flowed automatically into the glass from the tap with accompanying sound effects after virtually grabbing it and moving it under the tap.

- Opening and closing a window. Another task was to open and close the ICU room window by grabbing and pulling its handle using a controller.

We made use of the freely available characters in the Microsoft Rocketbox Avatar library[3] to create our NPCs (cf. Fig. 5.2). This library includes 115 different characters and is pre-rigged, enabling the use of animations for idle, walk, and talk based on an animation-state machine. The animations used for the NPCs in this experiment were downloaded from the Adobe Inc.-owned character platform Mixamo®[4]. The voice lines required for our storyline were recorded with the help of students. Figure 5.3 visualizes a schematic overview of the experimental setup for the user study.

Procedure

At the beginning of the experiment, the participants were provided with a written guide that explained how to use the controllers and the tasks they needed to perform. It was also mentioned that the time and execution of the tasks were not recorded to prevent any impact on the stress levels of the participants. Once the participants read the manual, they put on the Zephyr Bioharness® and the Groove GSR (see Figure 3.15). Then, they wore the VR HMD while the experimenter loaded the tutorial scene. Before the experiment started, we recorded a baseline (BL) of the physiological measures and participants filled out the pre-experiment PSQ20. On average, the participants spent 14:43 minutes (SD=1:36) in the scenario.

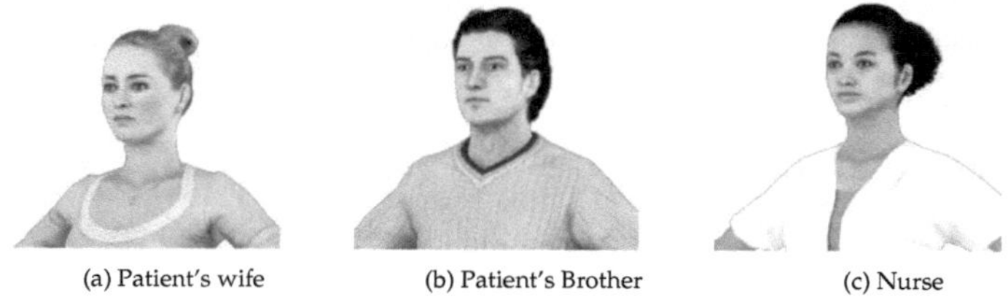

(a) Patient's wife   (b) Patient's Brother   (c) Nurse

Figure 5.2: Rocketbox characters used in our application and their role.

---

[3] https://github.com/microsoft/Microsoft-Rocketbox, last accessed Oct 31st, 2023
[4] https://www.mixamo.com, last accessed Oct 31st, 2023

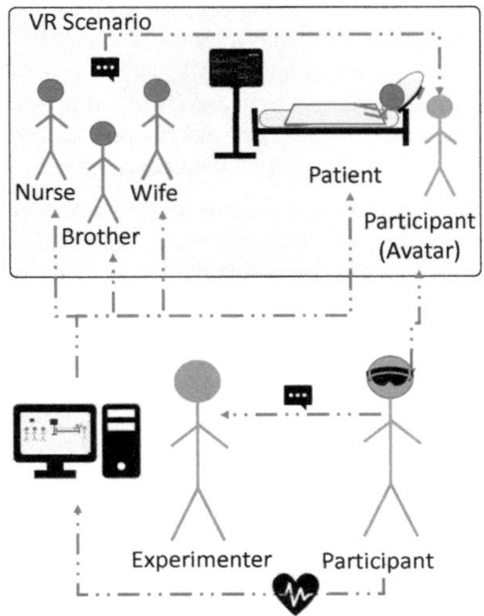

Figure 5.3: A schematic overview of the experiment setup.

Participants

For our study, we recruited a total of 16 participants (6f, 10m, 0d). The age range of the participants was between 21 to 60 years (m=29.2 years, SD=10.8). Half of the participants had prior experience in intensive care. Before participating in the experiment, we instructed all subjects to abstain from consuming alcohol and caffeine for a day before and after the experiment. We also asked them to avoid strenuous physical activity 24 hours before the experiment. There was no monetary compensation offered for participation in the study, and none of the participants had any prior experience with VR.

Data Analysis

We had to exclude cardiac data from three participants and EDA data from a fourth participant due to faulty wiring in the measuring hardware, but have taken into consideration the remaining data sets from those four participants. The objective data was filtered for outliers by removing values that were either above or below the 1.5-fold IQR distance from the upper and lower quartile.

All participants were presented with PSQ20 and a 7-point Likert item before and after the experiment, while the IPQ was filled out by the participants after they had completed the VR scenario. We used the formula $A_i \rightarrow A_{i+1} = \frac{(X_{i+1} - X_i) * 100}{X_i}$ to calculate changes in subjective stress levels between different acts and groups. To test H_1, we filtered the data and calculated the average per participant per act. These averages were then used as a basis for further statistical analysis.

Answers to the questionnaires are available as pre- and post-hoc and do not allow insights into stress changes between acts. We processed the PSQ20 as instructed by [FRA+09] and averaged the total score, the Likert item, as well as the IPQ, results over all subjects. All data underwent normal distribution tests using the Shapiro-Wilk test. Objective data was tested on a per-act/per-group basis. The selection of subsequent significance tests (ANOVA/t-test or Kruskal-Wallis/Mann-Whitey-U test) depended on the results of the Shapiro-Wilk tests. We only report significant results for Act C, which is the relevant act to answer our research question.

5.4 Results

In this section, we present the results of the study described above. We begin by reporting on the objective results and continue with the subjective results. We further discuss the percentage changes that we consider relevant at the end of each respective result section.

5.4.1 Objective Measures

In the following, the results of the calculations for the objective measures are described. We report on HR, HRV, EDA, and RF.

Heart Rate

Regarding the HR data, we did not find significant differences between Act A in groups α and γ by means of an ANOVA (α: F(1,14)=0.018, p=0.896; γ: F(1,18)=0.453, p=0.51). The same applied to the calculated ANOVA testing BL as well as Acts B and C (BL: F(1,11)=1.71, p=0.217; ActB: F(1,11)=1.44, p=0.256; ActC: F(1,11)=3.42, p=0.092).

The Kruskal-Wallis test performed for group β revealed no difference (β:H=0.419, p=0.936). A Kruskal-Wallis test in Act A showed a significant difference (H=6.23, p<0.05). The subsequent Mann-Whitney-U-Test resulted in a significant difference between groups α and β ($\alpha \mid \beta$: U=16, p<0.05 $\alpha \mid \gamma$: U=7, p=0.556; $\beta \mid \gamma$: U=2, p=0.063).

Heart Rate Variability

To compare the HRV among acts within groups α and γ an ANOVA was conducted. The results showed no significant differences between the acts in either group (α: F(1,14)=0.114, p=0.741; γ: F(1,18)=0.558, p=0.465). Similarly, the Kruskal-Wallis test conducted for participants from group β did not show any significant differences (β: H=0.287, p=0.962). BL and Act B were also compared between groups, but no significant differences were found (BL: F(1,11)=0.902, p=0.363; ActB: F(1,11)=0.926, p=0.36). Additionally, there were no significant differences found between groups in Act C (F(1,11)=1.72, p=0.217).

Electrodermal Activity

The calculated ANOVA for group α (F(1,18)=0.233, p=0.635) as well as the computed Kruskal-Wallis test for groups β and γ did not show significant changes in EDA data between the acts (β: H=0.419, p=0.936: γ: H=1.82, p=0.611). Further, there were no differences between groups in the last act (H=1.36, p=0.507).

Respiration Frequency

R_F in the groups α and β between acts A and B were tested via an ANOVA. The results showed no significant difference (α: F(1,14)=4.094, p=0.063; β: F(1,14)=2.79, p=0.117). For group γ, however, the result of the ANOVA was significant (γ: F(1,18)=9.62, p<0.01). The subsequent pair-wise t-test resulted in significant differences between the BL and all other acts (BL | ActA: t(10)=-5.487, p<0.01; BL | ActB: t(10)=-4.496, p<0.05; BL | ActC: t(10)=-3.55, p<0.05), as well as between act B and C (ActB | ActC: t(10)=3.703, p<0.05). There were no significant differences between the groups in Act C (F(1,11)=0.223, p=0.646).

Percentual Changes

Table 5.2 holds the average percentage changes of the objective measures over all participants (mean of means) for BL. HR has a significantly higher value in group α compared to group β, and HRV has a significantly lower one, respectively. HRV decreases in groups α and γ from the baseline. In α the reduction becomes less pronounced from act to act (ActA: -4.5%, ActC: -2.0%), while it gets stronger in group γ (ActA: -2.6%, ActC: -4.5%). Moreover, the average increase in EDA from Act B to Act C is more in the negative range at higher intensity levels (α: 2.0%; β: -8.01%; γ: -10.7%), i.e. the skin resistance becomes less, as participants secrete sweat in response to the stressor. In general, a large difference in results is observed when measuring EDA. For RF, a significant difference is shown between groups α and γ, with α having a higher increase to baseline measurement (103.9%) than γ (77.3%). Considering the mean percentage changes of HR, there is an increase for groups β and γ in act C compared to the BL (β: 0.6%; γ: 4.4%). Group α depicts a decrease of -0.5%. It can be observed that there is a higher increase in HR with increasing inten-

Table 5.2: Average percentage increase and SDs of objective measures between baseline measure and the three acts.

Measure	Group	Average (SD) Change in %		
		BL→A	BL→B	BL→C
HR	α	4.1 (4.5)	3.3 (3.8)	-0.5 (2.4)
	β	-1.2 (5.5)	-1.4 (9.0)	0.6 (8.7)
	γ	2.1 (4.5)	3.6 (6.1)	4.4 (8.7)
HRV	α	-4.5 (3.6)	-3.5 (4.3)	-2 (1.1)
	β	0.1 (5.6)	0.5 (8.5)	-1.6 (8.7)
	γ	-2.6 (5.6)	-4.0 (5.8)	-4.5 (7.9)
EDA	α	-17.6 (17.1)	-21.8 (15.3)	-21.4 (11.7)
	β	-5.2 (26.2)	-13.4 (28.1)	-18.8 (31.7)
	γ	-15.0 (21.0)	-21.7 (22.3)	-29.9 (25.5)
R_F	α	103.9 (49.3)	106.7 (48.5)	76.5 (66.9)
	β	104.8 (55.4)	78.6 (39.9)	64.7 (41.2)
	γ	77.3 (37.5)	91.3 (51.1)	70.9 (45.9)

sity. With regards to RF, there is generally a lower mean at BL than in the following activities, except in the comparisons α: BL | ActA and BL | ActB (103.9% to 106.7%) and γ: BL | ActA and BL | ActB (77.3% to 91.3%).

5.4.2 Subjective Measures

In the following, we report on the subjective measures. We demonstrate results from the PSQ20, the Likert item, the IPQ as well as the percentage changes in stress levels.

PSQ20

The Shapiro-Wilk test showed a normal distribution for the total scores, and a subsequent ANOVA. showed a significant difference in the post hoc comparison ($F(1,14)=4.86$, $p<0.05$). The non-pairwise t-test between the experimental groups α, β, and γ revealed higher stress in groups β and γ (α | β: $t(8)=-2.92$, $p<0.05$; α | γ: $t(9)=-2.36$, $p<0.05$). We did not find a significant difference between groups β and γ ($t(9)=0.264$, $p=0.798$).

Data for all sub-scales was normally distributed. An ANOVA did not show significant differences between the groups post experiment comparisons in any sub-scale except Demands: $F(1,14)=22.3$, $p<0.01$ (Worries: $F(1,14)=1.48$, $p=0.24$; Tension: $F(1,14)=1.56$, $p=0.23$; Joy: $F(1,14)=2.86$, $p=0.123$). The subsequent non-pairwise t-tests between all groups should a significant decrease in groups β and γ over α (α |

β: t(6)=-3.64, p<0.05; α | γ: t(9)=-6.24, p<0.01), but not between β and γ: t(7)=-0.98, p=0.36.

Likert Item

The results of the study show that there was a significant difference between the groups in terms of self-rated stress level (F(1,14)=5.30, p<0.05). Participants in groups β and γ reported experiencing significantly higher stress levels than those in group α (α | β: t(8)=-2.77, p<0.05; α | γ: t(9)=-2.42, p<0.05). However, there was no significant difference in stress levels reported between the β and γ groups (β | γ: t(9)=0.084, p=0.935). Figure 5.4 illustrates these results in a graph. For the raw scores, see Table 5.3.

IPQ

The Shapiro-Wilk test indicated that the IPQ sub-scales SP and REAL followed a normal distribution, whereas the remaining sub-scales did not. Although there was no significant difference in spatial presence between the groups (F(1,14)=0.574, p=0.472), participants from group γ rated the realism significantly higher than those in group α (t(8.68)=-2.5, p<0.05). The sub-scales G and INV did not show any sig-

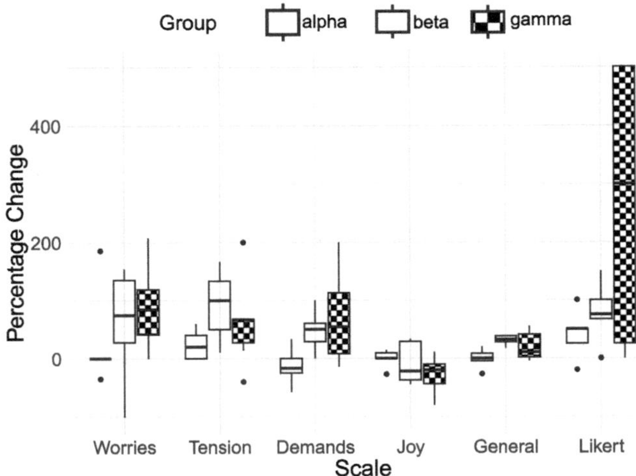

Figure 5.4: Box plots showing results of subjective measures, higher scores mean higher stress levels.

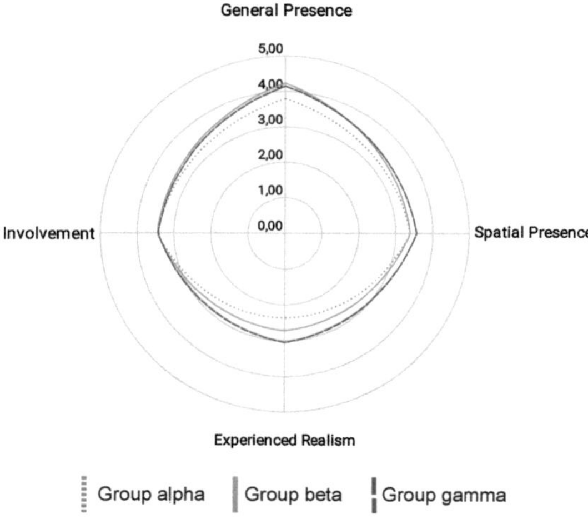

Figure 5.5: Radar chart showing IPQ results in each group.

nificant differences between the groups (G: H=2.54, p=0.28; INVH=0.57, p=0.75). The IPQ results are presented graphically in Figure 5.5.

Percentual Changes

Table 5.3 displays the means and standard deviations of changes in both the PSQ20 and the Likert item. Both subjective measures indicate a higher mean in the intensity of the stress level, associated with a higher intensity of the moral stressor (PSQ20 total score: β: 46.1%, γ: 69.3%; Likert item: β: 78.3%, γ: 308%). In contrast, the control group α did not show an increase in the stress reaction according to the PSQ20 (46.1%), and reported a smaller increase as per the Likert item (41%). This data highlights that the emotional stressor presented in a VE has a significant effect on the groups β and γ, as measured through qualitative user feedback.

5.5 Discussion and Findings

In this section, we discuss and classify our results based on the study's hypothesis H_1. Moreover, we examine whether a higher intensity of the stressor in the generated scenario resulted in a greater stress response.

Table 5.3: Average increase and SDs in subjective stress measures (∗ denotes p<0.05, ∗∗ denotes p<0.05).

Measure	Group	Means (SD).		Mean Increase in %
		Pre	Post	
PSQ20 General	α	26.3 (10.5)	26.3 (11.8)	-3.15
	β	33.7 (8.0)	48.0 (11.6)∗	46.1
	γ	28.3 (9.3)	45.8 (69.3)∗	69.3
PSQ20 Worries	α	20 (13.3)	21.3 (11.9)	6.5
	β	22.7 (15.3)	37.3 (22.9)	64.3
	γ	18.9 (9.81)	35.6 (19.6)	23.14
PSQ20 Tension	α	28 (17.3)	32 (19.7)	22.55
	β	32 (16.6)	54.7 (11.9)	70.93
	γ	31.1 (10.9)	47.8 (22.9)	53.69
PSQ20 Joy	α	74.4 (19.1)	73.3 (20)	-1.48
	β	52 (8.69)	45.3 (11.9)	-12.88
	γ	71.1 (13.1)	51.1 (24.1)	-28.13
PSQ20 Demands	α	32 (11)	25.3 (5.58)∗	-20.9
	β	32 (9.89)	45.3 (11)∗∗	41.56
	γ	34.4 (11.5)	51.1 (8.07)	48.54
Likert	α	2.8 (1.6)	3.4 (1.1)	41.0
	β	3.2 (0.8)	5.4 (1.1)	78.3
	γ	1.7 (0.8)	5.3 (1.5)	308.0

5.5.1 Objective Measures

Considering the objective data, we find a trend of measures pointing to a stronger stress response with increasing intensity level, see Table 5.2. The measured increase in the breathing frequency in Act A possibly resulted from the initial confrontation with the VE. Participants had to first become familiar with interacting and speaking with the characters. Also, uncertainty may have resulted in nervousness and symptoms of stress.

In general, the objective measurements indicate that there are no substantial differences between the groups and their stress responses. However, the HR and EDA data trends reveal that the measured stress levels tend to increase at higher intensity levels of the moral stressor. On the other hand, subjective measures show significantly higher stress levels at post-measurement in the groups β and γ than in α. Although no significant difference is found between groups β and γ, group γ shows higher percentage increases. Considering Goyals statement on the reliability of objective and subjective measures, we assume that the validity of the PSQ20 and the Likert question outweighs that of the sensors [GSVP16].

5.5.2 Subjective Measures

Based on our obtained results which are summarized in Table 5.1, we conclude that the intensity of the stressor had a measurable impact on our participants. The results of the PSQ20 and the Likert item demonstrate that the absence of relatives at diagnosis and further treatment (group α) did not lead to an increase in perceived stress. The intensity of the moral stressor was able to induce emotional stress in groups β and γ, with perceived stress being the strongest in group γ. These findings are in line with the findings of DeMaria et al. regarding calmer and more aggressive individuals [DJBM+10]. Our results further provide evidence that not only the presence of a stressor is measurable as indicated by Prachyabrued et al. [PWD+19b], but also its intensity. We further show that VR users not only feel empathy towards NPCs but are also influenced by their behavior.

The results of the IPQ indicate that the perceived realism increased significantly with each increase in stressor intensity in the sub-scale Real. Moreover, the increased level of the General sub-scale indicates higher stress levels, as shown by the PSQ20. This hints at a bidirectional relationship between presence and emotion, which was also demonstrated in [RMC+07]. Additionally, higher levels of stress led to higher levels of realism. Three participants who had professional experience in critical care noted that the presence of family members was very realistic, as they would be standing at the bedside while the nurse was attending to their tasks in the real world.

Considering these results shown above, we conclude that the results of the subjective measurements as well as the data trends of the objective measure support hypothesis H_1, which is why we accept it.

5.5.3 Limitations and Challenges

To provide more reliable and accurate conclusions about the sensory measurement results, it is recommended to conduct the study with a larger sample size. This will help to reduce the variability of the measured data and the impact of other factors that may affect the results. It is important to note that the physiological characteristics of individuals and their responses to stress are highly personalized, which means that the values of each participant can significantly influence the overall findings of the study.

Moreover, due to the limited number of participants in the study, it was not possible to make a comparison between the stress responses of nurses with those of the general population. The small sample size would have made it difficult to establish statistical significance between the two groups. Therefore, it was not possible to determine whether experience in intensive care had any effect on the stress response. The study found that ICU nurses who participated in the stress management training with the VR system were more confident in communicating with family members and acted as they would in their daily professional lives. Furthermore, those participants who were nurses mentioned that the shift handover used irregular wordings. Shift handovers follow a protocol, which the scenario used in this study did not consider. Coming studies should follow established standards more closely. However, some participants were uncertain when interacting with the characters, which could be a confounding factor.

Though none of the participants had prior experience with VR, younger participants found the controls easier, possibly due to their experience with video games. To gather accurate data, the demographic questionnaire should include questions about participants' experience with VR or video games. A lot of participants criticized the body movement as unreal, as avatars stood in a crooked position when idle and kept staring at the participants, as they were programmed to follow the movements. This came across as uncanny and should be improved in further research.

5.6 Summary

To investigate the effects of a moral stressor, we performed a literature analysis and subsequent expert interviews. We found "moral distress" to be a commonly cited emotional stressor. We then implemented a virtual scenario with dramaturgic elements following Field's three-act structure [Fie94].

In our study, we aimed to determine if higher levels of stress could result in a more significant stress response. We utilized both subjective and objective methods of measurement to assess the stress response. Although we found minimal differences in heart rate, heart rate variability, respiratory frequency, and electrodermal activity, we did find a higher stress response through subjective measurements using the PSQ20 and a single 7-point Likert scale question. Our study also revealed that NPCs communicating with pre-recorded speech fragments in virtual environments could induce a stress response. We found that virtual relatives could successfully represent the stressor developed for the script. Finally, we suggest that using a Wizard-of-Oz trial is a promising approach to implementing a stressor involving human interaction.

Upcoming research should investigate the possibilities of NPCs that are configurable in real-time so that bi-directional interactions between users and NPCs become possible. This gives experimenters great control over the situation. This can also be implemented through artificial intelligence, where the user's vitals and behavior in VR could be taken into account to determine the behavior of NPCs. In this way, aspiring nurses could be better prepared to handle emotional stressors, and to deal with patients' families. It is also of interest whether training conducted in this way has a similarly positive effect on training outcomes as has been shown by DeMaria et al. [DJBM+10].

6 Ecological Validation of the Virtual Intensive Care Unit

In the previous two chapters, we have shown that the VR-based stressor replicas we have investigated are capable of inducing stress in our experiment participants. However, due to the confounding factors of VR, we cannot infer that the effects are equal to their real-world counterparts, or that the VE environment is perceived as realistic. To make generalizable statements in this regard, we need to compare the effects of our VR scenario to a real-life situation, i.e. ensure the experiments' ecological validity.

In this chapter, we introduce the concept of ecological validity (see Section 6.1). Then, we present an updated scenario that we implemented according to user feedback collected in focus groups. The changes include a new storyline, more characters, and a wider range of tasks. To compare the effects of the stressors to a physical scenario, the complete storyline has also been transferred into the LIFE, as a stand-in for the status quo in schools. We present this new environment in Section 6.2. The study for the ecological validation is described in Section 6.3. We report the results in Section 6.4 and discuss them in Section 6.5.

6.1 Introduction

Because research in psychological and behavioral sciences is often carried out in a laboratory setting, the results of these cannot be generalized per se, a problem that is also known as the "real world or lab dilemma" [HHKH20]: Using controlled, simplified or sterile laboratory stimuli is necessary for conducting precise experimental manipulations of specific phenomena and reducing external influences, thus increasing internal validity. Yet, this approach has been criticized for lacking the contextual richness of real-world settings, limiting its generalizability and ecological validity. If research aims to predict real-life phenomena, it requires a balance between strict experimental protocols and including naturalistic, dynamic, and contextually embedded stimuli [KF20]. To counter this, researchers strive for high "ecological validity" in their experiments. Egon Brunswik developed and used the term ecological validity first in 1955 in the context of vision research [Bru49]. Since the 1970s, its meaning has shifted and has since then been commonly used to refer "to the extent to which the environment experienced by the subject in a scientific investigation has the properties it is supposed or assumed to have by the investigator" [LLCFL18], or in other terms to "the extent to which research findings would generalize to settings typical of everyday life" [Bau07]. As such, it shares ideas with other concepts such as representative design, realism, or external validity [LLCFL18, KSV15].

As we aim to create the real-life phenomenon of experiencing an ICU in VR, we would need to compare our VE with an ICU to get the most valid results. However, the high safety standards in a real ICU make it unfeasible to run the study in the actual environment. This necessitates the construction of a highly realistic test laboratory as a study environment as we must ensure that the stress induced is comparable to the levels that would be induced during training sessions in skills labs. As a high level of realism in simulators has a positive effect on knowledge retention [AA14], it is advantageous to make sure that the participants perceive the scenario and the overall simulation as real. Comments on missing features and lack of realism in certain details prompted us to re-create the scenario from Chapter 5, the details of which will be presented in the next section.

6.2 Improving the Scenario

Expert feedback received during the studies presented in Chapters 4 and 5 suggested that the storyline and the wording should be improved to better reflect the actual process of a shift handover, as well as the conditions in an ICU. The experts noted that the focus on possible consequences and repercussions in case of patient death should be increased.

We executed two consecutive focus groups in Oldenburg and Lübeck with six participants overall, all but one of whom were teaching staff with a nursing degree. Before the focus group work started, participants were shown a 15-minute demo of the current VR setup and were allowed to test it out for themselves. The goal of the focus groups was to create a life-like scenario that includes the present environment and stressors. Participants were told not to consider existing characters nor the current background scenario and could thus brainstorm without further restrictions. The focus groups were executed on two dates and took four hours each. The results of both focus groups were combined and produced a scenario based on true events. Details have been changed to protect the privacy of those portrayed. We have changed the names, gender, age and professions of the people involved.

6.2.1 Scenario

Like the first scenario, the resulting storyline is written following the three-act structure by Field (see Section 5.2). We paid close attention to details like expressions and wording from the profession. Medical information shared during conversations between characters fits the described injury. Brand names have been omitted, medication is referred to only by the name of the active ingredient. The scenario encompasses six different characters, all of whom have been given reasonable background stories that are revealed to the participants as the story unfolds throughout the experiment. Figure 6.1 shows portraits of all characters involved.

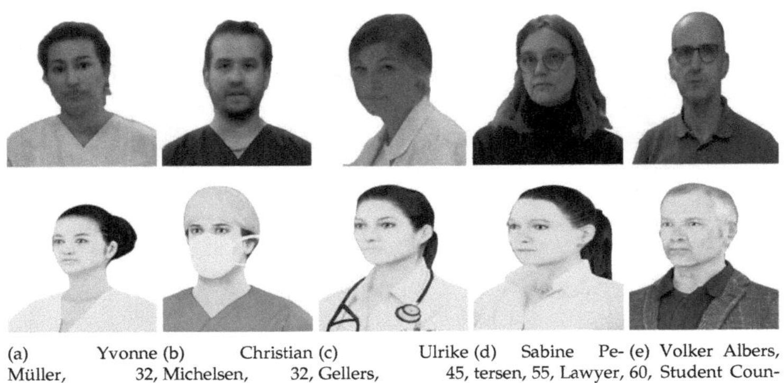

(a) Yvonne Müller, Intensive Care Nurse (b) Christian Michelsen, 32, Anesthesia Nurse (c) Ulrike Gellers, 32, Orthopaedic Surgeon (d) Sabine Petersen, 45, Patient's daughter (e) Volker Albers, 55, Lawyer, Patient's son / 60, Student Counselor, Patient's son

Figure 6.1: Portrait shots for all NPCs playing a role in the scenario, with the respective NPC 3D Model.

During the first act, the background story and medical history of the patient are given by a fellow nurse during a shift handover. The colleague (Yvonne, see Fig. 6.1a) informs participants that the elderly patient fell during an overnight stay and broke a hip but was not found by nursing staff immediately. Participants are being told that - against the internists' advice - the patient decides to have the surgery performed, as they have been told by surgical staff that keeping the broken bone untreated can be fatal. The nurse continues with the medication information given to the patient as well as their subjective pain levels, and finishes the handover by notifying the participant about the imminent arrival of the patient's adult children, implying difficult behavior towards medical and nursing staff. The nurse leaves the room, and participants are given several tasks.

The second act features two additional characters. An anesthesia nurse (cmp. Fig. 6.1b) informs the participant that the patient retracted their decision last minute and will not have the surgery performed. The anesthesia nurse also tells the participants about the patients' reasoning: "They said they had lived a long and fulfilled life and it is okay to go now". The nurse further tells participants that both the surgeon and the family of the patient have been informed and are on their way. Next, the surgeon (see Fig. 6.1c) enters the room and pleads with the patient, stating that the chance of dying due to the untreated fracture is quite high. The surgeon leaves the room and the experiment continues, as participants are required to run another battery of tasks. Two pieces of information are meant to induce moral distress in the participants: (a) they are part of the nursing staff and thus, by proxy, also responsi-

(a) Act 1 - Shift handover. The nurse informs the participant about the patient's case, their vitals, and who is involved.

(b) Act 2(a) - The patient is brought back and the anesthesia nurse tells the participant about their change of heart concerning the surgery.

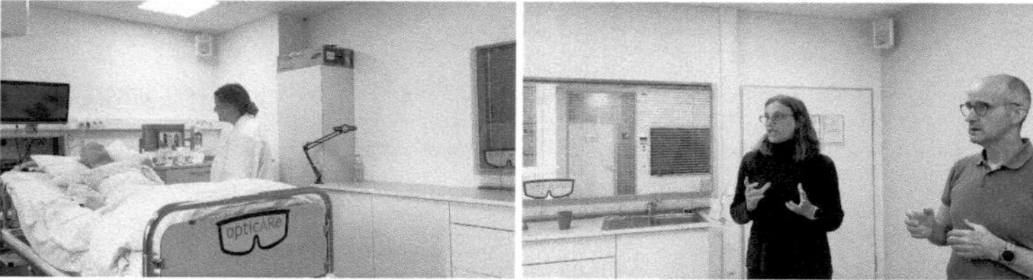

(c) Act 2(b) - The surgeon who was scheduled to perform the surgery reminds the patient of the consequences.

(d) Act 3 - The patient's family has arrived and now aggressively argues that the participant has to convince the patient to change their mind, as it is their fault the patient has a broken hip in the first place.

Figure 6.2: The storyline of our scenario in four shots.

ble for the patient's accident, and (b) they are now also informed about the patient's wishes.

In the third act, the patient's family (the daughter and son, cf. Figures 6.1d and 6.1e) enter the room and immediately start to put pressure on the participant by threatening legal action and putting them at fault. As the act unfolds, participants are given even more tasks, this time with the addition of a task interruption, during which the daughter yells: "Are you even doing your job? Just imagine this would be your father!". During the next task, participants are put under time pressure, while the son blames them: "This is all your fault! You have to convince our father to take the surgery!". Finally, the surgeon re-enters the room once more and asks the family to leave the ICU for the nurse (the participant) to be able to do their job. Both follow that request, stating that this incident will have consequences as they will talk to the surgeon general.

6.2.2   Tasks

We added more tasks in this scenario to offer more variation and subsequently increase engagement and realism. In addition to the ones presented in the last two chapters, participants now were asked to:

1. run a blood gas analysis

2. check the patient's urine flow

3. check the patient's body temperature

(1) A blood gas analysis (BGA) gives medical staff the required information about the content of O2, CO2, pH, and the acid-base balance of arterial blood. It is a common procedure for patients receiving ventilation [Lan23]. The completion of the BGA requires using a syringe to draw blood from a port on the patient's right arm. The syringe is then emptied into a device that analyses the blood and prints the results on a screen and a piece of paper.

(2) Checking the patient's urine throughput as well as the color provides information on the kidney's functionality and health. The urine bag is usually hung under the bed and is connected to the bladder via a catheter.

(3) Using the body temperature, one may conclude inflammatory processes in the body. Several illnesses cause characteristic changes in body temperature. Ear thermometers are a common device, they measure the body temperature via the drumhead in a quick manner.

Counterbalanced task lists were prepared and worked through in sequences during those phases in which the scenario did not feature any NPCs. The third act differs from this, as the combination of stressors necessitated the NPC's presence.

6.3   Study Design

The study was designed as a mixed-methods, between-subjects study. Participants experienced the same scenario in two different environments (experiment conditions) - a skills lab setup in LIFE, and the virtual version using a Pico 4 HMD[1] (VR). In this study, we did not only want to measure the stress-inducing capabilities but also the perceived realism in each environment. To this end, we employed a questionnaire to assess the realism of clinical simulations quantitatively (ProRealSim, [CMPMSI+23]). As we have already provided evidence about the stress-inducing qualities of the VE, and because we apply the same stressors equally in both conditions, we investigate the following hypotheses.

---

[1] https://www.picoxr.com/uk/products/pico4, last accessed January 16th, 2024

H_1: There is no difference in the stress levels in our participants post-experiment between the virtual environment and the skills lab.

Furthermore, as virtual environments are commonly viewed as ecologically valid [Par15, PS23], and since we have seen high ratings on the IPQ for our vICU in the two previous studies and gotten positive feedback about some aspects of the realism, we further hypothesize the following:

H_2: There is no difference in realism between the virtual environment and the skills lab environment.

To investigate these hypotheses, we set up both environments to be as similar as possible.

LIFE

To run the experiment in LIFE and offer the tasks described in the previous section, we set up different devices and screens in the laboratory. While some tasks were ported solely to screen-based Android devices, others were executed by a combination of make-shift devices and screens. Figure 6.3 shows exemplary different task stations.

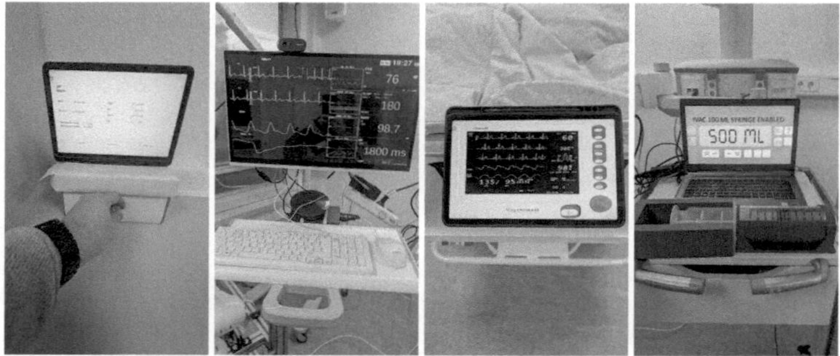

(a) The blood gas analysis device. Participants in one task are being asked to empty the syringe in the hole and receive the calculated pH value after tapping "Start Analysis" on the display.

(b) The vitals requested in one task are being displayed on a monitor that is part of the ceiling-mounted supply unit in LIFE.

(c) The second patient monitor alerts participants about a drop in heart rate and thus interrupts their current task.

(d) The syringe task is realized using a laptop mimicking the perfusors' display and a 3D-printed mount for the syringe.

Figure 6.3: Exemplary task setups for the experiment condition "LIFE".

The location of all tasks as well as other points of interest were kept the same over both experimental setups, see Figure 6.4 for the vICU. The figure is also representative of the study setup in LIFE.

VR

We made adjustments to the VR environment to accommodate the additional tasks. We added required devices, such as the in-ear thermometer, the BGA device, and the urine bag to the locations outlined in Figure 6.4. The VR part of the study was executed in the MIRACLE where participants used a combination of physical walking and controller-based teleportation.

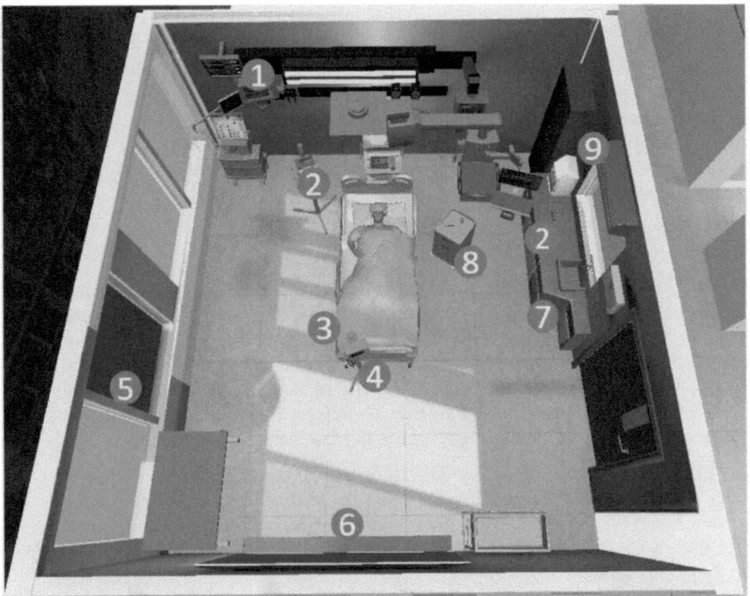

Figure 6.4: Bird perspective of the virtual ICU with points of interest for task completions: 1) Read vitals 2) Refill medication (left) and swap syringe (right) 3) Read urine flow 4) Acknowledge alarm 5) Open window 6) Task screen 7) Fill a glass of water 8) Check body temperature 9) Run blood gas analysis.

Additional Characters

Depending on the condition, the characters of the scenario were either embodied through 3D characters from the Microsoft Rocketbox or by amateur actresses and actors, as depicted in Figure 6.1. Performers were given the script and their role texts to prepare for their roles. Interactions with the participant and other NPCs were recorded in LIFE on a smartphone (Google Pixel 6, Android 14) and tripod setup. Depending on the role, actors and actresses were also outfitted with a costume. Performers were not reimbursed.

Further, virtual characters were improved over those from Chapter 5, as we used more realistic body movements as well as facial movements when speaking. We asked amateur voice actors to pre-record the speaking parts. While the interactions are still unilateral, we have ensured more purposeful wording as well as higher quality recordings, both in audio quality and acting. The sentences spoken by the NPCs include medically and situational relevant information.

Participants

For this study, we invited 13 participants (age m=40.92, SD=13.55), 12 of whom had a professional background in nursing, and one was a medical doctor. The average working experience was 15 years. Participants were recruited through advertising in educational facilities, inter-project contact, and personal relationships. Participants were compensated with 15 € per hour. Only a few participants had prior experience with VR.

Data Recording and Analysis

We used the Zephyr belt to collect physiological data as in the previous studies. Data was tested for normal distribution using Shapiro-Wilk and the hypotheses were tested with either the t-test or the Wilcox test, depending on the result of the Shapiro-Wilk test. We recorded HR, HRV, as well as V_T and RF in a 3-minute standing baseline and calculated the average for each measure. As the experimental phase is significantly longer than the baseline, we focused the analysis on the last three minutes of the experimental phase, where the three stressors coincide.

We had to remove the physiological data of one participant due to a Bluetooth connection error. Further, one participant was unable to finish the VR condition due to strong feelings of nausea. Their data have also been removed from the pool of data for the LIFE environment.

The subjective stress measures were collected pre- and post-experiment, and the realism questionnaire was filled out after the participants had finished each scenario. The IPQ was additionally answered in the VR condition. The IPQ items do not apply to the skills lab condition, so we did not collect them. As in the previous studies, differences are calculated in percent to make results comparable, i.e.

$[(Condition - Baseline) * 100]/Baseline$. Significance tests, however, have been applied to raw data instead of percent changes.

6.4 Results

In this section, we present the results of the data analysis. For brevity, we will use the following abbreviations for the environment variables "clinical skills lab" (CSL) and "virtual reality" (VR), and for the data recording times "baseline" (BL) and "during the scenario" (SO).

6.4.1 Stress Measures

Below we show the changes in stress levels in our participants as measured using the approach developed in the previous studies.

Objective Measures

The check for normal distributions of recorded physiological data from the CSL_{BL} and CSL_{SO} conditions showed that data from HR and RF were normally distributed, data for HRV and V_T were not ($V_{T_{BL}}$: W=0.691, p<0.01; $V_{T_{SO}}$: W=0.717, p<0.01; HRV_{BL}: W=0.836, p<0.05; HRV_{SO}: W=0.634, p<0.01). Except for RF, no changes in physiological measures between the CSL_{BL} and CSL_{SO} were significant (HR: t(11)=0.88, p=0.396; HRV: V=24, p=0.266; V_T: V=26, p=0.339; RF: t(11)=-10.5, p<0.01).

In the VR condition, no data except for RF in both conditions were normally distributed (HR_{BL}: W=0.759, p<0.01; HR_{SO}: W=0.679, p<0.01; HRV_{BL}: W=0.355, p<0.01; HRV_{SO}: W=0.353, p<0.01; $V_{T_{BL}}$: W=0.579, p<0.01; $V_{T_{SO}}$: W=0.88, p<0.01). Significance tests for differences between VR_{BL} and VR_{SO} recordings show a significant increase only in RF (t(10) = -5.289, p<0.01). All other increases were not significant (HR: V=29, p=0.765; HRV: V=28, p=0.7; V_T: V=23, p=0.413).

There is no statistically significant difference in the post-hoc comparisons of the physiological data. Please refer to Table 6.1 for a summary of percentual changes of both the subjective and the objective measures as well as the post-hoc significance tests.

Subjective Measures

In the CSL_{BL} measure all scales of the PSQ20 were normally distributed, but the replies to the Likert item were not (W=0.674, p<0.01). In CSL_{SO}, all measures were normally distributed. Calculations for VR_{BL} demonstrate that the Tension (W=0.817, p<0.05) and Worries (W=0.856, p<0.05) sub-scales were not normally distributed, and neither were the replies for the Likert item (W=0.859, p<0.05). The remain-

Table 6.1: Percentual changes for each environment, pre- to post hoc, and significance tests for post-hoc differences between environments. Bold text shows significance.

	CSL	VR	Difference post-hoc
HR	-4.10%	0.68%	**V=27, p=0.637**
HRV	21.58%	6.68%	V-43, p=0.413
RF	104.88%	54.65%	t(9)=1.873, p=0.09
V_T	2.06%	0.53%	V=20, p=0.492
PSQ20	28.76%	24.54%	t(12)=0.125, p=0.9
Likert	52.56%	112.82%	t(12)=-1.82, p=0.09

ing sub-scales were normally distributed. Post-experiment, all data was normally distributed.

A comparison of the BL measures between VR and CSL conditions showed, that except for the Joy sub-scale, no significant differences between the conditions exist. Hence, we calculated an ANCOVA for the Joy sub-scale when comparing the environments post-experiment. We used ANCOVA because it allows us to compare group means while statistically controlling for the effects of other variables (in this case, the BL measure, since it is significant). After checking for an impact of the experimental conditions (VR and CSL) using ANCOVA while controlling for BL, we did not find evidence for a significant difference between the two experimental conditions in the Joy sub-scale (F=0.007, p=0.936). A non-significant p-value for the two experimental conditions suggests no difference in group means post hoc.

To test H_1, we compared the post-experiment measures of each environment with one another. The results of our calculations show that all post-experiment measures are distributed normally, and further do not differ from each other in a statistically significant way, as shown by the subsequent t-tests (cmp. Table 6.1). Box plots visualizing the results are outlined in Figure 6.5.

6.4.2 Perceived Realism and Presence

This subsection presents the results of the realism questionnaire and the IPQ that were answered by participants after each condition.

Realism Questionnaire ProRealSim

The ProRealSim has three dimensions, each describing an aspect of a simulation. A Global Realism score is calculated by applying weights to each dimension: $GlobalRealism = (0.5*\text{Simulated Participant})+(0.2*\text{Simulator})+(0.3*\text{Scenography})$. The box plot in Figure 6.6 shows the distributions and the differences between conditions. For the calculation of the dimensions, we have removed items due to their inapplicability to either condition (smell, non-consumables, touch, odor).

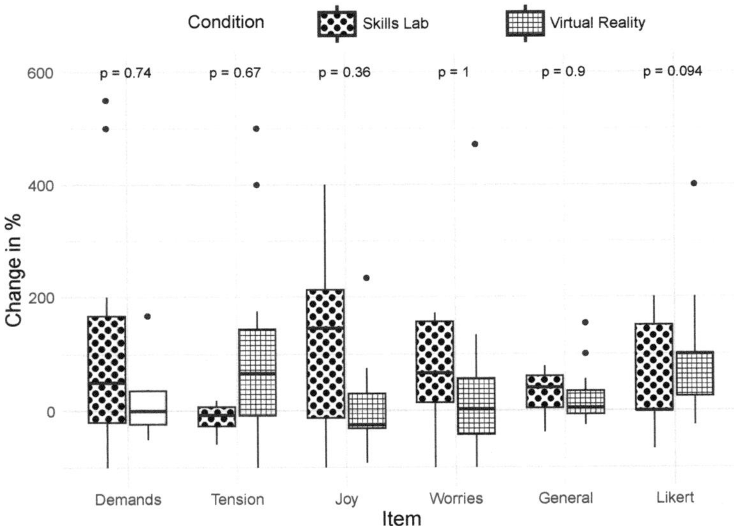

Figure 6.5: Box plot showing the percentual changes between pre- and post-experiment of the subjective stress measures in both conditions, as well as the p-values for the post-experiment comparison.

In the VR condition, all dimensions and the Global Realism were normally distributed. In CSL, the dimension Simulator and the Global Realism were not (Simulator: $W=0.78$, $p<0.05$, Global Realism: $W=0.81$, $p<0.05$). When comparing the dimensions between the conditions, we see there are no statistical differences for any dimension, see Table 6.2.

We have calculated global accuracy and naturality scores, even though this was not intended by the original authors. We did so by applying the same weights we used when calculating the global realism. Concerning the Accuracy Score, we report a non-normal distribution in VR ($W=0.85$, $p<0.05$). The Wilcox test shows no significant difference ($V=49$, $p=0.47$). The second score we calculated was the Naturality Score. Data for the scale was normally distributed in VR, but not in the CSL condition ($W=0.85$, $p<0.05$). The subsequent Wilcox test does not show a significant difference between conditions in the naturality score. All results for the realism questionnaire are depicted in Figure 6.7. Concerning descriptive statistics and the significance tests, please refer to Table 6.2.

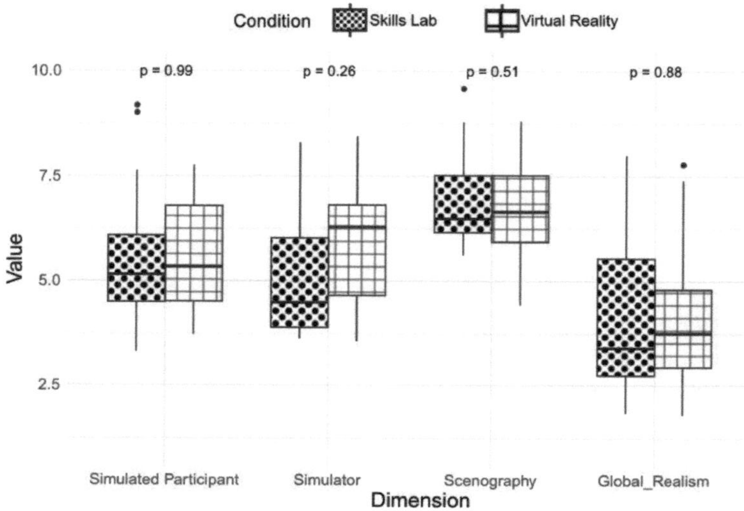

Figure 6.6: Boxplot showing the scores for all realism sub-scores for both environments.

Table 6.2: Descriptive statistics and results of significance tests between the CSL and VR conditions.

| Dimension | Mean (SD) | | Result of post-hoc |
	VR	CSL	Significance test
Simulated Participant	5.63 (1.38)	5.63 (1.97)	t(11)= -0.004, p = 0.997
Simulator	6.03 (1.59)	5.27 (1.83)	V = 54, p = 0.266
Scenography	6.61 (1.32)	6.94 (1.24)	t(11)= -0.67, p = 0.512
Global Realism	6 (1.25)	5.95 (1.66)	t(10) = 0.15, p = 0.881
Score			
Accuracy	4.41 (2.02)	4.31 (1.97)	V=49, p=0.47
Naturality	4.3 (1.9)	4.21 (1.96)	V=30.5, p=0.86

Igroup Presence Questionnaire

After participants had finished the VR condition, we asked them to fill out the IPQ. The General Presence in the environment was rated at 5.3 out of 7 (SD=1.65). Both the sub-scale Spatial Presence and Involvement scored 4.8 (SD$_{SP}$=1.45, SD$_{I}$=1.5)

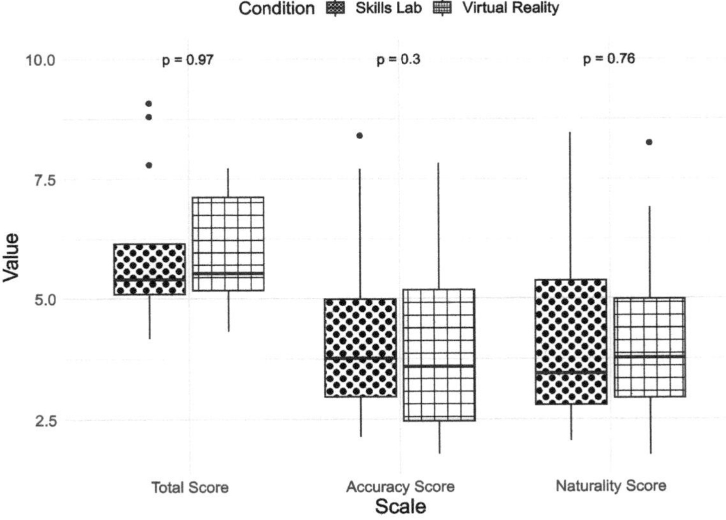

Figure 6.7: Boxplot showing the scores for all realism sub-scores for both environments.

and the Realism sub-scale was rated at 4.2 (SD=1.61). All scores are displayed in Figure 6.8.

6.4.3 Semi-structured Interviews

After participants finished both conditions, we invited them to partake in a semi-structured interview. The focus of the interview revolved around their memories of the use of role-plays and skills labs during their apprenticeship, and what they thought of both of our environments in comparison. Other items in the interview dealt with the question of whether participants could imagine using VR in education, especially as a tool for exams.

Most participants had used skills labs in their apprenticeship, except for three participants (professional experience > 30 years), who all stated that skills labs just were not part of their education during their schooling. We learned that the term "skills lab" was used to describe a broad range of learning environments, starting with a mannequin on a nursing bed (P9, P10) on the one end of the spectrum over temporarily re-purposed classrooms (P2, P7, P12) and highly specialized, highly re-

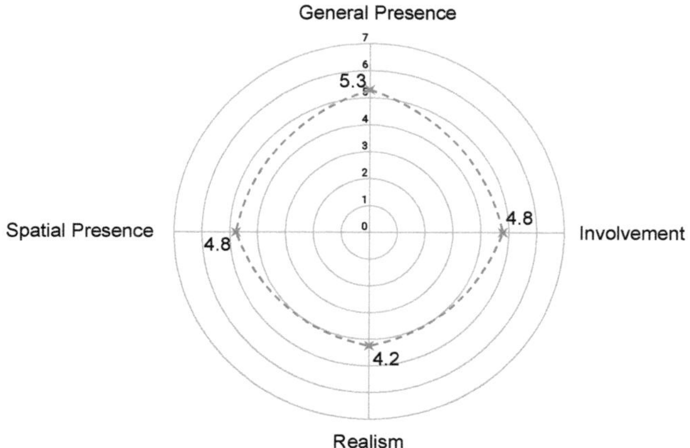

Figure 6.8: Radar chart with the scores of the IPQ, for the VR condition.

alistic rooms (P5, P6, P8). The general consensus was that LIFE was a more realistic depiction of an ICU than what participants were used to (e.g. P1, P5, P8).

While participants were accustomed to role-playing, they were divided as a group concerning learning success through role-play. Participants noted that "it is a hit or miss and depends on your fellow students" (P7) or that "it is hard to forget the actual person behind the role" (P12). Another participant said that it "depends on my mood and energy on a daily basis. Sometimes they hit too close to home and then decision making becomes difficult" (P2), showing that role-play can also have a private, emotional aspect.

Three participants preferred the VR scenario over the CSL scenario (P3, P4, P10), due to the higher visual realism of some devices, e.g. monitors or the BGA device. The storyline and wordings were rated as cohesive and authentic (P4, P6), although some equipment was missing, e.g. a syringe collection container to safely dispose of used needles (P8). Participants believe that VR could be a useful tool in education due to the ability to take it home to learn (P2) or do practical homework (P5) with "more time to learn things and not make a fool of oneself in front of peers" (P7). The "sheer limitless applications" (P1) for different scenarios like "communication or violence prevention" (P12), and the opportunity "to try out new devices" (P3), were also viewed as positive aspects.

Others were more critical of the system: "Of course it is suitable for all activities that have to be carried out in a certain sequence, such as sterilization of the workplace, but even there, subtleties such as the contact time have to be taken into account. Everything that has to do with empathy and interpersonal interaction in general is better learned directly with [real] patients" (P6). Only one participant would opt for VR to take an exam, because "patients are told that they are part of an exam and start behaving picture perfect" (P10). Others would use it as part of exam preparation or as a pre-exam, while others put the patient into focus because one has to communicate, even in a non-verbal manner (P5), or noted missing haptics in VR (P3).

6.5 Discussion and Findings

In this study, we aimed for an ecological validation of the vICU by comparing it to a skills lab and thus contribute to the third research question of this thesis: To what extent are VR stress and real stress comparable when using a full simulation?

After implementing the same scenario in both surroundings, including tasks and additional characters, we had participants work through both environments while recording their stress levels and collecting information on the perceived realism. The objective results are, except for R_F, not statistically significant. We attribute this difference to the walking required during the scenario as opposed to the standing still during the baseline recording. However, comparing the scenario phases of both conditions with each other, we see no statistically significant differences between them.

The ratings of the PSQ20 sub-scales Worries, Tension were affected through the scenario in the CSL condition, as well as the General Score of the PSQ20. However, in the subjective measures, the single Likert item only showed a significant increase in the VR condition. Furthermore, the VR condition includes distinct outliers that influence the calculations.

The evaluation of the stress-inducing capabilities of both environments with our target group showed that each environment seems to have a different effect on the subjects. We believe that the mixed results of this study can explained by the high experience of the participants in this study compared to the previous two. As the research in Chapters 4 and 5 has shown, the virtual representations of the investigated stressors are capable of increasing stress levels. The assumption of the work experience having an influence is backed by some participants, stating aspects like "When I came in here, I felt right at home" or "The sounds were quite real. My cooker bonnet would have annoyed me more" (P2). We also believe the small change in physiological measures is due to the high work experience, too. Participants stayed very calm under both stressors, making a point of not missing steps or working hastily. Considering the results, especially taking into account the ratings in the Likert item, we conclude that the stress reaction does not depend on the simulation environment and thus accept H_1.

A second focus of this study was put on realism. The realism measures in both environments score very similarly in all dimensions and scores of the ProRealSim questionnaire, thereby we accept H_2. As the scales of the questionnaire seek to evaluate the simulations in comparison to reality, both environments have room for improvement. For the dimensions, the authors define scores between 3.5 and 5 as "low", scores between 5 and 7 as "average", and scores above 7 as "high" (> 8.5 is very high). Thus, most participants rated the Scenography as average/high. This dimension received the best ratings of all dimensions. It comprises items about the environment (sound, smell, lighting), as well as consumable and non-consumable items. Thus, the received scores attest to the realism of the artificial environments we have created, both in VR and the skills lab. The dimension Simulated participant evaluates the characters that were part of our storyline. This dimension includes the conceptual, emotional, and physical characterization of the NPCs (height, weight, cultural and professional backgrounds, emotions, etc.). Participants were less in agreement for the VR condition, some gave better scores than others. In the CSL condition, the spread was less, but so was the median. We believe that the 3D model NPCs were perceived as more real than the video recordings of the actors, as they were not video recordings. The third dimension, Simulator, shows the strongest differences between the two conditions (0.76 in mean difference). This dimension includes items on the vital signs (if shown, e.g. on a monitoring device), physical characteristics (e.g. size in single-organ simulators or model fidelity in devices), sounds from the simulator (as opposed to sounds in the environment) etc. The VR condition scores higher in this dimension, which can be explained, in part, by the use of 3D models of actual devices in VR. vs lo-fi paper replica in the CSL. This was mainly due to financial constraints in our experimental setup but reflects the conditions in the skills labs used by schools. Nevertheless, many participants noted that the CSL environment was already much better than what they were used to from their education. Because VR has been rated equally as high as the CSL, we conclude that the ecological validation in terms of perceived realism of the environment and scenario was successful.

These results are specific to our environment and scenario, which have been designed in close collaboration with the target group from the beginning. When creating similar storylines, developers should focus on implementing as many medical details as possible. Further, the graphical design does not have to be photorealistic. With the processing capabilities of the current generation of stand-alone VR devices in mind, this is an advantage. Rendering technologies such as ray tracing are still reserved for powerful and expensive graphic cards.

Considering the positive remarks of our participants and the successful ecological validation, we believe that VR has great potential in creating realistic, stressful scenarios that can help aspiring nurses to learn coping strategies to deal with occupational stress.

7 Conclusion and Future Work

In this chapter, we draw conclusions about the content of this thesis, reflect on it, and discuss discuss future research venues. Section 7.1 summarizes the content of the dissertation. Further, the scientific contributions to the research questions are described, highlighted, and critically reflected upon in Section 7.2. Moreover, we outline design recommendations that we deduct from our overall findings in Section 7.3. The chapter concludes with our ideas for future research projects in the field of stress generation in VR (see Section 7.4) and finishes with closing notes (cf. Section 7.5).

7.1 Synopsis

This thesis contains the results of several user studies with the overall research goal of creating stressful scenarios in VR to aid in stress resilience training for nurses utilizing stress inoculation. As a result of our literature review on the current use of VR in nursing education, we learned that while the concept of applying VR as part of training is already applied in other professions, it is just starting to gain traction in nursing (see Chapter 2). Through executing shadowing sessions in educational and professional environments, as well as through focus groups, expert interviews, and an online survey, we have collected requirements for a VR-based training software (see Chapter 3). Based on these requirements, we developed VR scenarios to research specific stressors nurses are commonly exposed to in the ICU. These stressors have been selected in close collaboration with nursing staff. The replicas focus on the stressor categories Performance, Physical, and Social as defined by Kaluza et al. [Kal18]. We have investigated the stress-inducing capabilities of these stressors, both in isolation (see Chapters 4 and 5) as well as in combination (see Chapter 6). The study presented in Chapter 6 further aimed to ecologically validate the virtual scenario and environment. Our results show that not only do the stressor implementations tend to increase the subjects' stress level in a virtual as well as a skills lab environment, but also that our vICU is perceived as being just as real as the skills lab environment on which it is based.

Finally, to support researchers, we also contribute recommendations on the configuration of a mixed reality laboratory, based both on our initial setup as well as the upgrades and improvements we implemented during our research.

7.2 Contributions to the Research Questions

Our work contributes to the overall research goal by providing answers to the research questions defined in Chapter 1. To this end, we employed qualitative and quantitative studies to first understand the context of use and then execute experimental research, investigating the stress response of our users and the presence and realism. Furthermore, we present details on what future research should look like to facilitate effective VR-based SIT (see Chapter 7.4).

7.2.1   RQI: What are the requirements for VR software to be used as a stress management tool in nursing training?

We investigated the professional environment as a first step toward creating stressful VR scenarios. Combining the results of literature analysis, ethnographic research, and expert interviews, we have synthesized several requirements for the VR system. Based on these requirements, we have designed a 3D model of an ICU and used the software first on wired HMDs. Through several iterations, we have updated the program to run on wireless, self-sufficient VR HMDs. We thus meet the requirements for mobility and independent use. Not only are these devices mobile, but by eventually moving away from vendor-specific HMDs, we enable both educational institutions to adopt a Bring-Your-Own-Device approach. This can potentially remove the need to purchase hardware, which increases cost efficiency. Keeping the scenario software up to date with the increasing capabilities in newer hardware improves graphics, audio, and tracking and thus helps to keep user engagement high and additionally decreases errors.

Throughout the experiments, the VE and the nursing scenario were rated as presence-inducing. We believe that close cooperation with nurse practice instructors and other teaching staff is paramount in creating realistic and believable simulations for students to learn with.

7.2.2   RQ II: How can different occupational stressors from the nursing profession be replicated in VR and what effect do they have on users?

The stressors we have created a virtual counterpart for have been carefully selected from the various stressors that can be found in the ICU. The selection process included a literature analysis and subsequent focus groups which then resulted in the choices "Time Pressure", "Task Interruption" and "Moral Distress". Using the game engine Unity3D, we embedded the stressors into the VE as obstructions that kept participants from finishing the tasks provided to them by the experimenters. These tasks have also been carefully selected and implemented based on the collected information from shadowing sessions as well as focus groups.

We created the virtual replicas of stressors from both the Performance and the Physical stressor category using visual and audible representations of the non-virtual stressors. "Time Pressure" represents the Performance category and was conveyed as a simple timer countdown displayed in the signal color red and appeared when a task was given. Even though participants were told that there were no negative consequences other than the fact that a mistake was logged, the effect was strong enough to increase their stress levels. While we could have added tactile feedback in the controllers or an additional auditive signal to inform about the time pressure, we decided against that as it would not have corresponded to the real world.

The "Task Interruption" belongs to the Physical category. In contrast to "Time Pressure", we implemented it as an auditive signal, alerting participants about the patient's blood pressure moving outside of the pre-set threshold. Subjects were asked to acknowledge the alarm and then finish the previous task. As described in the literature, participants skipped sub-steps of the interrupted task and had thus more logged errors. Additionally, this stressor was also capable of eliciting a measurable stress response. Comparing the NASA-TLX results between the "Time Pressure" and the "Task Interruption" shows significant differences in some, but not all sub-scales, suggesting characteristic effects of each stressor on the task load.

The third stressor "Moral Distress" belongs to the stressor category Social Stress [Kal18]. Moral distress represents one of the most cited stressors affecting ICU nurses. We employed Field's three-act structure for storytelling to design a scenario that puts participants into a moral dilemma (in our case, having to fulfill family requests against one's morals) and embed it into the VE. We used artificial 3D characters from the Rocketbox Library to embody the patient's family and other characters required in the scenario. By changing the outcome of the scenario by varying events of act three, we created different intensities of the stressor (α, β, and γ, increasing) and tested those intensities in a between-groups study. Subjective evaluations show a significant increase between the levels α and β, as well as between α and γ. Interestingly, participants of the γ group rated the generated presence during the experiment higher than the other two, indicating a link between emotion and presence.

The presented studies show that the stressors have a significant effect on the subjective stress levels of our participants. By keeping the realism high, e.g. by using known alarm sounds or requesting the correct order of sub-steps, we were able to induce stress in our experimental settings.

7.2.3   RQ III: To what extent are VR stress and real stress comparable when using a full simulation?

The third research question aimed at the validation of our stressors. The goal of this ecological validation is to ensure that the effects of our VR-based stressors are of similar strength as they would be in reality. For safety and practical reasons, it was not possible to run the validation study in an ICU. Because of this, we utilized a skills lab for the comparison. This furthermore better reflects the current state of education, as schools include simulation training in clinical skills labs as part of their theoretical education.

By implementing a scenario that encompasses all stressors from the previous chapters (see Chapters 4 and 5) in both VR and the CSL, we were able to validate the effects of the stressors as well as the simulation as a whole, utilizing a realism questionnaire for clinical simulation [CMPMSI+23]. The scenario tested includes an improved storytelling approach, with the medical case being based on true events. The new scenario includes more roles and improved conversations. While conversations were still one-sided without the possibility for participants to react, they have been redesigned in collaboration with experts to increase accuracy and improve medical language. In the VR part of this study, the additional roles have been added from the Rocketbox Library, and further enhanced by adding facial movements when speaking. Voice lines were recorded by research staff. For the CSL part, roles were recorded with amateur actors on video and were played on the wall-mounted monitor in LIFE during the study to establish the storyline. Furthermore, more tasks have been added in both environments to increase engagement and decrease diminishing returns from repeating tasks over and over.

The results of this study show that the stress reaction in both conditions is similar. Even though we see a much stronger increase in the Likert item in the VR condition, we attribute this to the added mental load that VR inherently brings with it. The similar rating in the PSQ20 underlines this, as the Likert item is a very general inquiry on stress, whereas the PSQ20 asks more specific questions. These results show that both environments share the same stress-inducing capabilities. Concerning the perceived realism, and thus the main focus of RQ3, we show that the VR environment was graded as real as our skills lab, which participants described as more real than the skills labs they are used to from their own training and education. Considering both the quantitative and qualitative results of the inquiry on perceived realism, this study strongly indicates the applicability of VR as a mobile skills lab in nursing education, both in terms of stress induction as well as realism. Further research must be undertaken to investigate the effects of VR on learning and knowledge retention.

7.2.4 Limitations

Although we followed a scientific methodology in investigating our research questions, we could not avoid certain limitations. These must be taken into account when interpreting the results, as they prevent us from making completely generalizable statements.

Sample Size

Investigating our research questions with the HCD process in mind, we targeted mainly (aspiring) nurses as prospective study participants. Despite advertising our studies in several hospitals and educational institutions, we were not able to recruit a large group of participants. There may be several reasons for this, for example, an already heavy workload or that additional participation in scientific studies may be discouraging. Furthermore, comments in interviews indicate that especially older nurses are not interested in adding more technology to their profession. Lastly, the timing of our research coincided with the COVID-19 pandemic, where social interaction was brought to a minimum, which was even more the case for healthcare personnel.

Nevertheless, in such a challenging situation, we were able to recruit subjects from the health sector because we complied with the health requirements and carried out everything according to regulations. Even though the number of participants could have been larger in some cases, the studies conducted were able to provide answers to the research questions in this dissertation.

Ecological validity

As we researched safety-critical environments, it was challenging to design ecologically valid experiments. Nevertheless, it is important to keep in mind that the clinical environment we used (LIFE) was perceived as more realistic in comparison to the skills labs participants were used to. Even though we were not able to recreate an actual ICU, we are confident that the fidelity of both of our environments outperforms the status quo in most education facilities in terms of realism, as shown in Chapter 6. Additionally, despite us having investigated only a sample of the stressors that are inherent to the profession and the environment, we are optimistic that the results obtained from studies in this thesis can contribute to finding viable solutions and improving the present status of nursing education. The combination of the stressors we implemented is capable of inducing stress, both in LIFE and the virtual ICU. We believe that embedding these solutions into an SIT-style intervention can contribute to holistic stress prevention training.

7.3 Key Insights and Design Rationale

In this section, we highlight the influence of various factors on the experiments and outline how these can be considered in the best way possible.

7.3.1 Hardware Choices

When implementing VR experiments for stress training, careful consideration of hardware choices is necessary. First, both wired and wireless headsets have advantages that must be evaluated. Wireless devices offer enhanced freedom of movement, contributing to a more immersive experience at a lower cost, while wired devices provide consistent connectivity and prevent potential latency issues and allow for higher computational power, for example for realistic lighting or the integration of artificial intelligence. Furthermore, nausea mitigation is a critical concern, demanding design choices such as high refresh rates, low latency, and optimal field of view. As an additional measure, eye-tracking could be used as a tool to gain insight into user attention and subsequent decision-making. These hardware selections collectively contribute to the overall success of VR stress training experiments, ensuring a comprehensive and effective approach to skill development in a simulated environment.

7.3.2   VR Complexities

VR is a relatively new addition to the amount of devices we interact with. We found that participants had difficulties distinguishing between buttons and their purpose, e.g. grasp (controller shaft) vs. activate (trigger). Ensuring that button mapping is simple and in line with established standards is important. In addition, we suggest supporting users in an introductory phase by highlighting objects of interest to reduce mental demands. If the available space allows, we recommend disabling teleportation in VR, as it often leads to confusion and disorientation among our participants.

Nursing tasks are highly standardized. One has to make an effort to keep the established processes, i.e. the order of things, in VR and not focus so much on haptic or tactile feedback. Current VR controllers are not able to replicate syringes correctly, for example, so trying to implement this only adds to the confusion. This is where using hand tracking and investigating how it affects the user experience could prove beneficial. Instead of paying much attention to the granular details when performing tasks, we suggest using the capabilities of VR to convey information (signal tones and sounds, lights, timers, etc.). As a VR developer, one can further reduce interaction complexity by using bounding boxes to constrain and automate interactions between devices (e.g. syringe and BGA device).

7.3.3   Experience Matters

We often noticed a difference in our users when it came to their reactions to stressors or interactions with VR. In the first study (Chapter 4), participants had an average age of 29, while in the third user study (Chapter 6), the average age was 40 and they had significantly more work experience. The average physiological stress response was lower in the third study, as the nurses remained calmer when performing tasks under the influence of stressors. On the other hand, younger participants had fewer problems with operating controllers and interacting or moving in the virtual space, but at the same time showed stronger reactions to stressors. This demonstrates that stress is a very subjective matter and that both the professional experience and VR skills of the target users should be taken into account when designing simulation scenarios.

7.3.4 Reality Comparison

By confirming the validity of the scenario and environment, it is possible to ensure that the skills and behaviors observed in VR simulations closely match those required in real environments. This increases the transferability of the observed stress reactions from the virtual environment to real-life situations.

It should also be emphasized that research conducted in ecologically valid VR simulations leads to more meaningful results. The findings are more predictive of behavior in the real world and are more translatable to other scenarios. This supports the generalizability of research results. This is particularly important in areas such as healthcare, where interventions and training programs need to be applicable to a variety of scenarios.

7.4 Future Research

While this work examined the feasibility of stress inoculation and its effects on participants' stress levels successfully, several research opportunities opened up that should be investigated by researchers and practitioners alike. In the following, we describe several aspects that warrant further investigation in the future.

7.4.1 Additional Stressors

We have investigated the effect of three specific stressors in this thesis. These have been selected based on expert input and literature and were used as representations for their category. More stressors from all categories should be investigated to gain a more complete picture. One could, for example, add increasing consequences in case of failure for the category Performance Stressors. We have not yet investigated Bodily Stressors, but considering the amount of physical work nurses do, e.g. through walking (average for steps and distance: 9.360 steps or 5.79km [CC22]), this should also be included in future research. Using omnidirectional treadmills, such as the KatWalk V2[1] or Disney's HoloTile[2] and adding a second virtual ICU to include caring for more than a single patient could be a fitting simulation. Further, incorporating physical and heavy props using mixed reality would allow, for instance, the simulation of e.g. pushing beds or lifting patients.

7.4.2 Interaction

One of the most interesting questions that emerged during our research is the influence of the way people interact in and with the VE. On the one hand, it is important

---

[1] https://www.kat-vr.com/products/kat-walk-c-2-core, last accessed January 16th, 2024
[2] https://www.youtube.com/watch?v=68YMEmaF0rs&t=213s, last accessed January 22nd, 2024

to research how much the mental load of using VR controllers interferes with the stress level, and whether hand-tracking or mixed-reality props will change the outcome of our studies. On the other hand, in our studies, the social interaction with the NPCs was designed unilaterally, as voice lines were pre-recorded and both NPCs and participants were unable to react to each other. Researchers could either prepare different pathways for conversations and enable trainers to select them, e.g. via the tablet application, or train a generative AI to take on the role of the NPC. By combining text-to-speech technology with a large language model, scenarios could achieve higher realism because NPCs could react to questions or statements by participants. Furthermore, this way scenarios would never repeat twice in the exact same way, which could be beneficial for simulation training.

7.4.3 Multi-User Scenarios

During our interviews, experts mentioned that nurses often have to work together with each other or medical staff. This can create stress as well, for example through social and professional hierarchies which play an important role, or through the delegation of tasks within a team. Researchers should investigate how these can be converted into VR, how de-escalation strategies can be taught in a multi-user VR scenario, and what effects these have on the stress levels of students. VR also removes the need to be physically present and allows people to participate in simulations from a distance. For example, specialized training can be provided without the necessity for the expert to be on-site.

7.4.4 Scenario Editor

Employing professional developers to create more scenarios or make changes to existing ones can be very time-consuming and expensive. It is in the interest of teaching staff to be able to create and adapt scenarios to the mandatory curriculum. This includes research into the specific requirements for this type of software, such as feature sets, generalizability, and ultimately usability. Furthermore, building on the RCD (see Chapter 3), a scenario editor would give more granular control to teaching staff and enable them to react to the participants' actions and behavior in the best possible way.

7.4.5 Integration into Education

Having stressful VR scenarios for education at one's disposal is important, but it is equally important to integrate them into nursing education and investigate the long-term effects. Thus, research should investigate the impact on long-term stress resilience and possible cross-interactions with knowledge retention. Future research should also consider the different stakeholders that need to be involved in order to achieve successful integration (e.g. different state ministries, headmasters of nursing schools, technical departments of educational facilities, etc.). This task is not only a research activity but should also be approached as a practical step to ensure that knowledge transfer can be realized.

7.4.6 Mixed Reality Approaches

The most modern VR headsets use a technology called video see-through to show the wearer of an HMD their real surroundings. This technology allows developers to overlay information in the real world, just like one would do with AR. However, the considerably larger field of view in these VR headsets makes it a much better fit for so-called mixed reality. It is possible to show recorded people playing a role, medical devices, and additional information in these headsets. As such, MR can aid in device familiarisation or be used to create dynamic environments that adapt to the situations trained in.

7.5 Closing Notes

Stress is, by its nature, a very individual concept. Many factors play a role and this is why it is important to allow for custom learning journeys. With VR, we have the right tools at hand. The research results from this dissertation not only help nurses and nursing students, but they also help patients. In our last study, P13 gave a statement (see front matter) that we want to reiterate here: "VR creates routine, routine creates certainty, certainty creates trust." (translated from the original German quote: "VR schafft Routine, Routine schafft Sicherheit, Sicherheit schafft Vertrauen"). In saying this, P13 emphasized the importance of the underlying goal: by enabling students to repeat simulations as much as they want on their terms, they can internalize procedures, helping them to be more confident in their tasks and routines. This, in turn, improves the relationship between nurses and their patients.

With increasing technological advances in the VR space, we believe that more realistic scenarios can be developed in collaboration between teaching staff and developers. These can cover a broader range of stressors, environments, and even multi-user scenarios to further support the education of aspiring nurses. Thus, VR training can not only help them to better understand the working environment but can also prepare them for one of the most stressful jobs of all by learning and developing different coping mechanisms.

Figures

Tables

Bibliography

[AA14]   Aqel, Ahmad A. ; Ahmad, Muayyad M.: High-Fidelity Simulation
            Effects on CPR Knowledge, Skills, Acquisition, and Retention in
            Nursing Students. In: Worldviews on Evidence-Based Nursing 11
            (2014), Nr. 6, 394–400. https://onlinelibrary.wiley.com/doi/
            abs/10.1111/wvn.12063

[AA15]   Al-Abtah, Jallal: Pflege. 2. korrigierter Nachdruck. Stuttgart :
            Georg Thieme Verlag KG, 2015 (I care - Lehrbücher für Fachberufe
            im Gesundheitswesen)

[AGSM⁺15]   Andreatta, Marta ; Glotzbach-Schoon, Evelyn ; Mühlberger, An-
            dreas ; Schulz, Stefan M. ; Wiemer, Julian ; Pauli, Paul: Initial and
            sustained brain responses to contextual conditioned anxiety in hu-
            mans. In: Cortex 63 (2015), S. 352–363

[Ass13]   Association, American P.: Diagnostic and statistical manual of
            mental disorders: DSM-5™, 5th ed. Arlington, VA, US : American
            Psychiatric Publishing, Inc., 2013 (Diagnostic and statistical manual
            of mental disorders: DSM-5™, 5th ed.)

[Aus]   Ausbildungs- und Prüfungsverordnung für die Pflege-
            berufe.   https://www.bundesgesundheitsministerium.de/
            ausbildungs-und-pruefungsverordnung-pflegeberufe

[AV13]   Armony, Jorge (Hrsg.) ; Vuilleumier, Patrik (Hrsg.): The Cam-
            bridge handbook of human affective neuroscience. Cambridge ;
            New York : Cambridge University Press, 2013

[AVS⁺20]   Alexandrovsky, Dmitry ; Volkmar, Georg ; Spliethver, Maximilian
            ; Finke, Stefan ; Herrlich, Marc ; Döring, Tanja ; Smeddinck, Jan D.
            ; Malaka, Rainer: Playful User-Generated Treatment: A Novel
            Game Design Approach for VR Exposure Therapy. In: Proceed-
            ings of the Annual Symposium on Computer-Human Interaction
            in Play. New York, NY, USA : Association for Computing Machin-
            ery, 2020 (CHI PLAY '20), S. 32–45

[Bau07]   Baumeister, Roy F.: Encyclopedia of social psychology. Bd. 1. Sage,
            2007

[BBH16]   Brundage, Shelley B. ; Brinton, James M. ; Hancock, Adri-
            enne B.: Utility of virtual reality environments to examine phys-
            iological reactivity and subjective distress in adults who stutter.
            In: Journal of Fluency Disorders 50 (2016), December, S. 85–95.
            http://dx.doi.org/10.1016/j.jfludis.2016.10.001. – DOI
            10.1016/j.jfludis.2016.10.001

[BC06]   Braun, Virginia ; Clarke, Victoria: Using thematic analysis in psychology. In: Qualitative Research in Psychology 3 (2006), Januar, Nr. 2, S. 77–101. http://dx.doi.org/10.1191/1478088706qp063oa. – DOI 10.1191/1478088706qp063oa

[BC23]   Brown, Lynn G. ; Chidume, Tiffani: Don't forget about role play: An enduring active teaching strategy. In: Teaching and Learning in Nursing 18 (2023), Januar, Nr. 1, S. 238–241. http://dx.doi.org/10.1016/j.teln.2022.09.002. – DOI 10.1016/j.teln.2022.09.002

[BDR⁺17]   Blome, Tim ; Diefenbach, Alexander ; Rudolph, Stefan ; Bucher, Kristina ; Mammen, Sebastian von: VReanimate — Non-verbal guidance and learning in virtual reality. In: 2017 9th International Conference on Virtual Worlds and Games for Serious Applications (VS-Games), 2017, S. 23–30

[BDU⁺05]   Buerhaus, Peter I. ; Donelan, Karen ; Ulrich, Beth T. ; Norman, Linda ; Williams, Mamie ; Dittus, Robert: Hospital RNs' and CNOs' perceptions of the impact of the nursing shortage on the quality of care. In: Nursing Economics 23 (2005), Nr. 5, S. 214–221

[BEW⁺21]   Bolinski, Felix ; Etzelmüller, Anne ; Witte, Nele A. J. D. ; Beurden, Cecile v. ; Debard, Glen ; Bonroy, Bert ; Cuijpers, Pim ; Riper, Heleen ; Kleiboer, Annet: Physiological and Self-reported Arousal in Virtual Reality Versus Face-to-face Emotional Activation and Cognitive Restructuring in University Students: a Crossover Experimental Study Using Wearable Monitoring. In: Behaviour Research and Therapy 142 (2021), May, S. 103877. http://dx.doi.org/10.1016/j.brat.2021.103877. – DOI 10.1016/j.brat.2021.103877

[BHB⁺18]   Bosse, Tibor ; Hartmann, Tilo ; Blankendaal, Romy A. ; Dokter, Nienke ; Otte, Marco ; Goedschalk, Linford: Virtually Bad: A Study on Virtual Agents that Physically Threaten Human Beings. In: Proceedings of the 17th International Conference on Autonomous Agents and MultiAgent Systems. Richland, SC : International Foundation for Autonomous Agents and Multiagent Systems, July 2018 (AAMAS '18), S. 1258–1266

[BJKB15]   Bevan, Ann L. ; Joy, Rosalyn ; Keeley, Sarah ; Brown, Petra: Learning to nurse: combining simulation with key theory. In: British Journal of Nursing 24 (2015), August, Nr. 15, S. 781–785. http://dx.doi.org/10.12968/bjon.2015.24.15.781. – DOI 10.12968/bjon.2015.24.15.781. – Publisher: Mark Allen Group

[BKEE18]   Butt, Ann L. ; Kardong-Edgren, Suzan ; Ellertson, Anthony: Us-
            ing game-based virtual reality with haptics for skill acquisition. In:
            Clinical Simulation in Nursing 16 (2018), S. 25–32

[BKM84]   Bloom, Benjamin S. ; Karthwohl, David R. ; Massia, BB: Taxonomy
            of Educational Objectives, Handbook 2, Affective Domain. New
            York: Addison Wesley, 1984

[BMC15]   Bertram, Johanna ; Moskaliuk, Johannes ; Cress, Ulrike: Virtual
            training: Making reality work? In: Computers in Human Behav-
            ior 43 (2015), Februar, S. 284–292. http://dx.doi.org/10.1016/
            j.chb.2014.10.032. – DOI 10.1016/j.chb.2014.10.032

[BN16]   Bugaj, T. J. ; Nikendei, C.: Practical Clinical Training in Skills
            Labs: Theory and Practice. In: GMS Journal for Medical Educa-
            tion 33 (2016), August, Nr. 4, S. Doc63. http://dx.doi.org/10.
            3205/zma001062. – DOI 10.3205/zma001062

[Boe81]   Boehm, Barry W.: Software engineering economics. Englewood
            Cliffs, N.J : Prentice-Hall, 1981 (Advances in Computing Science
            and Technology Series)

[Bro96]   Brooke, John: Sus: a "quick and dirty"usability. In: Usability eval-
            uation in industry 189 (1996), Nr. 3, S. 189–194

[Bro19a]   Brown, Joset E.: Graduate Nurses' Perception of the Ef-
            fect of Simulation on Reducing the Theory-Practice Gap. 5
            (2019). http://dx.doi.org/10.1177/2377960819896963. – DOI
            10.1177/2377960819896963

[Bro19b]   Brown, Joset E.: Graduate Nurses' Perception of the Effect of Sim-
            ulation on Reducing the Theory-Practice Gap. In: Sage Open Nurs-
            ing 5 (2019), S. 2377960819896963

[Bru49]   Brunswick, E: Ecological validity of potential cues and their uti-
            lization in perception. In: Systematic and Representative Design of
            Psychological Experiments (1949)

[Can29]   Cannon, Walter B.: Bodily Changes in Pain, Hunger, Fear and
            Rage. 2. New York : Appleton, 1929

[CBH+06]   Connolly, Charlene ; Bleich, Michael R. ; Hatcher, Barbara J. ; Davis,
            Kathleen ; Hewlett, Peggy O. ; Hill, Karen S.: Wisdom at work: The
            importance of the older and experienced nurse in the workplace.
            (2006)

[CC22]   Chang, Hyoung E. ; Cho, Sung-Hyun: Nurses' steps, distance traveled, and perceived physical demands in a three-shift schedule. In: Human Resources for Health 20 (2022), Dezember, Nr. 1, S. 1–11. http://dx.doi.org/10.1186/s12960-022-00768-3. – DOI 10.1186/s12960–022–00768–3. – Number: 1 Publisher: BioMed Central

[CCS10]   Carver, Charles S. ; Connor-Smith, Jennifer: Personality and Coping. In: Annual Review of Psychology 61 (2010), Nr. 1, S. 679–704. http://dx.doi.org/10.1146/annurev.psych.093008.100352. – DOI 10.1146/annurev.psych.093008.100352

[CG09]   Chin, Jeffrey ; Gamson, William: Assessment in Simulation and Gaming: A Review of the Last 40 Years. In: Simulation & Gaming - Simulat Gaming 40 (2009), Juli, S. 553–568. http://dx.doi.org/10.1177/1046878109332955. – DOI 10.1177/1046878109332955

[CHO+17]   Cho, Dongrae ; Ham, Jinsil ; Oh, Jooyoung ; Park, Jeanho ; Kim, Sayup ; Lee, Nak-Kyu ; Lee, Boreom: Detection of Stress Levels from Biosignals Measured in Virtual Reality Environments Using a Kernel-Based Extreme Learning Machine. In: Sensors 17 (2017), Oktober, Nr. 10, S. 2435. http://dx.doi.org/10.3390/s17102435. – DOI 10.3390/s17102435

[CJH+02]   Coiera, Enrico W. ; Jayasuriya, Rohan a. ; Hardy, Jennifer ; Bannan, Aiveen ; Thorpe, Max E.:   Communication Loads on Clinical Staff in the Emergency Department. In: Medical Journal of Australia 176 (2002), Nr. 9, S. 415–418

[CJH+19]   Clifford, Rory M S. ; Jung, Sungchul ; Hoermann, Simon ; Lindeman, Robert W. ; Billinghurst, Mark: Creating a Stressful Decision Making Environment for Aerial Firefighter Training in Virtual Reality. In: Proceedings of 2019 IEEE Conference on Virtual Reality and 3D User Interfaces (VR). Osaka, Japan : IEEE, 2019, S. 181–189

[CKG97]   Cohen, Sheldon ; Kessler, Ronald C. ; Gordon, Lynn U.: Measuring Stress: A Guide for Health and Social Scientists. New York, NY : Oxford University Press, 1997

[CL20]   Crosswell, Alexandra D. ; Lockwood, Kimberly G.:   Best practices for stress measurement: How to measure psychological stress in health research. In: Health Psychology Open 7 (2020), Juli, Nr. 2. http://dx.doi.org/10.1177/2055102920933072. – DOI 10.1177/2055102920933072

[CLMM12]   Céline Gélinas ; Lise Fillion ; Marie-Anik Robitaille ; Manon Truchon: Stressors Experienced by Nurses Providing End-of-Life Palliative Care in the Intensive Care Unit. In: Canadian Journal of

Nursing Research Archive (2012), 18-39. `https://cjnr.archive.mcgill.ca/article/view/2337`

[CMPMSI+23] Coro-Montanet, Gleyvis ; Pardo Monedero, María J. ; Sánchez Ituarte, Julia ; Wagner Porto Rocha, Helena ; Gomar Sancho, Carmen: Numerical Assessment Tool to Measure Realism in Clinical Simulation. 20 (2023), Nr. 3, S. 2247. `http://dx.doi.org/10.3390/ijerph20032247`. – DOI 10.3390/ijerph20032247

[CTMS18] Chatzigianni, Dimitra ; Tsounis, Andreas ; Markopoulos, Nikolaos ; Sarafis, Pavlos: Occupational Stress Experienced by Nurses Working in a Greek Regional Hospital: A Cross-Sectional Study. In: Iran J Nurs Midwifery Res 23 (2018), Nr. 6, 450–457. `Https://www.ncbi.nlm.nih.gov/pmc/articles/PMC6178576/`

[CWZ17] Cao, Zhengcao ; Wang, Yamin ; Zhang, Liang: Real-time Acute Stress Facilitates Allocentric Spatial Processing in a Virtual Fire Disaster. In: Scientific Reports 7 (2017), December, Nr. 1, S. 14616. `http://dx.doi.org/10.1038/s41598-017-14910-y`. – DOI 10.1038/s41598–017–14910–y

[CYL+13] Corbett, Brendan ; Yamaguchi, Takehiko ; Liu, Shijing ; Huang, Lixiao ; Bahn, Sangwoo ; Nam, Chang S.: Influence of Haptic Feedback on a Pointing Task in a Haptically Enhanced 3D Virtual Environment. In: Kurosu, Masaaki (Hrsg.): Human-Computer Interaction. Interaction Modalities and Techniques. Berlin, Heidelberg : Springer Berlin Heidelberg, 2013, S. 561–567

[CZGZ20] Chen, Na ; Zhao, Ming ; Gao, Kun ; Zhao, Jun: The Physiological Experimental Study on the Effect of Different Color of Safety Signs on a Virtual Subway Fire Escape-An Exploratory Case Study of Zijing Mountain Subway Station. In: International Journal of Environmental Research and Public Health 17 (2020), August, Nr. 16, S. 5903. `http://dx.doi.org/10.3390/ijerph17165903`. – DOI 10.3390/ijerph17165903

[DBGJ] Dörner, Ralf (Hrsg.) ; Broll, Wolfgang (Hrsg.) ; Grimm, Paul (Hrsg.) ; Jung, Bernhard (Hrsg.): Virtual und Augmented Reality (VR / AR): Grundlagen und Methoden der Virtuellen und Augmentierten Realität. Heidelberg, German : Springer (eXamen.press). `http://dx.doi.org/10.1007/978-3-642-28903-3`. `http://dx.doi.org/10.1007/978-3-642-28903-3`

[DCBL18] Dey, Arindam ; Chen, Hao ; Billinghurst, Mark ; Lindeman, Robert W.: Effects of Manipulating Physiological Feedback in Immersive Virtual Environments. In: Proceedings of the 2018 Annual Symposium on Computer-Human Interaction in Play. New

York, NY, USA : Association for Computing Machinery, October 2018 (CHI PLAY '18), S. 101–111

[Der75]   Derogatis, Leonard R.:   Brief symptom inventory. In: European Journal of Psychological Assessment (1975)

[DGCP08]   Duffield, Christine ; Gardner, Glenn ; Catling-Paull, Christine: Nursing work and the use of nursing time. In: Journal of Clinical Nursing 17 (2008), Dezember, Nr. 24, S. 3269–3274. `http://dx.doi.org/10.1111/j.1365-2702.2008.02637.x`. – DOI 10.1111/j.1365–2702.2008.02637.x

[DJBM⁺10]   Demaria Jr, Samuel ; Bryson, Ethan o. ; Mooney, Timothy J. ; Silverstein, Jeffrey H. ; Reich, David L. ; Bodian, Carol ; Levine, Adam I.:   Adding emotional stressors to training in simulated cardiopulmonary arrest enhances participant performance. In: Medical education 44 (2010), Nr. 10, 1006–1015. `http://dx.doi.org/10.1111/j.1365-2923.2010.03775.x`. – DOI 10.1111/j.1365–2923.2010.03775.x

[DLC⁺15]   Delahaye, Marcel ; Lemoine, Patrick ; Cartwright, Shanique ; Deuring, Gunnar ; Beck, Johannes ; Pflueger, Marlon ; Graf, Marc ; Hachtel, Henning: Learning aptitude, spatial orientation and cognitive flexibility tested in a virtual labyrinth after virtual stress induction. In: BMC Psychology 3 (2015), December, Nr. 1, 22. `http://dx.doi.org/10.1186/s40359-015-0080-5`. – DOI 10.1186/s40359–015–0080–5. – ISSN 2050–7283

[DLMZ16]   Diemer, Julia ; Lohkamp, Nora ; Mühlberger, Andreas ; Zwanzger, Peter: Fear and physiological arousal during a virtual height challenge—effects in patients with acrophobia and healthy controls. In: Journal of Anxiety Disorders 37 (2016), January, S. 30–39. `http://dx.doi.org/10.1016/j.janxdis.2015.10.007`. – DOI 10.1016/j.janxdis.2015.10.007

[DMK20]   Das, Souvik ; Maiti, J. ; Krishna, O. B.:   Assessing Mental Workload in Virtual Reality Based EOT Crane Operations: A Multi-Measure Approach.   In: International Journal of Industrial Ergonomics 80 (2020), November, S. 103017. `http://dx.doi.org/10.1016/j.ergon.2020.103017`. – DOI 10.1016/j.ergon.2020.103017

[DMSS19]   Drews, Frank A. ; Markewitz, Boaz A. ; Stoddard, Gregory J. ; Samore, Matthew H.:   Interruptions and Delivery of Care in the Intensive Care Unit. In: Human Factors 61 (2019), Juni, Nr. 4, S. 564–576. `http://dx.doi.org/10.1177/0018720819838090`. – DOI 10.1177/0018720819838090

[DMTC$^+$19] Darbyshire, Julie L. ; Müller-Trapet, M ; Cheer, J ; Fazi, FM ; Young, JD: Mapping Sources of Noise in an Intensive Care Unit. In: Anaesthesia 74 (2019), Nr. 8, S. 1018–1025

[DPLB17] Dey, Arindam ; Piumsomboon, Thammathip ; Lee, Youngho ; Billinghurst, Mark: Effects of Sharing Physiological States of Players in a Collaborative Virtual Reality Gameplay. In: Proceedings of the 2017 CHI Conference on Human Factors in Computing Systems. New York, NY, USA : Association for Computing Machinery, May 2017 (CHI '17), S. 4045–4056

[Dre19] Drews, Frank A.: The frequency and impact of task interruptions in the ICU. In: Human Factors 61 (2019), Mai, Nr. 4, S. 564–576. http://dx.doi.org/10.11177/0018702819838090. – DOI 10.11177/0018702819838090

[EAHB15] Ewertsson, Mona ; Allvin, Renée ; Holmström, Inger K. ; Blomberg, Karin: Walking the bridge: Nursing students' learning in clinical skill laboratories. 15 (2015), Nr. 4, S. 277–283. http://dx.doi.org/10.1016/j.nepr.2015.03.006. – DOI 10.1016/j.nepr.2015.03.006

[ECK05] Elpern, Ellen H. ; Covert, Barbara ; Kleinpell, Ruth: Moral distress of staff nurses in a medical intensive care unit. In: American journal of critical care : an official publication, American Association of Critical-Care Nurses 14 (2005), Nr. 6, S. 523–530

[ELL16] Elliman, James ; Loizou, Michael ; Loizides, Fernando: Virtual reality simulation training for student nurse education. In: 2016 8th international conference on games and virtual worlds for serious applications (VS-games) IEEE, 2016, S. 1–2

[Epp12a] Epp, Kirstin: Burnout in critical care nurses: a literature review. In: Dynamics 23 (2012), Nr. 4, S. 25–31

[Epp12b] Epp, Kirstin: Burnout in Critical Care Nurses: A Literature Review. In: Dynamics 4 (2012), Nr. 23, S. 25–31

[FBJ$^+$13] Farquharson, Barbara ; Bell, Cheryl ; Johnston, Derek ; Jones, Martyn ; Schofield, Pat ; Allan, Julia ; Ricketts, Ian ; Morrison, Kenny ; Johnston, Marie: Nursing Stress and Patient Care: Real-Time Investigation of the Effect of Nursing Tasks and Demands on Psychological Stress, Physiological Stress, and Job Performance: Study Protocol. In: J Adv Nurs 69 (2013), Oktober, Nr. 10, 2327–2335. http://dx.doi.org/10.1111/jan.12090. – DOI 10.1111/jan.12090

[FBS$^+$18] Finseth, Tor ; Barnett, Neil ; Shirtcliff, Elizabeth A. ; Dorneich, Michael C. ; Keren, Nir: Stress Inducing Demands in Virtual

Environments. In: Proceedings of the Human Factors and Ergonomics Society Annual Meeting 62 (2018), September, Nr. 1, S. 2066–2070. http://dx.doi.org/10.1177/1541931218621466. – DOI 10.1177/1541931218621466. – Publisher: SAGE Publications Inc

[FHF⁺18]   Freeman, Daniel ; Haselton, Polly ; Freeman, Jason ; Spanlang, Bernhard ; Kishore, Sameer ; Albery, Emily ; Denne, Megan ; Brown, Poppy ; Slater, Mel ; Nickless, Alecia: Automated psychological therapy using immersive virtual reality for treatment of fear of heights: a single-blind, parallel-group, randomised controlled trial. In: The Lancet Psychiatry 5 (2018), August, Nr. 8, S. 625–632. http://dx.doi.org/10.1016/S2215-0366(18)30226-8. – DOI 10.1016/S2215-0366(18)30226-8

[Fie94]   Field, Syd: Screenplay: The Foundations of Screenwriting. Dell Publishing Company, 1994 (A Dell Trade paperback). https://books.google.de/books?id=WzdvPwAACAAJ

[Fin17]   Fink, George: Stress: Concepts. In: Definition and History: Reference Module in Neuroscience and Biobehavioral Psychology (2017), S. 1–9

[FKD⁺18a]   Finseth, Tor T. ; Keren, Nir ; Dorneich, Michael C. ; Franke, Warren D. ; Anderson, Clayton C. ; Shelley, Mack C.: Evaluating the Effectiveness of Graduated Stress Exposure in Virtual Spaceflight Hazard Training. In: Journal of Cognitive Engineering and Decision Making 12 (2018), Dezember, Nr. 4, S. 248–268. http://dx.doi.org/10.1177/1555343418775561. – DOI 10.1177/1555343418775561. – Publisher: SAGE Publications

[FKD⁺18b]   Finseth, Tor T. ; Keren, Nir ; Dorneich, Michael C. ; Franke, Warren D. ; Anderson, Clayton C. ; Shelley, Mack C.: Evaluating the Effectiveness of Graduated Stress Exposure in Virtual Spaceflight Hazard Training. In: Journal of Cognitive Engineering and Decision Making 12 (2018), December, Nr. 4, S. 248–268. http://dx.doi.org/10.1177/1555343418775561. – DOI 10.1177/1555343418775561. – Publisher: SAGE Publications

[FM10]   Freeman, Nicholas ; Muraven, Mark: Don't interrupt me! Task interruption depletes the self's limited resources. In: Motivation and Emotion 34 (2010), September, Nr. 3, S. 230–241. http://dx.doi.org/10.1007/s11031-010-9169-6. – DOI 10.1007/s11031-010-9169-6

[FO15]   Freina, Laura ; Ott, Michela: A Literature Review on Immersive Virtual Reality in Education: State of the Art and Perspectives. In:

Proceedings of the 11th International Scientific Conference "eLearning and Software for Education". Bucharest, RO : Carol | National Defence University Publishing House, April 2015, S. 133–141

[FPETNFP+18] Ferrandini Price, Mariana ; Escribano Tortosa, Damián ; Nieto Fernandez-Pacheco, Antonio ; Perez Alonso, Nuria ; Cerón Madrigal, José J. ; Melendreras-Ruiz, Rafael ; García-Collado, Ángel J. ; Pardo Rios, Manuel ; Juguera Rodriguez, Laura: Comparative study of a simulated incident with multiple victims and immersive virtual reality. In: Nurse Education Today 71 (2018), December, S. 48–53. http://dx.doi.org/10.1016/j.nedt.2018.09.006. – DOI 10.1016/j.nedt.2018.09.006

[FRA+09] Fliege, H. ; Rose, M. ; Arck, P. ; Levenstein, S. ; Klapp, B. F.: PSQ - Perceived Stress Questionnaire. In: Diagnostica 47 (2009). http://dx.doi.org/10.23668/psycharchives.2889. – DOI 10.23668/psycharchives.2889

[FSG+15] Farra, Sharon L. ; Smith, Sherrill ; Gillespie, Gordon L. ; Nicely, Stephanie ; Ulrich, Deborah L. ; Hodgson, Eric ; French, DeAnne: Decontamination training: With and without virtual reality simulation. In: Advanced emergency nursing journal 37 (2015), Nr. 2, S. 125–133

[FSZ+20] Fadeev, Kirill A. ; Smirnov, Alexey S. ; Zhigalova, Olga P. ; Bazhina, Polina S. ; Tumialis, Alexey V. ; Golokhvast, Kirill S. u. a.: Too real to be virtual: Autonomic and EEG responses to extreme stress scenarios in virtual reality. In: Behavioural neurology 2020 (2020)

[FTA19] Fusaro, M. ; Tieri, G. ; Aglioti, S. M.: Influence of cognitive stance and physical perspective on subjective and autonomic reactivity to observed pain and pleasure: An immersive virtual reality study. In: Consciousness and Cognition 67 (2019), January, S. 86–97. http://dx.doi.org/10.1016/j.concog.2018.11.010. – DOI 10.1016/j.concog.2018.11.010

[FZSBC90] Foxall, Martha J. ; Zimmerman, Lani ; Standley, Roberta ; Bene Captain, Barbara: A Comparison of Frequency and Sources of Nursing Job Stress Perceived by Intensive Care, Hospice and Medical-Surgical Nurses. In: Journal of Advanced Nursing 15 (1990), Nr. 5, S. 577–584. http://dx.doi.org/10.1111/j.1365-2648.1990.tb01857.x. – DOI 10.1111/j.1365–2648.1990.tb01857.x

[GBW+16] Górski, Filip ; Buń, Paweł ; Wichniarek, Radosław ; Zawadzki, Przemysław ; Hamrol, Adam: Effective design of educational virtual reality applications for medicine using knowledge-engineering techniques. In: EURASIA Journal of Mathematics, Science and Technology Education 13 (2016), Nr. 2, S. 395–416

[GDM11] Gibbons, Chris ; Dempster, Martin ; Moutray, Marianne: Stress, coping and satisfaction in nursing students: Stress, coping and satisfaction in nursing students. In: Journal of Advanced Nursing 67 (2011), März, Nr. 3, 621–632. http://dx.doi.org/10.1111/j.1365-2648.2010.05495.x. – DOI 10.1111/j.1365–2648.2010.05495.x. – 00262

[GGG⁺19] Giannakakis, Giorgos ; Grigoriadis, Dimitris ; Giannakaki, Katerina ; Simantiraki, Olympia ; Roniotis, Alexandros ; Tsiknakis, Manolis: Review on psychological stress detection using biosignals. In: IEEE Transactions on Affective Computing (2019), S. 1–1. http://dx.doi.org/10.1109/TAFFC.2019.2927337. – DOI 10.1109/TAFFC.2019.2927337

[GHP⁺19] Gupta, Kunal ; Hajika, Ryo ; Pai, Yun S. ; Duenser, Andreas ; Lochner, Martin ; Billinghurst, Mark: In AI We Trust: Investigating the Relationship between Biosignals, Trust and Cognitive Load in VR. In: 25th ACM Symposium on Virtual Reality Software and Technology. New York, NY, USA : Association for Computing Machinery, November 2019 (VRST '19), S. 1–10

[GJ21] Grabowski, A. ; Jach, K.: The use of virtual reality in the training of professionals: with the example of firefighters. In: Computer Animation and Virtual Worlds (2021). http://dx.doi.org/10.1002/cav.1981. – DOI 10.1002/cav.1981

[GL20] Grassini, Simone ; Laumann, Karin: Questionnaire Measures and Physiological Correlates of Presence: A Systematic Review. In: Frontiers in Psychology 11 (2020), S. 349. http://dx.doi.org/10.3389/fpsyg.2020.00349. – DOI 10.3389/fpsyg.2020.00349

[GSVP16] Goyal, Aishwarya ; Singh, Shailendra ; Vir, Dharam ; Pershad, Dwarka: Automation of Stress Recognition Using Subjective or Objective Measures. In: Psychological Studies 61 (2016), Nr. 4, S. 348–364. http://dx.doi.org/10.1007/s12646-016-0379-1. – DOI 10.1007/s12646–016–0379–1

[GTA81] Gray-Toft, Pamela ; Anderson, James G.: The Nursing Stress Scale: Development of an instrument. 3 (1981), Nr. 1, S. 11–23. http://dx.doi.org/10.1007/BF01321348. – DOI 10.1007/BF01321348

[GWKJ19] Gujjar, Kumar R. ; Wijk, Arjen van ; Kumar, Ratika ; Jongh, Ad de: Efficacy of virtual reality exposure therapy for the treatment of dental phobia in adults: A randomized controlled trial. In: Journal of Anxiety Disorders 62 (2019), 100–108. `http://dx.doi.org/10.1016/j.janxdis.2018.12.001`. – DOI 10.1016/j.janxdis.2018.12.001

[GWM+19] Gradl, Stefan ; Wirth, Markus ; Mächtlinger, Nico ; Poguntke, Romina ; Wonner, Andrea ; Rohleder, Nicolas ; Eskofier, Bjoern M.: The Stroop Room: A Virtual Reality-Enhanced Stroop Test. In: 25th ACM Symposium on Virtual Reality Software and Technology. New York, NY, USA : Association for Computing Machinery, November 2019 (VRST '19), 1–12

[Ham96] Hammond, Kenneth R.: Human judgement and social policy: Irreducible uncertainty, inevitable error, unavoidable injustice. New York, NY, US : Oxford University Press, 1996 (Human judgement and social policy: Irreducible uncertainty, inevitable error, unavoidable injustice)

[Har06] Hart, Sandra G.: Nasa-Task Load Index (NASA-TLX); 20 Years Later. In: Proceedings of the Human Factors and Ergonomics Society Annual Meeting 50 (2006), Nr. 9, S. 904–908. `http://dx.doi.org/10.1177/154193120605000909`. – DOI 10.1177/154193120605000909

[Har10] Harder, B. N.: Use of Simulation in Teaching and Learning in Health Sciences: A Systematic Review. In: Journal of Nursing Education 49 (2010), Nr. 1, 23–28. `http://dx.doi.org/10.3928/01484834-20090828-08`. – DOI 10.3928/01484834–20090828–08

[HDRS+13] Happell, Brenda ; Dwyer, Trudy ; Reid-Searl, Kerry ; Burke, Karena J. ; Caperchione, Cristina M. ; Gaskin, Cadeyrn J.: Nurses and Stress: Recognizing Causes and Seeking Solutions. In: Journal of Nursing Management 21 (2013), Mai, Nr. 4, 638–647. `http://dx.doi.org/10.1111/jonm.12037`. – DOI 10.1111/jonm.12037

[Hei92] Heilig, Morton L.: EL Cine del Futuro: The Cinema of the Future. In: Presence: Teleoperators and Virtual Environments 1 (1992), Januar, Nr. 3, 279–294. `http://dx.doi.org/10.1162/pres.1992.1.3.279`. – DOI 10.1162/pres.1992.1.3.279. – ISSN 1054–7460

[HEK20] Hirt, Christian ; Eckard, Marcel ; Kunz, Andreas: Stress generation and non-intrusive measurement in virtual environments using eye tracking. In: Journal of Ambient Intelligence and Humanized Computing 11 (2020), December, Nr. 12, S. 5977–5989. `http://dx.doi.org/10.1007/s12652-020-01845-y`. – DOI 10.1007/s12652-020-01845-y

[HHKH20] Holleman, Gijs A. ; Hooge, Ignace T. C. ; Kemner, Chantal ; Hessels, Roy S.: The 'Real-World Approach' and Its Problems: A Critique of the Term Ecological Validity. 11 (2020). https://www.frontiersin.org/articles/10.3389/fpsyg.2020.00721

[HKM+14] Hartanto, Dwi ; Kampmann, Isabel L. ; Morina, Nexhmedin ; Emmelkamp, Paul G. M. ; Neerincx, Mark A. ; Brinkman, Willem-Paul: Controlling Social Stress in Virtual Reality Environments. In: PLoS ONE 9 (2014), March, Nr. 3. http://dx.doi.org/10.1371/journal.pone.0092804. – DOI 10.1371/journal.pone.0092804

[HM00] Healy, Christine M. ; McKay, Michael F.: Nursing stress: the effects of coping strategies and job satisfaction in a sample of Australian nurses. In: Journal of Advanced Nursing 31 (2000), Nr. 3, 681–688. http://dx.doi.org/10.1046/j.1365-2648.2000.01323.x. – DOI 10.1046/j.1365-2648.2000.01323.x

[HN15] Helton, William S. ; Näswall, Katharina: Short Stress State Questionnaire: Factor Structure and State Change Assessment. In: European Journal of Psychological Assessment 31 (2015), June, Nr. 1, S. 20–30. http://dx.doi.org/10.1027/1015-5759/a000200. – DOI 10.1027/1015-5759/a000200

[HRP13] Harder, Nicole ; Ross, Carolyn J. ; Paul, Pauline: Student Perspective of Roles Assignment in High-Fidelity Simulation: An Ethnographic Study. In: Clinical Simulation in Nursing 9 (2013), Nr. 9, S. 329–334. http://dx.doi.org/10.1016/j.ecns.2012.09.003. – DOI 10.1016/j.ecns.2012.09.003

[HS88] Hart, Sandra G. ; Staveland, Lowell E.: Development of NASA-TLX (Task Load Index): Results of empirical and theoretical research. In: Advances in Psychology Bd. 52. Moffet Field, CA, NY : Elsevier, 1988, S. 139–183

[HTLTMLM17] Higuera-Trujillo, Juan L. ; López-Tarruella Maldonado, Juan ; Llinares Millán, Carmen: Psychological and physiological human responses to simulated and real environments: A comparison between Photographs, 360° Panoramas, and Virtual Reality. In: Applied Ergonomics 65 (2017), November, 398–409. http://dx.doi.org/10.1016/j.apergo.2017.05.006. – DOI 10.1016/j.apergo.2017.05.006

[ICCG] Ippoliti, Elena ; Casale, Andrea ; Calvano, Michele ; Guadagnoli, Francesca: Giving Form to Absence: Experiences in Representation, Communication, and Narration for the Places and Community of Amatrice. http://dx.doi.org/10.4018/978-1-5225-6936-7.ch014. In: Analysis, Conservation, and Restoration of Tangible and Intangible Cultural Heritage. Hershey,

PA, USA : IGI Global. – DOI 10.4018/978–1–5225–6936–7.ch014, 329–365

[ISO19]   ISO: ISO 9241-210:2019: Ergonomics of human-system interaction — Part 210: Human-centred design for interactive systems. Berlin, Germany : Deutsches Institut für Normung, 2019. – 33 S.

[Jer15]   Jerald, Jason: The VR Book: Human-Centered Design for Virtual Reality. New York, NY, USA : Association for Computing Machinery and Morgan I& Claypool, 2015

[JPKC⁺18]   Jongeneel, Alyssa ; Pot-Kolder, Roos ; Counotte, Jacqueline ; Gaag, Mark van d. ; Veling, Wim: Self-esteem moderates affective and psychotic responses to social stress in psychosis: A virtual reality study. In: Schizophrenia Research 202 (2018), December, 80–85. http://dx.doi.org/10.1016/j.schres.2018.06.042. – DOI 10.1016/j.schres.2018.06.042. – ISSN 0920–9964

[Jul11]   Julian, Laura J.: Measures of Anxiety: State-Trait Anxiety Inventory (STAI), Beck Anxiety Inventory (BAI), and Hospital Anxiety and Depression Scale-Anxiety (HADS-A). In: Arthritis Care Res 63 (2011), November, Nr. S11, S467–S472. http://dx.doi.org/10.1002/acr.20561. – DOI 10.1002/acr.20561

[Kal18]   Kaluza, Gert: Stressbewältigung: Trainingsmanual Zur Psychologischen Gesundheitsförderung. Heidelberg, Germany : Springer Berlin Heidelberg, 2018 (Psychotherapie: Praxis). http://dx.doi.org/10.1007/978-3-662-55638-2. http://dx.doi.org/10.1007/978-3-662-55638-2

[KBBNZ20]   Krisch, Kirra A. ; Bandarian-Balooch, Siavash ; Neumann, David L. ; Zhong, John: Eliciting and attenuating reinstatement of fear: Effects of an unextinguished CS. In: Learning and Motivation 71 (2020), August, 101650. http://dx.doi.org/10.1016/j.lmot.2020.101650. – DOI 10.1016/j.lmot.2020.101650

[KBL19]   Kim, Aelee ; Bae, Hayoung ; Lee, Kyoungmin: Effects of Tactile Perception on Emotion and Immersion to Film Viewing in a Virtual Environment. In: 25th ACM Symposium on Virtual Reality Software and Technology. Parramatta NSW Australia : ACM, November 2019, 1–3

[KCE⁺14]   Kniffin, Tracey C. ; Carlson, Charles R. ; Ellzey, Antonio ; Eisenlohr-Moul, Tory ; Beck, Kelly B. ; McDonald, Renee ; Jouriles, Ernest N.: Using Virtual Reality to Explore Self-Regulation in High-Risk Settings. In: Trauma, Violence, & Abuse 15 (2014), Oktober, Nr. 4, S.

310–321. http://dx.doi.org/10.1177/1524838014521501. – DOI 10.1177/1524838014521501

[KD02]   Kim, Jeansok J. ; Diamond, David M.: The stressed hippocampus, synaptic plasticity and lost memories. In: Nature Reviews Neuroscience 3 (2002), Nr. 6, S. 453–462. http://dx.doi.org/10.1038/nrn849. – DOI 10.1038/nrn849

[KDG⁺21]   Krampe, Henning ; Denke, Claudia ; Gülden, Jakob ; Mauersberger, Vivian-Marie ; Ehlen, Lukas ; Schönthaler, Elena ; Wunderlich, Maximilian M. ; Lütz, Alawi ; Balzer, Felix ; Weiss, Björn ; Spies, Claudia D.: Perceived Severity of Stressors in the Intensive Care Unit: A Systematic Review and Semi-Quantitative Analysis of the Literature on the Perspectives of Patients, Health Care Providers and Relatives. In: Journal of Clinical Medicine 10 (2021), August, Nr. 17, S. 3928. http://dx.doi.org/10.3390/jcm10173928. – DOI 10.3390/jcm10173928

[KF20]   Kothgassner, Oswald D. ; Felnhofer, Anna: Does virtual reality help to cut the Gordian knot between ecological validity and experimental control? In: Annals of the International Communication Association 44 (2020), Juli, Nr. 3, S. 210–218. http://dx.doi.org/10.1080/23808985.2020.1792790. – DOI 10.1080/23808985.2020.1792790

[KGG⁺21]   Kothgassner, Oswald D. ; Goreis, Andreas ; Glenk, Lisa M. ; Kafka, Johanna X. ; Beutl, Leon ; Kryspin-Exner, Ilse ; Hlavacs, Helmut ; Palme, Rupert ; Felnhofer, Anna: Virtual and real-life ostracism and its impact on a subsequent acute stressor. In: Physiology & Behavior 228 (2021), January, S. 113205. http://dx.doi.org/10.1016/j.physbeh.2020.113205. – DOI 10.1016/j.physbeh.2020.113205

[KKA73]   Kleinknecht, Ronald A. ; Klepac, Robert K. ; Alexander, Leib D.: Origins and Characteristics of Fear of Dentistry. In: The Journal of the American Dental Association 86 (1973), April, Nr. 4, S. 842–848. http://dx.doi.org/10.14219/jada.archive.1973.0165. – DOI 10.14219/jada.archive.1973.0165

[KM00]   Kirkcaldy, B. D. ; Martin, T.: Job Stress and Satisfaction Among Nurses: Individual Differences. In: Stress Medicine 16 (2000), Nr. 2, S. 77–89. http://dx.doi.org/10.1002/(SICI)1099-1700(200003)16:2<77::AID-SMI835>3.0.CO;2-Z. – DOI 10.1002/(SICI)1099–1700(200003)16:2<77::AID–SMI835>3.0.CO;2–Z

[KPFF⁺14]   Kleven, Nils F. ; Prasolova-Førland, Ekaterina ; Fominykh, Mikhail ; Hansen, Arne ; Rasmussen, Guri ; Sagberg, Lisa M. ; Lindseth,

Frank: Training nurses and educating the public using a virtual operating room with Oculus Rift. In: 2014 International Conference on Virtual Systems & Multimedia (VSMM) IEEE, 2014, S. 206–213

[KPGW16]   Kumar, Arunesh ; Pore, Prasad ; Gupta, Sachin ; Wani, Aziz O.: Level of stress and its determinants among Intensive Care Unit staff. 20 (2016), Nr. 3, S. 129–132. http://dx.doi.org/10.4103/0019-5278.203137. – DOI 10.4103/0019–5278.203137

[KPH93]   Kirschbaum, Clemens ; Pirke, Karl-Martin ; Hellhammer, Dirk: The 'Trier Social Stress Test' – A Tool for Investigating Psychobiological Stress Responses in a Laboratory Setting. In: Neuropsychobiology 28 (1993), S. 76–81. http://dx.doi.org/10.1159/000119004. – DOI 10.1159/000119004

[KRGF+15]   Kleinsmith, Andrea ; Rivera-Gutierrez, Diego ; Finney, Glen ; Cendan, Juan ; Lok, Benjamin: Understanding Empathy Training with Virtual Patients. In: Computers in human behavior 52 (2015), S. 151–158. http://dx.doi.org/10.1016/j.chb.2015.05.033. – DOI 10.1016/j.chb.2015.05.033

[KSV15]   Kieffer, Suzanne ; Sangiorgi, Ugo ; Vanderdonckt, Jean: ECOVAL: A Framework for Increasing the Ecological Validity in Usability Testing. Bd. 2015. 2015. http://dx.doi.org/10.1109/HICSS.2015.61. http://dx.doi.org/10.1109/HICSS.2015.61

[KvC21]   Krupić, Dino ; Zuro, Barbara ; Corr, Philip J.: Anxiety and threat magnification in subjective and physiological responses of fear of heights induced by virtual reality. In: Personality and Individual Differences 169 (2021), February, 109720. http://dx.doi.org/10.1016/j.paid.2019.109720. – DOI 10.1016/j.paid.2019.109720

[KZA+20]   Kennard, Maxwell ; Zhang, Haihan ; Akimoto, Yuki ; Hirokawa, Masakazu ; Suzuki, Kenji: Effects of Visual Biofeedback on Competition Performance Using an Immersive Mixed Reality System. In: 2020 IEEE International Conference on Systems, Man, and Cybernetics (SMC). Toronto, Ontario, Canada : IEEE, 2020, S. 3793–3798

[LA10]   Laal, Marjan ; Aliramaie, Nasrin: Nursing and Coping With Stress. In: Public Health 2 (2010), Nr. 5

[Lan23]   Lang, Hartmut: Blood Gas Analysis (BGA). Version: 2023. http://dx.doi.org/10.1007/978-3-662-64196-5_27. In: Lang, Hartmut (Hrsg.): Out-of Hospital Ventilation : An Interdisciplinary Perspective on Landscape and Health. Berlin, Heidelberg : Springer, 2023. – DOI 10.1007/978–3–662–64196–5_27, 333–359

[LB17]   Loranger, Claudie ; Bouchard, Stéphane: Validating a Virtual Envi-
                ronment for Sexual Assault Victims. In: Journal of Traumatic Stress
                30 (2017), April, Nr. 2, S. 157–165. http://dx.doi.org/10.1002/
                jts.22170. – DOI 10.1002/jts.22170

[LD08]   Lee, K. J. ; Dupree, Claretta Y.: Staff Experiences With End-of-Life
                Care in the Pediatric Intensive Care Unit. In: Journal of Palliative
                Medicine 11 (2008), September, Nr. 7, 986–990. http://dx.doi.
                org/10.1089/jpm.2007.0283. – DOI 10.1089/jpm.2007.0283

[LF87]   Lazarus, Richard S. ; Folkman, Susan: Transactional theory and re-
                search on emotions and coping. In: European Journal of personality
                1 (1987), Nr. 3, S. 141–169

[LFH]   Lazar, Jonathan ; Feng, Jinjuan H. ; Hochheiser, Harry: Research
                Methods in Human-Computer Interaction. 2. Cambridge, MA,
                USA : Morgan Kaufmann

[LKHI21]   Lee, Minha ; Kolkmeier, Jan ; Heylen, Dirk ; IJsselsteijn, Wijnand:
                Who Makes Your Heart Beat? What Makes You Sweat? Social Con-
                flict in Virtual Reality for Educators. In: Frontiers in Psychology 12
                (2021). http://dx.doi.org/10.3389/fpsyg.2021.628246. – DOI
                10.3389/fpsyg.2021.628246

[LLCFL18]   Labonte-LeMoyne, Elise ; Courtemanche, François ; Fredette, Marc
                ; Léger, Pierre-Majorique: How Wild Is Too Wild: Lessons
                Learned and Recommendations for Ecological Validity in Physio-
                logical Computing Research:. In: Proceedings of the 5th Interna-
                tional Conference on Physiological Computing Systems. Seville,
                Spain : SCITEPRESS - Science and Technology Publications, 2018,
                S. 123–130

[LLG+20]   Laurent, Alexandra ; Lheureux, Florent ; Genet, Magali ; Mar-
                tin Delgado, Maria C. ; Bocci, Maria G. ; Prestifilippo, Alessia ;
                Besch, Guillaume ; Capellier, Gilles: Scales Used to Measure Job
                Stressors in Intensive Care Units: Are They Relevant and Reliable?
                A Systematic Review. In: Frontiers in Psychology 11 (2020), März,
                S. 245. http://dx.doi.org/10.3389/fpsyg.2020.00245. – DOI
                10.3389/fpsyg.2020.00245

[LLRJ15]   Levy, Fanny ; Leboucher, Pierre ; Rautureau, Gilles ; Jouvent,
                Roland: E-virtual reality exposure therapy in acrophobia: A pi-
                lot study. In: Journal of Telemedicine and Telecare 22 (2015), June,
                Nr. 4, 215–220. http://dx.doi.org/10.1177/1357633X15598243.
                – DOI 10.1177/1357633X15598243

[LMPG+16]   Labrague, Leodoro ; McEnroe-Petitte, Denise ; Gloe, Donna ; Thomas, Loretta ; Papathanasiou, Ioanna ; Tsaras, Konstantinos: A Literature Review on Stress and Coping Strategies in Nursing Students. In: Journal of Mental Health 25 (2016), Dezember. http://dx.doi.org/10.1080/09638237.2016.1244721. – DOI 10.1080/09638237.2016.1244721

[LPV+93]   Levenstein, S. ; Prantera, C. ; Varvo, v. ; Scribano, M.L. ; Berto, E. ; Luzi, C. ; Andreoli, A.: Development of the Perceived Stress Questionnaire: A New Tool for Psychosomatic Research. In: Journal of Psychosomatic Research 37 (1993), Januar, Nr. 1, 19–32. http://dx.doi.org/10.1016/0022-3999(93)90120-5. – DOI 10.1016/0022–3999(93)90120–5. – ISSN 00223999

[LTFL+16]   Lavoie-Tremblay, Mélanie ; Feeley, Nancy ; Lavigne, Geneviève L. ; Genest, Christine ; Robins, Stéphanie ; Fréchette, Julie: Neonatal Intensive Care Unit Nurses Working in an Open Ward: Stress and Work Satisfaction. 35 (2016), Nr. 3, S. 205–216. http://dx.doi.org/10.1097/HCM.0000000000000122. – DOI 10.1097/HCM.0000000000000122

[MAF+19]   Martens, Marieke A. ; Antley, Angus ; Freeman, Daniel ; Slater, Mel ; Harrison, Paul J. ; Tunbridge, Elizabeth M.: It Feels Real: Physiological Responses to a Stressful Virtual Reality Environment and Its Impact on Working Memory. In: Journal of Psychopharmacology (Oxford, England) 33 (2019), October, Nr. 10, S. 1264–1273. http://dx.doi.org/10.1177/0269881119860156. – DOI 10.1177/0269881119860156

[Mai18]   Mai, Christian: The Usage of Presence Measurements in Research: A Review. In: Proceedings of the International Society for Presence Research, 2018, S. 21–22

[MAS18]   Mousas, Christos ; Anastasiou, Dimitris ; Spantidi, Ourania: The effects of appearance and motion of virtual characters on emotional reactivity. In: Computers in Human Behavior 86 (2018), September, S. 99–108. http://dx.doi.org/10.1016/j.chb.2018.04.036. – DOI 10.1016/j.chb.2018.04.036

[May15]   Mayring, Philipp: Qualitative Content Analysis: Theoretical Background and Procedures. In: Bikner-Ahsbahs, Angelika (Hrsg.) ; Knipping, Christine (Hrsg.) ; Presmeg, Norma (Hrsg.): Approaches to Qualitative Research in Mathematics Education: Examples of Methodology and Methods. Springer Netherlands, 2015, S. 365–380

[MB92]   Marteau, Theresa M. ; Bekker, Hilary: The development of a six‐item short‐form of the state scale of the Spielberger

State—Trait Anxiety Inventory (STAI). In: British Journal of Clinical Psychology 31 (1992), September, Nr. 3, 301–306. `http: //dx.doi.org/10.1111/j.2044-8260.1992.tb00997.x`. – DOI 10.1111/j.2044–8260.1992.tb00997.x

[MBS+20]   Mostajeran, Fariba ; Balci, Melik B. ; Steinicke, Frank ; Kuhn, Simone ; Gallinat, Jurgen: The Effects of Virtual Audience Size on Social Anxiety during Public Speaking. In: 2020 IEEE Conference on Virtual Reality and 3D User Interfaces (VR). Atlanta, GA, USA : IEEE, March 2020, 303–312

[MC98]   Mattick, Richard P. ; Clarke, J.Christopher: Development and validation of measures of social phobia scrutiny fear and social interaction anxiety. In: Behaviour Research and Therapy 36 (1998), April, Nr. 4, 455–470.   `http://dx.doi.org/10.1016/S0005-7967(97) 10031-6`. – DOI 10.1016/S0005–7967(97)10031–6

[MCZS20]   Misztal, Sebastian ; Carbonell, Guillermo ; Zander, Lysann ; Schild, Jonas: Intensifying Stress Perception Using Visual Effects in VR Games. In: International Conference on the Foundations of Digital Games. New York, NY, USA : Association for Computing Machinery, September 2020 (FDG '20), S. 1–4

[Mei77]   Meichenbaum, Donald: Stress-Inoculation Training. Version: 1977. `http://dx.doi.org/10.1007/978-1-4757-9739-8_6`.   In: Cognitive-Behavior Modification: An Integrative Approach. Boston, MA : Springer US, 1977 (The Springer Behavior Therapy Series). – DOI 10.1007/978–1–4757–9739–8_6, S. 143–182

[Men20]   Mendelson, Tamar: Stress, emotional. In: Encyclopedia of behavioral medicine. Springer, 2020, S. 2170–2172

[MGL+19]   Mosquera, Chanelle ; Galvan, Bonita ; Liu, Ellen ; De Vito, Ross ; Ting, Perry ; Costello, Enrica L. ; Wood, Zoë J.: ANX dread: a virtual reality experience to explore anxiety during task completion. In: Proceedings of the 14th International Conference on the Foundations of Digital Games. New York, NY, USA : Association for Computing Machinery, August 2019 (FDG '19), S. 1–5

[MGS+20]   Malta, Loretta S. ; Giosan, Cezar ; Szkodny, Lauren E. ; Altemus, Margaret M. ; Rizzo, Albert A. ; Silbersweig, David A. ; Difede, JoAnn: Predictors of involuntary and voluntary emotional episodic memories of virtual reality scenarios in Veterans with and without PTSD. In: Memory (Hove, England) 28 (2020), July, Nr. 6, S. 724–740. `http://dx.doi.org/10.1080/09658211.2020.1770289`. – DOI 10.1080/09658211.2020.1770289

[MHF15]   Mellalieu, Stephen ; Henton, Sheldon ; Fletcher, David: A competitive anxiety review: Recent directions in sport psychology research. In: Literature Reviews in Sport Psychology. 2015, S. 1–45

[MHS+03]   Morrison, Wynne E. ; Haas, Ellen C. ; Shaffner, Donald H. ; Garrett, Elizabeth S. ; Fackler, James C.: Noise, Stress, and Annoyance in a Pediatric Intensive Care Unit:. In: Critical Care Medicine 31 (2003), Januar, Nr. 1, S. 113–119. http://dx.doi.org/10.1097/00003246-200301000-00018. – DOI 10.1097/00003246–200301000–00018

[MJM12]   Mealer, Meredith ; Jones, Jacqueline ; Moss, Marc: A Qualitative Study of Resilience and Posttraumatic Stress Disorder in United States ICU Nurses. In: Intensive Care Medicine 38 (2012), September, Nr. 9, S. 1445–1451. http://dx.doi.org/10.1007/s00134-012-2600-6. – DOI 10.1007/s00134–012–2600–6

[MK94]   Milgram, Paul ; Kishino, Fumio: A taxonomy of mixed reality visual displays. In: IEICE TRANSACTIONS on Information and Systems 77 (1994), Nr. 12, S. 1321–1329

[MLO10]   Muschalla, Beate ; Linden, Michael ; Olbrich, Dieter: The relationship between job-anxiety and trait-anxiety–a differential diagnostic investigation with the Job-Anxiety-Scale and the State-Trait-Anxiety-Inventory. 24 (2010), Nr. 3, S. 366–371. http://dx.doi.org/10.1016/j.janxdis.2010.02.001. – DOI 10.1016/j.janxdis.2010.02.001

[MLSRGR+16] Montero-López, Eva ; Santos-Ruiz, Ana ; García-Ríos, M. C. ; Rodríguez-Blázquez, Raúl ; Pérez-García, Miguel ; Peralta-Ramírez, María I.: A virtual reality approach to the Trier Social Stress Test: Contrasting two distinct protocols. In: Behavior Research Methods 48 (2016), März, Nr. 1, S. 223–232. http://dx.doi.org/10.3758/s13428-015-0565-4. – DOI 10.3758/s13428–015–0565–4

[MMCK20]   Min, Seulki ; Moon, Jung-Geun ; Cho, Chul-Hyun ; Kim, Gerard J.: Effects of Immersive Virtual Reality Content Type to Mindfulness and Physiological Parameters. In: 26th ACM Symposium on Virtual Reality Software and Technology. New York, NY, USA : Association for Computing Machinery, November 2020 (VRST '20), S. 1–9

[MMP+18]   Mills, Brennen W. ; Miles, Alecka K. ; Phan, Tina ; Dykstra, Peggy M. ; Hansen, Sara S. ; Walsh, Andrew S. ; Reid, David N. ; Langdon, Claire: Investigating the extent realistic moulage impacts on immersion and performance among undergraduate paramedicine students in a simulation-based trauma scenario: a pilot study. In: Simulation in Healthcare 13 (2018), Nr. 5, S. 331–340

[MN85]   Meichenbaum, Donald ; Novaco, Ray: Stress Inoculation: A Preventative Approach. In: Issues in Mental Health Nursing 7 (1985), Januar, Nr. 1-4, S. 419–435. http://dx.doi.org/10.3109/01612848509009464. – DOI 10.3109/01612848509009464

[MRB03]   McGrath, A. ; Reid, N. ; Boore, J.: Occupational Stress in Nursing. In: International Journal of Nursing Studies 40 (2003), Juli, Nr. 5, S. 555–565. http://dx.doi.org/10.1016/S0020-7489(03)00058-0. – DOI 10.1016/S0020-7489(03)00058-0. – 00384

[MSA17]   McCurdie, Tara ; Sanderson, Penelope ; Aitken, Leanne M.: Traditions of research into interruptions in healthcare: A conceptual review. In: International Journal of Nursing Studies 66 (2017), Januar, S. 23–36. http://dx.doi.org/10.1016/j.ijnurstu.2016.11.005. – DOI 10.1016/j.ijnurstu.2016.11.005

[MSB+07]   Mealer, Meredith L. ; Shelton, April ; Berg, Britt ; Rothbaum, Barbara ; Moss, Marc: Increased Prevalence of Post-traumatic Stress Disorder Symptoms in Critical Care Nurses. In: American Journal of Respiratory and Critical Care Medicine 175 (2007), April, Nr. 7, S. 693–697. http://dx.doi.org/10.1164/rccm.200606-735OC. – DOI 10.1164/rccm.200606-735OC

[MSP+13]   Matthews, Gerald ; Szalma, James ; Panganiban, April R. ; Neubauer, Catherine ; Warm, Joel S.: Profiling task stress with the dundee stress state questionnaire. In: Psychology of stress: New research 1 (2013), S. 49–90

[MSRS]   Moro, Christian ; Stromberga, Zane ; Raikos, Athanasios ; Stirling, Allan: Combining virtual (Oculus Rift & Gear VR) and augmented reality with interactive applications to enhance tertiary medical and biomedical curricula. In: SA '16: SIGGRAPH ASIA 2016 Symposium on Education: Talks. Macau, China : ACM Press, S. 1–2

[MSU16]   Meraner, V. ; Sperner-Unterweger, B.:   Patienten, Ärzte und Pflegepersonal auf Intensivstationen : Psychologische und psychotherapeutische Interventionen.   In: Der Nervenarzt 87 (2016), Nr. 3, S. 264–268.   http://dx.doi.org/10.1007/s00115-016-0098-9. – DOI 10.1007/s00115-016-0098-9

[Muh15]   Muhanna, Muhanna A.:   Virtual reality and the CAVE: Taxonomy, interaction challenges and research directions. In: Journal of King Saud University - Computer and Information Sciences

27 (2015), Juli, Nr. 3, 344–361. http://dx.doi.org/10.1016/j. jksuci.2014.03.023. – DOI 10.1016/j.jksuci.2014.03.023

[MWE19]   Mertens, Gaëtan ; Wagensveld, Patrick ; Engelhard, Iris M.: Cue conditioning using a virtual spider discriminates between high and low spider fearful individuals. In: Computers in Human Behavior 91 (2019), February, S. 192–200. http://dx.doi.org/10.1016/j. chb.2018.10.006. – DOI 10.1016/j.chb.2018.10.006

[NBR13]   Nanji, Karen C. ; Baca, Kirsten ; Raemer, Daniel B.: The effect of an olfactory and visual cue on realism and engagement in a health care simulation experience. In: Simulation in Healthcare 8 (2013), Nr. 3, S. 143–147

[NH06]   Nørgaard, Mie ; Hornbæk, Kasper: What Do Usability Evaluators Do in Practice? An Explorative Study of Think-Aloud Testing. In: Proceedings of the 6th Conference on Designing Interactive Systems. New York, NY, USA : Association for Computing Machinery, 2006 (DIS '06), 209–218

[NKRB+20]   Nakarada-Kordic, I. ; Reay, S. ; Bennett, G. ; Kruse, J. ; Lydon, A. M. ; Sim, J.: Can virtual reality simulation prepare patients for an MRI experience? In: Radiography 26 (2020), August, Nr. 3, 205–213. http://dx.doi.org/10.1016/j.radi.2019.11.004. – DOI 10.1016/j.radi.2019.11.004

[OBW18]   Oh, Catherine S. ; Bailenson, Jeremy N. ; Welch, Gregory F.: A Systematic Review of Social Presence: Definition, Antecedents, and Implications. In: Frontiers in Robotics and AI 5 (2018), S. 114. http://dx.doi.org/10.3389/frobt.2018.00114. – DOI 10.3389/frobt.2018.00114

[ÖLH93]   Öhman, Arne ; Lewis, Michael ; Haviland, M: Handbook of emotions. In: Handbook of Emotions 3 (1993), S. 709–729

[Par15]   Parsons, Thomas D.: Virtual Reality for Enhanced Ecological Validity and Experimental Control in the Clinical, Affective and Social Neurosciences. In: Frontiers in Human Neuroscience 9 (2015). https://www.frontiersin.org/articles/10. 3389/fnhum.2015.00660

[PBW06]   Plaumann, Martina ; Busse, Anja ; Walter, Ulla: Grundlagen zu Stress. Version: 2006. http://dx.doi.org/10.1007/ 3-540-32662-6_2. In: Weißbuch Prävention 2005/2006: Stress? Ursachen, Erklärungsmodelle und präventive Ansätze. Berlin, Heidelberg : Springer, 2006. – DOI 10.1007/3–540–32662–6_2, 3–12

[PCR+13]   Pallavicini, Federica ; Cipresso, Pietro ; Raspelli, Simona ; Grassi,
             Alessandra ; Serino, Silvia ; Vigna, Cinzia ; Triberti, Stefano ; Vil-
             lamira, Marco ; Gaggioli, Andrea ; Riva, Giuseppe: Is virtual re-
             ality always an effective stressors for exposure treatments? Some
             insights from a controlled trial. In: BMC psychiatry 13 (2013),
             S. 52. http://dx.doi.org/10.1186/1471-244X-13-52. – DOI
             10.1186/1471–244X–13–52

[Pfl23]   Pflegeberufegesetz.   https://www.
             bundesgesundheitsministerium.de/pflegeberufegesetz.
             Version: 2023

[PFSFL18]   Prasolova-Førland, Ekaterina ; Steinsbekk, Aslak ; Fominykh,
             Mikhail ; Lindseth, Frank: Practicing interprofessional team com-
             munication and collaboration in a smart virtual university hospi-
             tal. In: Smart Universities: Concepts, Systems, and Technologies 4
             (2018), S. 191–224

[PLJS20]   Park, Sang H. ; Lee, Pyoung J. ; Jung, Timothy ; Swenson, Alasdair:
             Effects of the Aural and Visual Experience on Psycho-Physiological
             Recovery in Urban and Rural Environments. In: Applied Acous-
             tics 169 (2020). http://dx.doi.org/10.1016/j.apacoust.2020.
             107486. – DOI 10.1016/j.apacoust.2020.107486

[PLS+21]   Plotzky, Christian ; Lindwedel, Ulrike ; Sorber, Michaela ; Loessl,
             Barbara ; Kø"Nig, Peter ; Kunze, Christophe ; Kugler, Christiane
             ; Meng, Michael: Virtual Reality Simulations in Nurse Educa-
             tion: A Systematic Mapping Review. In: Nurse Education Today
             101 (2021), Juni, S. 104868. http://dx.doi.org/10.1016/j.nedt.
             2021.104868. – DOI 10.1016/j.nedt.2021.104868

[PMB+21]   Page, Matthew J. ; McKenzie, Joanne E. ; Bossuyt, Patrick M. ;
             Boutron, Isabelle ; Hoffmann, Tammy C. ; Mulrow, Cynthia D. ;
             Shamseer, Larissa ; Tetzlaff, Jennifer M. ; Akl, Elie A. ; Brennan,
             Sue E. u. a.: The PRISMA 2020 statement: an updated guideline for
             reporting systematic reviews. In: British Medical Journal 372 (2021)

[PPM22]   Petersen, Gustav B. ; Petkakis, Giorgos ; Makransky,
             Guido: A study of how immersion and interactivity drive
             VR learning.   179 (2022).   http://dx.doi.org/https:
             //doi.org/10.1016/j.compedu.2021.104429. –   DOI
             https://doi.org/10.1016/j.compedu.2021.104429

[PS23]   Personeni, Gabin ; Savescu, Adriana: Ecological validity of virtual
             reality simulations in workstation health and safety assessment. In:
             Frontiers in Virtual Reality 4 (2023). https://www.frontiersin.
             org/articles/10.3389/frvir.2023.1058790

[PTP+07]   Poncet, Marie C. ; Toullic, Philippe ; Papazian, Laurent ; Kentish-
             Barnes, Nancy ; Timsit, Jean-Francçois ; Pochard, Frédéric ;
             Chevret, Sylvie ; Schlemmer, Benoît ; Azoulay, Élie: Burnout
             Syndrome in Critical Care Nursing Staff.   175 (2007), Nr. 7,
             S. 698–704. http://dx.doi.org/10.1164/rccm.200606-806OC. –
             DOI 10.1164/rccm.200606–806OC

[PWD+19a]   Prachyabrued, Mores ; Wattanadhirach, Disathon ; Dudrow,
             Richard B. ; Krairojananan, Nat ; Fuengfoo, Pusit: Toward Virtual
             Stress Inoculation Training of Prehospital Healthcare Personnel: A
             Stress-Inducing Environment Design and Investigation of an Emo-
             tional Connection Factor. In: 2019 IEEE Virtual Reality (VR). Osaka,
             Japan : IEEE, March 2019, S. 671–679

[PWD+19b]   Prachyabrued, Mores ; Wattanadhirach, Disathon ; Dudrow,
             Richard B. ; Krairojananan, Nat ; Fuengfoo, Pusit: Toward Vir-
             tual Stress Inoculation Training of Prehospital Healthcare Person-
             nel: A Stress-Inducing Environment Design and Investigation of an
             Emotional Connection Factor. In: Teather, Rob (Hrsg.) ; Itoh, Yuta
             (Hrsg.) ; Gabbard, Joe (Hrsg.): Proceedings, 26th IEEE Conference
             on Virtual Reality and 3D User Interfaces. Piscataway, NJ : IEEE,
             2019, S. 671–679

[QNBB19]   Quintana, Pamela ; Nolet, Kévin ; Baus, Oliver ; Bouchard,
             Stéphane: The Effect of Exposure to Fear-Related Body Odorants
             on Anxiety and Interpersonal Trust Toward a Virtual Character. In:
             Chemical Senses 44 (2019), Oktober, Nr. 9, S. 683–692. http://dx.
             doi.org/10.1093/chemse/bjz063. – DOI 10.1093/chemse/bjz063

[RAPJK+06]   Rajendra Acharya, U. ; Paul Joseph, K. ; Kannathal, N. ; Lim,
             Choo M. ; Suri, Jasjit S.:   Heart rate variability: a review.
             In: Medical & Biological Engineering & Computing 44 (2006),
             Dezember, Nr. 12, S. 1031–1051. http://dx.doi.org/10.1007/
             s11517-006-0119-0. – DOI 10.1007/s11517–006–0119–0

[RF11]   Rodrigues, Vitor Manuel Costa P. ; Ferreira, Andreia Susana De S.:
             Stressors in Nurses Working in Intensive Care Units. In: Re-
             vista Latino-Americana De Enfermagem 19 (2011), August, Nr. 4.
             http://dx.doi.org/10.1590/S0104-11692011000400023. – DOI
             10.1590/S0104–11692011000400023

[RHK15]   Ruskin, Keith J. ; Hueske-Kraus, Dirk: Alarm Fatigue: Impacts
             on Patient Safety. 28 (2015). http://dx.doi.org/10.1097/ACO.
             0000000000000260. – DOI 10.1097/ACO.0000000000000260

[RKM+15]   Rothgang, Heinz ; Kalwitzki, Thomas ; Müller, Rolf ; Runte, Re-
            becca ; Unger, Rainer: Schwerpunktthema: Pflegen zu Hause.
            Asgard-Verlag-Service, 2015

[RM19]   Robitaille, Patrice ; McGuffin, Michael J.: Increased affect-arousal
            in VR can be detected from faster body motion with increased heart
            rate. In: Proceedings of the ACM SIGGRAPH Symposium on Inter-
            active 3D Graphics and Games. New York, NY, USA : Association
            for Computing Machinery, Mai 2019 (I3D '19), 1–6

[RMC+07]   Riva, Giuseppe ; Mantovani, Fabrizia ; Capideville, Claret S. ;
            Preziosa, Alessandra ; Morganti, Francesca ; Villani, Daniela ; Gag-
            gioli, Andrea ; Botella, Cristina ; Alcañiz, Mariano: Affective inter-
            actions using virtual reality: the link between presence and emo-
            tions. In: Cyberpsychology & behavior : the impact of the Internet,
            multimedia and virtual reality on behavior and society 10 (2007),
            Nr. 1, S. 45–56. http://dx.doi.org/10.1089/cpb.2006.9993. –
            DOI 10.1089/cpb.2006.9993

[Ros]   Rosseter, Robert: New Data Show Enrollment Declines in Schools
            of Nursing, Raising Concerns About the Nation's Nursing Work-
            force.   https://www.aacnnursing.org/news-data/all-news/
            new-data-show-enrollment-declines-in-schools-of\
            -nursing-raising-concerns-about-the-nations-nursing-\
            workforce

[RPF+19]   Reichenberger, Jonas ; Pfaller, Michael ; Forster, Diana ; Ger-
            czuk, Jennifer ; Shiban, Youssef ; Mühlberger, Andreas: Men
            Scare Me More: Gender Differences in Social Fear Condition-
            ing in Virtual Reality. In: Frontiers in Psychology 10 (2019), S.
            1617. http://dx.doi.org/10.3389/fpsyg.2019.01617. – DOI
            10.3389/fpsyg.2019.01617

[RPW+17]   Reichenberger, Jonas ; Porsch, Sonja ; Wittmann, Jasmin ; Zim-
            mermann, Verena ; Shiban, Youssef: Social Fear Conditioning
            Paradigm in Virtual Reality: Social vs. Electrical Aversive Condi-
            tioning. In: Frontiers in Psychology 8 (2017). http://dx.doi.org/
            10.3389/fpsyg.2017.01979. – DOI 10.3389/fpsyg.2017.01979

[RS10]   Russell, Carol ; Shepherd, John: Online role-play environ-
            ments for higher education. 41 (2010), Nr. 6, 992–1002. http:
            //dx.doi.org/10.1111/j.1467-8535.2009.01048.x. –   DOI
            10.1111/j.1467–8535.2009.01048.x

[RSS+20]   Rodrigues, Joã. ; Studer, Erik ; Streuber, Stephan ; Meyer, Nathalie
            ; Sandi, Carmen: Locomotion in Virtual Environments Pre-

dicts Cardiovascular Responsiveness to Subsequent Stressful Challenges. In: Nature Communications 11 (2020), December, Nr. 1, 5904. http://dx.doi.org/10.1038/s41467-020-19736-3. – DOI 10.1038/s41467–020–19736–3

[S⁺65]   Sutherland, Ivan E. u. a.: The ultimate display. In: Proceedings of the IFIP Congress Bd. 2 New York, 1965, S. 506–508

[SAP⁺19]   Schulz, Peter ; Alexandrovsky, Dmitry ; Putze, Felix ; Malaka, Rainer ; Schöning, Johannes: The Role of Physical Props in VR Climbing Environments. In: Proceedings of the 2019 CHI Conference on Human Factors in Computing Systems. New York, NY, USA : Association for Computing Machinery, Mai 2019 (CHI '19), S. 1–13

[SAS⁺80]   Suess, William M. ; Alexander, A. B. ; Smith, Deborah D. ; Sweeney, Helga W. ; Marion, Richard J.: The Effects of Psychological Stress on Respiration: A Preliminary Study of Anxiety and Hyperventilation. In: Psychophysiology 17 (1980), November, Nr. 6, S. 535–540. http://dx.doi.org/10.1111/j.1469-8986.1980.tb02293.x. – DOI 10.1111/j.1469–8986.1980.tb02293.x

[SATS17]   Suyanto, Erick M. ; Angkasa, Denny ; Turaga, Harfondy ; Sutoyo, Rhio: Overcome Acrophobia with the Help of Virtual Reality and Kinect Technology. In: Procedia Computer Science 116 (2017), January, S. 476–483. http://dx.doi.org/10.1016/j.procs.2017.10.062. – DOI 10.1016/j.procs.2017.10.062

[Sel50]   Selye, Hans: Stress and the general adaptation syndrome. In: British medical journal 1 (1950), Nr. 4667, S. 1383

[Sel76]   Selye, H: Stress in health and disease Butterworth's. In: Inc. Boston, MA (1976)

[SFR01]   Schubert, T ; Friedmann, F ; Regenbrecht, H: Igroup Presence Questionnaire. In: Teleoperators Virtual Environ. 41 (2001), S. 115–124

[SG12]   Sharma, Nandita ; Gedeon, Tom: Objective Measures, Sensors and Computational Techniques for Stress Recognition and Classification: A Survey. In: Computer Methods and Programs in Biomedicine 108 (2012), Nr. 3, 1287–1301. http://dx.doi.org/10.1016/j.cmpb.2012.07.003. – DOI 10.1016/j.cmpb.2012.07.003. – ISSN 01692607

[SKHH]   Schwind, Valentin ; Knierim, Pascal ; Haas, Nico ; Henze, Niels: Using Presence Questionnaires in Virtual Reality. In: Proceedings of the 2019 CHI Conference on Human Factors in Computing Systems. Glasgow, Scotland UK : ACM, S. 1–12

[SKM+20]   Stern, Yonatan ; Koren, Danny ; Moebus, Renana ; Panishev,
              Gabriella ; Salomon, Roy: Assessing the Relationship between
              Sense of Agency, the Bodily-Self and Stress: Four Virtual-Reality
              Experiments in Healthy Individuals.   In: Journal of Clinical
              Medicine 9 (2020), September, Nr. 9, S. 2931. http://dx.doi.org/
              10.3390/jcm9092931. – DOI 10.3390/jcm9092931

[Sla09]   Slater, Mel: Place illusion and plausibility can lead to realistic
              behaviour in immersive virtual environments. In: Philosophical
              Transactions of the Royal Society B: Biological Sciences 364 (2009),
              Nr. 1535, S. 3549–3557. http://dx.doi.org/10.1098/rstb.2009.
              0138. – DOI 10.1098/rstb.2009.0138

[SLASV09]   Slater, Mel ; Lotto, Beau ; Arnold, Maria M. ; Sanchez-Vives,
              Maria V.:   How we experience immersive virtual environments:
              the concept of presence and its measurement. In: Anuario de psi-
              cología 40 (2009), Nr. 2, S. 193–210

[SMS+20]   Scherz, Wilhelm D. ; MagañA, Victor C. ; Seepold, Ralf ; Madrid,
              Natividad M. ; Ortega, Juan A.:   Can Virtual Reality Be Used as a
              Significant Stressor for Studies Using ECG? In: Procedia Computer
              Science 176 (2020), Januar, S. 3255–3262. http://dx.doi.org/10.
              1016/j.procs.2020.09.123. – DOI 10.1016/j.procs.2020.09.123

[SN21]   Shorey, Shefaly ; Ng, Esperanza D.: The use of virtual reality simu-
              lation among nursing students and registered nurses: A systematic
              review. 98 (2021), 104662. http://dx.doi.org/10.1016/j.nedt.
              2020.104662. – DOI 10.1016/j.nedt.2020.104662

[Spe04]   Spencer, Donna: Card Sorting. In: Boxes and Arrows 7 (2004)

[Spi70]   Spielberger, Charles D.:   Manual for the State-Trait Anxietry, In-
              ventory. In: Consulting Psychologist (1970)

[Spi10]   Spielberger,   Charles   D.:   State-Trait   Anxiety   Inven-
              tory.   Version: Januar 2010.   http://dx.doi.org/10.1002/
              9780470479216.corpsy0943.   In: Weiner, Irving B. (Hrsg.) ;
              Craighead, W. E. (Hrsg.): The Corsini Encyclopedia of Psychology.
              Hoboken, NJ, USA : John Wiley & Sons, Inc., Januar 2010. – DOI
              10.1002/9780470479216.corpsy0943

[SRN+19]   Shaw, Emily ; Roper, Tessa ; Nilsson, Tommy ; Lawson, Glyn ;
              Cobb, Sue V. ; Miller, Daniel: The Heat is On: Exploring User Be-
              haviour in a Multisensory Virtual Environment for Fire Evacuation.
              In: Proceedings of the 2019 CHI Conference on Human Factors in
              Computing Systems. New York, NY, USA : Association for Com-
              puting Machinery, Mai 2019 (CHI '19), S. 1–13

[SRS+18]   Schweizer, Tina ; Renner, Fritz ; Sun, Dali ; Kleim, Birgit ; Holmes, Emily A. ; Tuschen-Caffier, Brunna: Psychophysiological reactivity, coping behaviour and intrusive memories upon multisensory Virtual Reality and Script-Driven Imagery analogue trauma: A randomised controlled crossover study. In: Journal of Anxiety Disorders 59 (2018), Oktober, 42–52. http://dx.doi.org/10.1016/j.janxdis.2018.08.005. – DOI 10.1016/j.janxdis.2018.08.005

[Ste92]   Steuer, Jonathan: Defining Virtual Reality: Dimensions Determining Telepresence. 42 (1992), Nr. 4, S. 73–93. http://dx.doi.org/10.1111/j.1460-2466.1992.tb00812.x. – DOI 10.1111/j.1460–2466.1992.tb00812.x

[SUQKA20]   Shewaga, Robert ; Uribe-Quevedo, Alvaro ; Kapralos, Bill ; Alam, Fahad: A Comparison of Seated and Room-Scale Virtual Reality in a Serious Game for Epidural Preparation. In: IEEE Transactions on Emerging Topics in Computing 8 (2020), Januar, Nr. 1, 218–232. http://dx.doi.org/10.1109/TETC.2017.2746085. – DOI 10.1109/TETC.2017.2746085

[SUS94]   Slater, Mel ; Usoh, Martin ; Steed, Anthony: Depth of Presence in Virtual Environments. In: Presence 3 (1994), January, S. 130–144. http://dx.doi.org/10.1162/pres.1994.3.2.130. – DOI 10.1162/pres.1994.3.2.130

[Sut02]   Sutcliffe, Alistair: User-centred requirements engineering. 1. publ. London Berlin Heidelberg New York Barcelona Hong Kong Milan Paris Singapore Tokyo : Springer, 2002

[SVBG21]   Sansó, Noemí ; Vidal-Blanco, Gabriel ; Galiana, Laura: Development and Validation of the Brief Nursing Stress Scale (BNSS) in a Sample of End-of-Life Care Nurses. 11 (2021), Nr. 2, 311–319. http://dx.doi.org/10.3390/nursrep11020030. – DOI 10.3390/nursrep11020030

[SWS21]   Sartain, Andrea F. ; Welch, Teresa D. ; Strickland, Haley P.: Utilizing Nursing Students for a Complex Role-Play Simulation. In: Clinical Simulation In Nursing 60 (2021), 74–77. http://dx.doi.org/10.1016/j.ecns.2021.06.009. – DOI 10.1016/j.ecns.2021.06.009

[SZMD20]   Shi, Yangming ; Zhu, Yibo ; Mehta, Ranjana K. ; Du, Jing: A neurophysiological approach to assess training outcome under stress: A virtual reality experiment of industrial shutdown maintenance using Functional Near-Infrared Spectroscopy (fNIRS). In: Advanced Engineering Informatics 46 (2020), Oktober, 101153. http://dx.doi.org/10.1016/j.aei.2020.101153. – DOI 10.1016/j.aei.2020.101153

[TDB+08]   Thompson, Carl ; Dalgleish, Len ; Bucknall, Tracey ; Estabrooks,
             Carole ; Hutchinson, Alison M. ; Fraser, Kim ; Vos, Rien de ; Bin-
             nekade, Jan ; Barrett, Gez ; Saunders, Jane: The Effects of Time
             Pressure and Experience on Nurses' Risk Assessment Decisions. 57
             (2008), Nr. 5

[TGCM19]   Tadayon, Ramesh ; Gupta, Chetan ; Crews, Debra ; McDaniel, Troy:
             Do Trait Anxiety Scores Reveal Information About Our Response
             to Anxious Situations? A Psycho-Physiological VR Study. In: Pro-
             ceedings of the 4th International Workshop on Multimedia for Per-
             sonal Health & Health Care. New York, NY, USA : Association for
             Computing Machinery, October 2019 (HealthMedia '19), S. 16–23

[TH07]   Teng, Ching-I. ; Huang, Li-Shia: Designing time-limited cyber
             promotions: effects of time limit and involvement. In: Cyberpsy-
             chology & Behavior: The Impact of the Internet, Multimedia and
             Virtual Reality on Behavior and Society 10 (2007), Februar, Nr. 1,
             S. 141–144. http://dx.doi.org/10.1089/cpb.2006.9979. – DOI
             10.1089/cpb.2006.9979

[THC10]   Teng, Ching-I ; Hsiao, Feng-Ju ; Chou, Tin-An: Nurse-perceived
             time pressure and patient-perceived care quality: Time pres-
             sure and care quality.   In: Journal of Nursing Management 18
             (2010), April, Nr. 3, S. 275–284. http://dx.doi.org/10.1111/j.
             1365-2834.2010.01073.x. – DOI 10.1111/j.1365–2834.2010.01073.x

[THPC17]   Tipton, Michael J. ; Harper, Abbi ; Paton, Julian F. R. ; Costello,
             Joseph T.:   The human ventilatory response to stress: rate or
             depth? In: The Journal of Physiology 595 (2017), September, Nr.
             17, 5729–5752. http://dx.doi.org/10.1113/JP274596. – DOI
             10.1113/JP274596

[TM07]   Trafton, J. G. ; Monk, Christopher A.: Task Interruptions. In: Re-
             views of Human Factors and Ergonomics 3 (2007), November, Nr.
             1, S. 111–126. http://dx.doi.org/10.1518/155723408X299852. –
             DOI 10.1518/155723408X299852

[TMG+18]   Tucker, A. ; Marsh, K. L. ; Gifford, T. ; Lu, X. ; Luh, P. B. ; Astur, R. S.:
             The effects of information and hazard on evacuee behavior in vir-
             tual reality. In: Fire Safety Journal 99 (2018), July, 1–11. http://dx.
             doi.org/10.1016/j.firesaf.2018.04.011. – DOI 10.1016/j.fire-
             saf.2018.04.011. – ISSN 0379–7112

[VCJ17]   Valentino, Kelvin ; Christian, Kevin ; Joelianto, Endra: Virtual real-
             ity flight simulator. In: Internetworking Indonesia Journal 9 (2017),
             Nr. 1, S. 21–25

[VE69]   Vreeland, Ruth ; Ellis, Geraldine L.:   Stresses on the Nurse in an Intensive-Care Unit.   In: AORN Journal 10 (1969), Nr. 3, 54–56. `http://dx.doi.org/10.1016/S0001-2092(08)70644-6`. –   DOI 10.1016/S0001–2092(08)70644–6

[VGC⁺13]   Villani, Daniela ; Grassi, Alessandra ; Cognetta, Chiara ; Toniolo, Davide ; Cipresso, Pietro ; Riva, Giuseppe: Self-help stress management training through mobile phones: An experience with oncology nurses.   In: Psychological Services 10 (2013), August, Nr. 3, 315–322. `http://dx.doi.org/10.1037/a0026459`. – DOI 10.1037/a0026459

[VR21]   Velana, Maria ; Rinkenauer, Gerhard: Individual-Level Interventions for Decreasing Job-Related Stress and Enhancing Coping Strategies Among Nurses: A Systematic Review. In: Frontiers in Psychology 12 (2021), Juli, 708696. `http://dx.doi.org/10.3389/fpsyg.2021.708696`. – DOI 10.3389/fpsyg.2021.708696

[WCH19]   Weiß, Sebastian ; Cobus, Vanessa ; Heuten, Wilko: Bedarfe für Virtual Reality Basierte Stress Trainings in der Pflege. In: Tagungsband Der Tagungsband Der 2. Clusterkonferenz 2019 – Innovative Technologien für Die Pflege. Berlin, Germany, 2019, S. 4

[WCT88]   Watson, David ; Clark, Lee A. ; Tellegen, Auke: Development and validation of brief measures of positive and negative affect: The PANAS scales. In: Journal of Personality and Social Psychology 54 (1988), Nr. 6, 1063–1070. `http://dx.doi.org/10.1037/0022-3514.54.6.1063`. – DOI 10.1037/0022–3514.54.6.1063

[WHG84]   West, Daniel J. ; Horan, John J. ; Games, Paul A.: Component analysis of occupational stress inoculation applied to registered nurses in an acute care hospital setting. In: Journal of Counseling Psychology 31 (1984), April, Nr. 2, S. 209–218. `http://dx.doi.org/10.1037/0022-0167.31.2.209`. – DOI 10.1037/0022–0167.31.2.209

[WM18]   Wilson, Graham ; McGill, Mark: Violent Video Games in Virtual Reality: Re-Evaluating the Impact and Rating of Interactive Experiences. In: Proceedings of the 2018 Annual Symposium on Computer-Human Interaction in Play. New York, NY, USA : Association for Computing Machinery, Oktober 2018 (CHI PLAY '18), 535–548

[Wol58]   Wolpe, Joseph: Psychotherapy by reciprocal inhibition. Palo Alto, CA, US : Stanford Univer. Press, 1958 (Psychotherapy by reciprocal inhibition.)

[Wol69]   Wolpe, Joseph.:   The practice of behavior therapy.   New York :
            Pergamon Press, 1969

[WS98]   Witmer, B. G. ; Singer, M.: Measuring Presence in Virtual Environ-
            ments: A Presence Questionnaire. In: Presence 7 (1998), Nr. 3, S.
            225–240. http://dx.doi.org/10.1162/105474698565686. – DOI
            10.1162/105474698565686

[WWH20]   Weiß, Sebastian ; Withöft, Ani ; Heuten, Wilko: aVRaid of Heights?
            - Exploring Integrated Non-Invasive Sensors For Stress Testing.
            In: 2020 IEEE International Conference on Healthcare Informatics
            (ICHI). Oldenburg, Germany : IEEE, November 2020, 1–10

[YBB22]   Yang, Jing ; Barde, Amit ; Billinghurst, Mark: Audio Augmented
            Reality: A Systematic Review of Technologies, Applications, and
            Future Research Directions. In: Journal of the Audio Engineering
            Society 70 (2022), Oktober, Nr. 10, 788–809. https://www.aes.org/
            e-lib/browse.cfm?elib=22008

[YYA+20]   Yin, Jie ; Yuan, Jing ; Arfaei, Nastaran ; Catalano, Paul J. ; Allen,
            Joseph G. ; Spengler, John D.:   Effects of biophilic indoor envi-
            ronment on stress and anxiety recovery: A between-subjects ex-
            periment in virtual reality.   In: Environment International 136
            (2020), March, 105427. http://dx.doi.org/10.1016/j.envint.
            2019.105427. – DOI 10.1016/j.envint.2019.105427

[ZWD19]   Zimmer, Patrick ; Wu, C. C. ; Domes, Gregor: Same same but dif-
            ferent? Replicating the real surroundings in a virtual trier social
            stress test (TSST-VR) does not enhance presence or the psychophys-
            iological stress response. In: Physiology & Behavior 212 (2019), De-
            cember. http://dx.doi.org/10.1016/j.physbeh.2019.112690.
            – DOI 10.1016/j.physbeh.2019.112690